AN ANTHOLOGY OF EROTIC VI

AN ANTHOLOGY OF
EROTIC VERSE

Edited by

Derek Parker

The Softback Preview

First published in Great Britain 1980
by Constable & Company Ltd
3 The Lanchesters,
162 Fulham Palace Road,
London W6 9ER

This edition published 1993 by
The Softback Preview
by special arrangement with
Derek Parker

Made and printed in Great Britain by
Biddles of Guildford and Kings Lynn

2 4 6 8 10 9 7 5 3 1

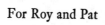
For Roy and Pat

CONTENTS

[8]

[15]

INTRODUCTION

This is an anthology of poems 'of or pertaining to the passion of love' (the *Oxford English Dictionary* definition of the word 'erotic'). Like every anthology, it aims to please, to entertain, to be enjoyed. There are of course deeply serious poems about sexual commitment and sexual behaviour. But on the whole, and for various reasons, erotic poetry is poetry of enjoyment: unsurprisingly, for – though over-serious protagonists of sexual freedom and over-earnest puritans alike seem often to overlook the fact – sex, as well as being a means of procreation and a means of 'knowing' one's partner, in the spiritual as well as the carnal sense, is or should be one of the most enjoyable activities known to humanity.

Erotic poetry celebrates that fact; and therefore is more often than not (as Lord Clark appositely said of the nude in art) likely to arouse or titillate the reader. With those critics who would suggest that some, or even much, of it is therefore pornographic, all one can do is agree. Some people will find this offensive. There are two poems here to which I would direct them: D. H. Lawrence (whose attitude to sex has been much misunderstood) has a fine and sane poem on 'bawdy' (p. 284), and the Italian poet Aldo Palazzeschi (p. 287) makes a rather different point, but makes it soundly, in his poem on 'Pornography'.

In addition, there is pornography and pornography. The *joie de vivre* and quality of the prose in Cleland's *Fanny Hill* is one thing; that of the Victorian pornographic magazine *The Pearl*, or of much modern pulp pornography, is quite another – the latter gloomily repetitive, unimaginative, and often illiterate. To deny that it can be aphrodisiac would be to deny that a scribbled drawing on a lavatory wall *can* be aphrodisiac; but it is usually sad stuff, and few people would argue that it can profitably be read for pleasure.

A great deal of the poetry assembled here was written for aphrodisiac purposes, and more or less overtly so. The law, for long periods of time, inhibited its publication and in some cases the authors themselves or their friends and editors did their best to hide it from the public eye. Much of it existed for years, even centuries, only in manuscript, in private libraries, or in the Private Case of the British Museum. It was certainly not available to the general reader; and it is only very recently that many quite innocent pieces of bawdy, let alone, say, Rochester's 'A Ramble in St James's Park', could be published. Victorian admirers of the Bowdlers looked aslant at Shakespeare's 'Venus and Adonis' – and from their point of view quite rightly: who would deny that Shakespeare would have been disappointed if his reader failed to catch something of the erotic charge between the two lovers in that poem? Who would argue that Ovid was not more concerned to titillate than to educate the reader of 'The Art of Love'? And certainly the purpose of the seventeenth-century collections of bawdy – such collections as *The Wit's Cabinet, Wit and Mirth, or Pills to Purge Melancholy*, and *Merry Drollery Complete* – was as much to arouse as to amuse.

Occasionally, to be sure, one is rather uneasily aware that the poets are writing to arouse themselves. Rochester is a case in point – his verses were written to amuse his hellraking friends (not the most sensitive or delicate-minded of men), but one catches in his tone something of the note of Swinburne's 'hidden' erotic poetry, the MS of whose twelve eclogues about corporal punishment, 'The Flogging Block' ('by Rufus Rodworthy, annotated by Barebum Birchingley'), is in handwriting so hurried, so vigorous, so frenzied, that its masturbatory purpose seems clear. Yet (as a short extract on pp. 263 shows) Swinburne was a poet considerable enough to make something readable even out of a masturbatory fantasy. The humour, however, is forced, if not unintentional; as to flagellation, Sir John Davies' 'In Francum' (p. 113) is more amusing and in a sense more honest.

Masturbation as such, incidentally, only rarely makes an appearance: there is a sly reference in Skythinos (p. 65); John Hopkins' 'To Amasia, Tickling a Gentleman' (p. 191) makes it fairly clear what kind of tickling is involved; but since I omitted a not very good poem of Rochester's on the subject, it is only Fleur Adcock in 'Against Coupling' (p. 342) who deals forthrightly with the subject,

The purpose of this anthology is not, however, to draw attention to the pathology of Swinburne's sexuality, or anyone else's; nor is it a didactic anthology. But while it may be that Ovid was not in the least concerned to educate his reader in 'The Art of Love', that is what, willy nilly, he did; and there is a sense in which many of these poems are 'educational'. Advice to the lovelorn, or the love-bemused, is often at the centre of them. Ovid's description of seduction techniques seems now rather obvious:

> *If dust be on her lap, or grains of sand,*
> *Brush both away with your officious hand.*
> *If none be there, yet brush that nothing hence,*
> *And still to touch her lap make some pretence . . .*

Simple stuff. But when he goes on to write about the importance of foreplay, he is dealing after all with an aspect of love-making that might well not have occurred to his young male readers; and his lines on simultaneous orgasm,

> *Raise to her heights the transports of your soul,*
> *And fly united to the happy goal*

have been paraphrased by innumerable sex manuals in the past thirty years or so. Other poets glance at that ideal in lovemaking: Guarini's shepherd, Thirsis, may have been somewhat surprised when his shepherdess cried

> *. . . Die not yet, I pray*
> *I'll die with thee if thou wilt stay*   (p. 71)

(the verb 'to die' was a synonym for orgasm for three centuries); but it is interesting that a number of male poets were concerned to put the woman's point of view. Dryden, later, made the same point in a song from *Marriage- -l a-Mode*, when Alexis

> *. . . found the fierce pleasure too hasty to stay,*
> *And his soul in the tempest just flying away,*

[23]

and Celia rebuked him for being unkind 'to leave me behind you, and die all alone'. The pair 'died' happily together (p. 153).

Women's fury at the male predilection for a quick dash to orgasm (so graphically described in the twentieth century: 'Wham, bam, thank you ma'am!') is a theme throughout the book, and there is a certain concern – not exclusively male – with premature ejaculation and impotence. Aphra Behn, one of the few women writers of erotic poetry, not unnaturally takes the view that these are an insult: her heroine Cloris is distraught:

> *The blood forsook the hinder place*
> *And strewed with blushes all her face,*
> *Which both disdain and shame expressed . . .* (p. 173)

Her lover Lysander, too, was not best pleased, and the lovers in many other poems share his feelings as he 'cursed his birth, his fate, his stars'.

One of Rochester's poems, 'The Imperfect Enjoyment', is entirely on the theme of premature ejaculation. It is of course a well known psychological fact that shame at the lack of an erection only exacerbates the problem. Ovid pointed this out:

> *. . . shame to perform it quailed me,*
> *And was the second cause why vigour failed me* (p. 56)

– though he unkindly went on to blame the girl ('Well, I believe she kissed not as she should').

As to straightforward impotence, this sometimes had its physiological causes (perhaps the pox, as in Sir John Harington's poem 'Against an Old Lecher', p. 86); sometimes psychological; the poets are often reduced simply to recording the fact without attempting to explain it, as Skythinos did in the second century AD (p. 65). Ovid blamed the woman:

> *Either she was foul, or her attire was bad,*
> *Or she was not the wench I wished t'have had –* (p. 55)

others simply moaned.

[24]

The male ego being what it is, there are more poems celebrating priapism than impotence – Robert Graves' 'Down, Wanton, Down' (p. 300) has a charm and humour lacking in Rochester's description of his phallus in 'The Imperfect Enjoyment', though the latter is, alas, entirely convincing:

> *When vice, disease and scandal lead the way*
> *With what officious haste dost thou obey!*
> *Like a rude, roaring hector in the streets*
> *Who scuffles, cuffs and jostles all he meets . . .*   (p. 204)

The modern view is generally more sympathetic, as in Vincent McHugh's 'Suite from Catullus' (p. 310), a splendid example of a poem of great charm on what not too long ago would have been an entirely unspeakable subject.

The determined woman reader in search of anti-male propaganda will, unfortunately, find much ammunition in these pages. There may not, these days, be quite so much female exasperation at the continual intimation that the male is naturally polygamous (as Herrick puts it – p. 121 – 'that man is poor/Who hath but one of many'), nor that it is the male who most acutely feels sexual tension (Sir Thomas Wyatt's 'Desire' – p. 70 – will now be accepted as applying equally to women). Perhaps in the end the indictment must insist more on selfishness, boastfulness and vanity rather than anything much more pejorative (though these are, of course, enough). There are few Rochesters, though one or two; the unpleasant music-hall joke about the man who never looks at a girl's face ('who looks at the mantelpiece while poking the fire?') is echoed here and there – for instance in Henry Hall's 'Song' (p. 211) 'who minds the sauce that must not eat?' And the line of male boasters runs direct from Catullus through to the twentieth century. 'You can expect to come nine times in nine minutes', the Roman told his mistress, Ipsithilla; 'promises, promises', she no doubt muttered. But Ovid, at least, and most of the poets here, recognised, unlike the Victorians, the woman's need for and right to sexual satisfaction.

Give 'em enjoyment, when the willing dame
Glows with desires, and burns with equal flame,

he writes in 'The Art of Love' (p. 52).

One does tend to feel that the male poet's conception of the sexually insatiable woman is invented for his own pleasure. It is not exclusive to the named poets: many of the ballads, when not concerned with peeping toms and lusty rustic youths, have at their centre an all too willing country girl who 'loves the sport', and who after her lover has died a number of deaths for her, is apt to declare:

> *. . . My joys do now begin:*
> *Oh, dearest, quickly to't again.* (p. 106)

Such ladies had remarkably little difficulty in curing impotence, if only temporarily:

> *. . . the nymph found her pleasure too great to restrain,*
> *And with kindness excessive, she killed me again.* (p. 230)

The frustration of the over-eager woman is most often a matter for farce; very occasionally, both real lust and real frustration are angrily seen, though on the whole it is only in the poems of our own time that real sensitivity is shown, as in Ronald McCuaig's remarkable poem 'The Commercial Traveller's Wife' (p. 317), or in Edna St Vincent Millay's sonnet (p. 294), in which perhaps for the first time a recognisable, truly liberated woman steps into sight.

There is no denying the fact that on the whole it is the male view of women that we see in these pages. What woman will be entirely happy, for instance, with the preoccupation of so many rampant male poets with extreme youth? Even allowing for fantasy, even after *Lolita* and the obscenity of teen-age sex magazines, we can only raise our eyebrows at Sedley's predilection for eleven-year-old girls, at Carew's plea

[26]

> *Give me a wench about thirteen,*
> *Already voted to the queen*
> *Of lust and lovers . . .* (p. 134)

and at Dryden's suggestion that a fourteen-year-old is probably crying: 'Take me, take me, some of you!' But at the other end of the scale, there is a deal of enthusiasm for age and experience: Philodemos extols the amorous techniques of Charito, ripened by lust for sixty years (p. 41), and an anonymous seventeenth-century poet tells of the 'lusty old woman' who seduces a youth under a hedge, then gives him five shillings 'to make a recruit'. And the professionals are always admired, from the very first poem in the book to the very last.

Shakespeare is not the only poet to find simple lust if not positively beastly, at least disturbing. Jonson, his contemporary, echoed the famous 'Sonnet CXXIX' in his own 'Fragment from Petronius':

> *Doing, a filthy pleasure is, and short –*
> *And done, we straight repent us of the sport.* (p. 117)

For every poet who takes sex as a simple pleasure (perhaps the most sympathetic and honest example of this point of view is in Sir Charles Sedley's 'On Fruition', p. 168), there is another who views it much more equivocally – and indeed while there are Rochesters to show the exquisite contempt for woman he demonstrates in 'A Whore' (p. 210), who shall blame them? Tom Pickard's 'Shag' (p. 344), a quite remarkable poem, mirrors Rochester's and his friends' attitudes in contemporary England, in a worrying, moving account of a gang-bang.

But these are on the whole, happily, undertones. By far the greater number of poems in the book are poems of persuasion, wooing, and triumph. The ceremonies of persuasion are given full weight: for, as John Oldmixon puts it in 'To Cloe' (p. 220):

> *. . . if I am never crossed,*
> *Half the pleasure will be lost,*

[27]

(though on the other hand Ovid tellingly recounts his irritation at having to go to endless trouble to engineer one brief meeting, p. 57). Andrew Marvell's 'To his Coy Mistress' is the most famous of the 'poems of persuasion'; but there are many others, such as Jonson's song 'To Celia' (p. 117). In some of them, the woman is extremely apt at temptation.

Between desire and fulfilment there are some splendid poems about sexual dreams: Herrick's 'The Vine' (p. 123) may surprise some readers who still think of him as a harmless country parson whose verses are of relentless prettiness, and mostly about ladies' feet; I like too Thomas Carew's conceit that dreams feed sexual pleasure to the soul:

> *And so our souls that cannot be embraced*
> *Shall the embraces of our bodies taste.*   (p. 128)

Antonio Machado pointed out that 'the truly erotic sensibility, in evoking the image of women, never omits to clothe it. The robing and disrobing: that is the true traffic of lust.' A majority of poets would probably agree, for time and time again we find the lady stripping for a bathe, or undressing for bed, conscious or unconscious of the swain in the bulrushes or the admirer behind the arras. Chapman's slow striptease of Corinna in 'Ovid's Banquet of Sense' (p. 77) is an early example in English poetry; many others follow, some much less polite. Even the respectable George Moore (p. 268) provides an example, with a splendidly sensual final couplet. Occasionally there is a mildly comic effect, as when an anonymous seventeenth-century poet describes one of Nell Gwyn's public appearances, at which Lord Buckhurst

> *. . . saw her roll . . . from side to side*
> *And through her drawers the powerful charm descried.* (p. 180)

These are not poems for those who believe, for one reason or another, that men should not enjoy looking at naked women. Chapman, again, put the pleasure well when Ovid peering into an arbour saw Corinna:

[28]

Now as she lay attired in nakedness
His eye did carve him on that feast of feasts . . .   (p. 79)

though perhaps the masterpiece in the *genre* is Donne's 'Elegy To His Mistress Going to Bed', where the unveiling leads naturally to a loving conclusion (and reassuringly love, as opposed to or as well as enjoyable sex, is the ideal most poets have in view, believing as Bertrand Russell put it, that 'Civilised people cannot fully satisfy their sexual instinct without love'). 'Full nakedness', exclaimed Donne, 'all joys are due to thee' (p. 119) and there are many celebrations of nudity, from Paulus' view (p. 66) that

> *. . . the lightest lawn*
> *is like the walls of Babylon*
> *when we lie together*

on to Herrick:

> *Give me my mistress as she is,*
> *Dressed in her naked simplicities.*   (p. 124)

Once the clothes are off, a few poets retire, carefully closing the bedroom door behind them. Others, however, remain, and for the most part get much closer to describing the mysteries of sexual love than any prose-writer. The image of the woman's body as a landscape is a familiar conceit, used perhaps most famously by Shakespeare in 'Venus and Adonis', in which Venus describes her body as a park (p. 90); but there are many other examples, such as Thomas Carew's 'A Rapture' (p. 127).

The male body is less often rhapsodised, chiefly of course because most of the erotic poets are men. There is a familiar passage in *The Song of Songs* (p. 67), and Marlowe's description of Leander (p. 97) – the latter stemming from Marlowe's homosexuality. Gerard Manley Hopkins' poem about Harry Ploughman, and Whitman's poetry, offer other examples; but for various reasons these poets were unable to express themselves fully, and there seems nothing in poetry to equal for sexual intensity that moving descrip-

[29]

tion of Fanny Hill looking at the naked body of her lover on the morning after her seduction, in Cleland's novel.

Finding good male homosexual poetry has proved difficult. The Greeks took life easily in this respect, but their poems were often little more than humorous squibs (Meleager's poem to Alexis, p. 40, is an exception). There are a few passages in *Don Leon*, George Colman's satire on Byron's *Don Juan* (still catalogued under 'Byron [*pseud*]' in the British Library catalogue) which show a certain tenderness (see the example I give, p. 242). But Colman's 'The Rodiad' is for the most part comic-cuts, and a great deal of Victorian and Edwardian homosexual poetry is sentimental rubbish; I have printed one or two poems a little above the average – see for instance Theodore Wratislaw's 'To a Sicilian Boy' (p. 267) (the last line of which echoes Oscar Wilde's verdict when a friend took him to a female brothel in Paris: 'Cold mutton!'). C. P. Cavafy is the great exception; apart from his love poems, there is his marvellously accurate evocation of furtive lust, 'To Remain' (p. 271).

There are many incidental pleasures to be found, reading through these poems. The social sidelights, for example, such as the extensive use made of London's parks and open spaces during the seventeenth and eighteenth centuries (cf. Rochester, p. 205, and John Gay, p. 223, who reveals that since courtiers have lost the taste for *al fresco* love-making, the price of closed carriages has risen alarmingly).

The anonymous ballads make one marvel, again and again, not only at the strong vein of sensuality (Baudelaire suggested that 'sexuality is the lyricism of the masses'), but at the liveliness and often the quality of the poetry. How splendidly 'The Lonely Maid' evokes awakening sexuality:

> *If dreams be true, then ride I can –*
> *I lack nothing but a man . . .* (p. 102)

and on the following page, what a charming idealised picture of rustic love. (Two later ballads, 'My Longing Desire' and 'The Sound Country Lass' (pp. 193/4), may be nearer the truth.) There is occasional scabrousness ('The Tenement', p. 175, is the one example I give from a vast number of similar verses); but simple, powerful eroticism seldom fails to bring out perennially memorable symbolism and strongly moving images, as in 'The Dream' (p. 182):

> *She lay all naked in her bed*
> *And I myself lay by;*
> *No veil nor curtain there was spread,*
> *No covering but I.*

The wit of these anonymous poets is often charming and, one can only say, cheeky. An established poet might hesitate to draw a picture of a bathing beauty for whom

> *Each fish did wish himself a man –*
> *About her all was drawn –*
> *And at the sight of her began*
> *To spread abroad his spawn* (p. 190)

or to worry about the social aspects of marrying a wife with no pubic hair ('Nae Hair On't', p. 226). Anon strides uninhibitedly on. And once again, there are interesting social sidelights: at least one edition of *Harris's List of Covent-Garden Ladies* (p. 238) had 'blurbs' in verse for the whores it advertised:

> *Then all her limbs unbound, her girdle loose,*
> *There's nothing you can ask her, she'll refuse.*

Occasionally, the anonymous poet is inspired to lines any poet would envy: what could be more beautiful than those in 'Arithmetic of the Lips' (p. 139):

> *Were the bright day no more to visit us,*
> *Oh, then for ever would I hold thee thus,*
> *Naked, enchained, empty of idle fear,*
> *As the first lovers in the garden were.*

I was somewhat bemused by the problem of the limerick; a very few seemed to merit presentation as classics of their kind. But after all, for some reason they are anti-erotic, anti-aphrodisiac – something to do with the form, maybe, because there is a long tradition of humour in erotic poetry. And some of that humour is first-rate: the wry exclamation of Cytherea, for instance, watching as Adonis dives into a river: 'O Jove! – why was I not a flood?' (p. 100); the deflating of courtly love in Sir John Davies' two poems 'A Lover Out of Fashion' and 'To His Mistress' (p. 114/5); Burns' lovely send-up of bucolic amorous balladry in 'Ode to Spring' (p. 239), and, of course, the poems of e. e. cummings, of which at least one (p. 295) is a classic. Some puns and jokes run through erotic poetry for centuries: the anonymous poem about 'Oyster Nan' (p. 196) contains precisely the same joke as the modern limerick about a couple in a different, but similar, situation:

> *A persistent young plumber named Lee*
> *Was plumbing his girl by the sea.*
> *Said she 'Stop your plumbing,*
> *There's somebody coming.'*
> *'I know,' said the plumber; 'it's me.'*

There is little point in making excuses about omissions or inclusions in anthologies. It will be obvious that I have included, for instance, only a small selection of poems in languages other than English (apart from the Greek and Latin, a happy hunting-ground for English poets for centuries). Those that are printed are poems which especially appealed to me, or which seemed to illustrate aspects of sexuality omitted elsewhere. There are a number of poems which will be unfamiliar, culled as they have been either from MSS or from very restricted collections. There are others which will be very familiar: Marvell's 'To His Coy Mistress' or Donne's 'To his Mistress Going to Bed' are included on the grounds on which, presumably, Beethoven's Fifth Symphony is included in the Promenade Concert series: someone will be reading them for the first time.

As to the omissions, some are accounted for by one reason, some by another. Chaucer's 'Wife of Bath' is missing because I did not feel that Chaucerian English could be reasonably included in an anthology for the general reader, and modern 'translations' all seem to me unsatisfactory. Other poems are excluded because meaningful extracts seem impossible. Tennyson's 'Maud', for instance, is surely a highly erotic poem; but a short extract could not hope to show this.

Critics will notice that I have repunctuated many early poems. I make no excuses for this: Elizabethan punctuation is notoriously of no help to a modern reader, and often actually obfuscates meaning. For similar reasons, I have usually spelt out words abbreviated in original texts, except where this would make a nonsense of the prosody. For instance, in Sir Robert Aytoun's 'To His Forsaken Mistress' (p. 115) I have left *th'art* for *thou art* in the first line, but spelt out *prayer* for *pray'r* in the third. I hope this will not be regarded as illogical, though some people may very properly argue that variations of pronunciation occasionally make it so.

DEREK PARKER, 1980

ACKNOWLEDGEMENTS

The author is grateful to the following authors and authors' estates in respect of the poems listed:

Adcock, Fleur: the author and the Oxford University Press for a poem from *High Tide in the Garden*.

Amis, Kingsley: the author and Messrs Jonathan Cape for poems from *A Look Round the Estate*.

Betjeman, Sir John: the author and John Murray (Publishers) Limited for a poem from the *Collected Poems*.

Comfort, Alex: the author and Eyre Methuen Ltd for poems from *Haste to the Wedding*.

Conder, Alan: Mrs F. H. Doris Cohen and the poet's estate for his translations of Baudelaire.

cummings, e. e.: Granada Publishing Limited for the poems from *Collected Poems*.

Cunliffe, Dave: the poet for his poem.

Duffy, Maureen: the poet and Weidenfeld & Nicolson Ltd, for poems from *The Venus Touch*.

Elliot, Alistair: the poet for his translation of a poem of Antipater of Thessalonika.

Ewart, Gavin: the poet for two poems from *Pleasures of the Flesh and An Imaginary Love Affair*; the poet and Victor Gollancz Ltd, for a poem from *Or Where a Young Penguin Lies Screaming*.

Graves, Robert: the poet and Messrs Cassell for two poems from *Poems About Love*.

Hacker, Marilyn: the author and Alan Ross Limited for a poem from *The London Magazine*.

Hobsbaum, Philip: the poet for his poem.

Hope, A. D.: the poet and Angus & Robertson (UK) Limited for a poem from *Collected Poems 1930–70*.

Lawrence, D. H.: the estate of the late Mrs Frieda Lawrence

[35]

Ravagli and Laurence Pollinger Ltd for poems from *Collected Poems*.

McCuaig, Ronald: the author and Angus & Robertson (UK) Ltd for poems from *The Ballad of Bloodthirsty Bessie and Other Poems*.

MacDiarmid, Hugh: the estate of the poet, and Macmillan Ltd for a poem.

Mansour, Joyce: the author and Alan Ross Ltd for a poem from *The London Magazine*.

Marshfield, Alan: the author for his translation from Rufinus.

Merwin, W. S.: the estate of Pablo Neruda and Jonathan Cape Ltd for a poem from *Selected Poems*; and Mr Merwin for his translation.

Michie, James: the poet and Granada Publishing Ltd, for his translation from Martial.

Millay, Edna St Vincent: Norma Millay Ellis and the poet's estate for a poem from the *Collected Poems* (1923, 1951).

Mitchell, Adrian: the poet and Cape Goliard Press for a poem from *Out Loud*.

Palazzeschi, Aldo: Arnoldo Mondadori Co. Ltd for a poem from *Via delle cento stelle*. Ronald Bottrall and the Anvil Press for the translation.

Pound, Ezra: Messrs Faber & Faber for poems from *Collected Shorter Poems*.

Scannell, Vernon: the poet for his poem.

Skelton, Robin: the author and Messrs Methuen for a translation of an anonymous Byzantine poet, from *Two Hundred Poems from the Greek Anthology*.

Smith, Stevie: James MacGibbon and the poet's estate for her poem.

Stewart, Douglas: the author and Angus & Robertson (UK) Ltd for a poem from *Collected Poems 1936-67*.

Swinburne, Algernon: William Heinemann Limited for permission to reprint an extract from *The Flogging Block*, courtesy of the British Library.

Symons, Arthur: William Heinemann Ltd for two poems.

Turnbull, Gael: the author and Jonathan Cape Ltd for a poem from *Scantlings*.

Turner, W. J.: Mrs Joan F. Lisle for a poem.
Williams, Jonathan: the poet for his poem.
Yeats, W. B.: M. B. Yeats and Macmillan Ltd for three poems.

The anonymous poems on pp 227 and 238, and the extract from John Wilkes' *The Essay on Women*, are reprinted by permission of the British Library.

Translations which are otherwise unacknowledged are by the Editor.

Despite many endeavours, the editor has failed to reach, or has received no replies from Oliver Bernard (a translation from Apollinaire), Paul Blackburn ('The Once-Over'), Pete Brown ('The Vision'), Vincent McHugh ('Suite from Catullus'), and Tom Pickard ('Shag'). He would be very pleased to hear of their whereabouts, so that the proper acknowledgement may be made.

AUTOMEDON
(c Roman Empire)

The Professional

That neat little Asiatic
acrobat who adopts
the most curious poses
is titillating to the fingertips.
I go for her. Not because
she knows every position
and every where to put
her feather hands, but because
she can get my poor withered
cock to stand. Doesn't mind
the shrunken skin.
She mouths it, teases
and clasps it,
and between her thighs
will warm up a stand
in Hell's frozen flames.

Demetrius the Fortunate

Demetrius, who teaches our boys their exercises,
Is certainly the lucky one. I dined with him yesterday.
One boy lay across his knees,
Another leaned over his shoulder; one poured wine,
Another served food – a handsome foursome, too.
I couldn't help a joke. 'Tell me,' I said,
'You've worked out some exercises for the night?'

ANON BYZANTINE POET

On a Small Bath

Do not ridicule the small.
Little things can charm us all.
Eros was not big at all.

(tr Robin Skelton)

ASKLEPIADES
(320 BC?–?)

Refreshment

A mouthful of snow is fine
                when summer has dried the mouth.
The airs of spring are fine
          to sailors when
winter is past. But finer
         is the single sheet over
two lovers as they
      sacrifice to Venus.

MELEAGER
(140 BC?–70 BC?)

Alexis

At noon
  on the street –
    Alexis.

Summer had rotted the fruit
  to a brown mess.
    Summer sun and the boy's look

Did my business.
   Night put out the sun.
      Your face devours my dreams.

Others find sleep a downy nest;
   mine burns me, taking
      the bright shape of your body.

PHILODEMOS
(c 110–30 BC)

Charito

So Charito has lived for three-score years.
Her thick, dense hair is still jet-black –
The white weight of her breasts needs no support –
Ambrosia breaks in beads on her taut skin –
Sheer lust shines out of her, sheer wanting it.
Lovers not nervous at such open passion:
Here's one ripened by it for sixty years.

Dialogue

'Hi, there.' 'Hi yourself.'
'What's your name?' 'What's yours?'
'Look, let's not get up-tight about this.'
'Right on.' 'Waiting for someone?'
'I have this regular guy.'
'What about some chow?'
'O.K.' 'O.K. – er – how much?'
'I'm promising nothing.'
'So promise nothing.' 'If you get me to bed
leave what you like on the mantelpiece.'
'O.K. What address? –
I'll call one evening.' 'I'm in the book.'
'When can you make it?' 'Whenever.'
'I want it now.' 'Your place, then.'

DIODORUS ZONAS
(c 100 BC?)

Tributes

A pomegranate just splitting, a peach just furry,
a fig with wrinkled flesh and juicy bottom,
a purple cluster (thick-berried well of wine),
nuts just skinned from their green peelings – these
the guardian of the fruit lays here for Priapus:
for this single shaft in the wilds, the seed of trees.

(tr Alistair Elliot)

TITUS LUCRETIUS CARUS
(c 99–55 BC)

Concerning the Nature of Love

Thus, therefore, he who feels the fiery dart
Of strong desire transfix his amorous heart,
Whether some beauteous boy's alluring face
Or lovelier maid with unresisted grace
From her each part the winged arrow sends,
From whence he first was struck, he thither tends.
Restless he roams, impatient to be freed
And eager to inject the sprightly seed.
For fierce desire does all his mind employ,
And ardent love assures approaching joy.
Such is the nature of that pleasing smart
Whose burning drops distil upon the heart
The fever of the soul shot from the fair
And the cold ague of succeeding care.
If absent, her idea still appears,
And her sweet name is chiming in your ears;
But strive those pleasing phantoms to remove,
And shun th'aerial images of love
That feed the flame; when one molests thy mind

Discharge thy loins on all the leaky kind –
For that's a wiser way than to restrain
Within thy swelling nerves that hoard of pain;
For every hour some deadlier symptom shows,
And by delay the gathering venom grows
When kindly applications are not used.
The scorpion, love, must on the wound be bruised.
On that one object 'tis not safe to stay,
But force the tide of thought some other way:
The squandered spirits prodigally throw
And in the common glebe of nature sow.
Nor wants he all the bliss that lovers feign
Who takes the pleasure and avoids the pain;
For purer joys in purer health abound,
And less affect the sickly than the sound.
When love its utmost vigour does employ,
Even then, 'tis but a restless wandering joy;
Nor knows the lover, in that wild excess,
With hands or eyes what first he would possess,
But strains at all, and fastening where he strains
Too closely presses with his frantic pains –
With biting kisses hurts the twining fair,
Which shows his joys imperfect, unsincere,
For stung with inward rage, he flings around
And strives t'avenge the smart on that which gave the wound.
But love those eager bitings does restrain,
And mingling pleasure mollifies the pain.
For ardent hope still flatters anxious grief,
And sends him to his foe to seek relief
Which yet the nature of the thing denies,
For love, and love alone of all our joys
By full possession does but fan the fire,
The more we still enjoy, the more we still desire.
Nature for meat and drink provides a space,
And when received they fill their certain place;
Hence thirst and hunger may be satisfied.
But this repletion is to love denied.

Form, feature, colour, whatsoe'er delight
Provokes the lover's endless appetite,
These fill no space, nor can we thence remove
With lips or hands or all our instruments of love:
In our deluded grasp we nothing find
But thin aerial shapes that fleet before the mind.
As he who in a dream with drought is cursed
And finds no real drink to quench his thirst
Runs to imagined lakes his heat to steep,
So love with phantoms cheats our longing eyes,
Which hourly seeing never satisfies.
Our hands pull nothing from the parts they strain
But wander o'er the lovely limbs in vain,
Nor when the youthful pair more closely join,
When hands in hands they lock, and thighs in thighs they twine,
Just in the raging foam of full desire
When both press on, both murmur, both expire,
They gripe, they squeeze, their humid tongues they dart,
As each would force their way to t'other's heart –
In vain: they only cruise about the coast,
For bodies cannot pierce, nor be in bodies lost,
As sure they strive to be when both engage
In that tumultuous momentary rage.
So tangled in the nets of love they lie,
Till man dissolves in that excess of joy.
Then when the gathered bag has burst its way
And ebbing tides the slackened nerves betray,
A pause ensues, and Nature nods a while,
Till with recruited rage new spirits boil;
And then the same vain violence returns,
With flames renewed th'erected furnace burns.
Again they in each other would be lost,
But still by adamantine bars are crossed.
All ways they try, successless all they prove
To cure the secret sore of lingering love.

(*from* The Fourth Book)
(tr John Dryden)

[44]

GAIUS VALERIUS CATULLUS
(c 84–54 BC)

XXXII

Dear Ipsithilla –
Here I am, full of food,
cock sticking right out of my tunic.
Do send me a note this afternoon
and invite me over, my love, my beauty,
Leave the door open, give everyone
the afternoon off, and *stay at home*.
Let 'em all wait.
When I arrive there won't be much delay –
you can expect to come nine times in nine minutes.
Actually, if you don't want to wait,
I could come over now . . . I've had lunch,
and by God, I'm ready!

LVI

Funny thing, Cato – you'll like this,
this'll make you laugh and love me even more.
Really, it's rather good.
You see, I came across this boy fucking this girl,
which rather got me going, so nodding to Venus
I got right up him with my own good staff.

LXXIV

Gellius' uncle was such a prude –
So hated even the mention of sex,
let alone the performance –
that Gellius happily fucked his aunt.
Uncle couldn't say a word.
In fact, Gellius could have fucked *him*
for that matter; he wouldn't have uttered!

LXXVIII

Gallus has two brothers,
one with a beautiful wife,

[45]

one with a handsome son.
Gallus, happily intriguing,
got the two lovelies between the same sheets.
All well, if not good; but what he forgot
is that he's a husband too. Ho! ho!

LXXXIX

How thin Gellius is!
Ah, well – such a kind mother,
such a compliant sister,
his uncle so forthcoming, and all those cousins . .
not much time, after all, to grow fat.
If he only kept clear of his deceased wife's sister
he'd still be thin as a rake.

LXXXV

I hate, I love. You may well ask why.
I couldn't tell you. But I feel it, and burn.

XV

Aurelius, my love and I hope this finds you
as it leaves us, and ask one small favour:
if you have ever in your life
wanted a love for once unpolluted,
please keep your hands off that one boy?
The *hoi polloi* don't worry me –
they go about their business
with their minds on themselves.
It's you and your cock worry me,
standing up for all the boys.
Well, wave it about as much as you like
and pretty well wherever:
just leave that one for me?
Not much to ask.
                    If you won't lay off,

and butt in with your usual techniques,
just remember what happens to adulterers:
I'll tie your feet, neatly apart,
and stuff mullet and radishes up your arse.

XVI

So I'm to bugger you and suck your cocks,
Furius and Aurelius, you pair of pouffes?
You think reading my poems,
I'm as randy as they are?
Hadn't you heard the poet should be chaste,
however pornographic his poems are?
Mine are pretty salty,
charming but not specially discreet,
and certainly provoke a certain itching –
not only in boys, but in men whose hairy genitals
need something unusual to work the miracle.
But reading of a thousand kisses
don't think I'm as effeminate as you.
So I'm to bugger you and suck your cocks?
Wrong, pair of pouffes, Furius and Aurelius.

MARCUS ARGENTARIUS
(c 1st Century BC/AD)

Lysidice

Take off those flimsy nets, Lysidice;
Don't twitch your bottom teasingly at me,
Walking about in your transparent dress
Although it suits you well, I must confess:
The muslin clings so tightly to your sides
It shows more of your body than it hides.
But if you find that an amusing trick
I'll drape a see-through veil over my prick.

[47]

Menophila

Hetero-sex is best for the man of a serious turn of mind,
But here's a hint, if you should fancy the other:
Turn Menophila round in bed, address her peachy behind,
And it's easy to pretend you're screwing her brother.

Heraclea

Your king, Heraclea, is sucking off
Young men: it's an open secret in the town.
How could you bring yourself to do it, though?
Did someone grab your plaits and force you down
To the act? Or is it just that, being named
After great Heracles, you feel that this
Entitles you, whenever it may arise,
To pay his club the tribute of a kiss?

(tr Fleur Adcock)

PUBLIUS OVIDIUS NASO
(43 BC–AD 17)

from *The Art of Love, Book One*

From Romulus the rise of plays began,
To his new subjects a commodious man
Who, his unmarried soldiers to supply,
Took care the Commonwealth should multiply
Providing Sabine women for his braves
Like a true king, to get a race of slaves.
His playhouse, not of Parian marble made,
Nor was it spread with purple sails for shade.
The stage with rushes or with leaves they strowed –

No scenes in prospect, no machining god.
On rows of homely turf they sat to see,
Crowned with the wreaths of every common tree.
There, while they sit in rustic majesty
Each lover had his mistress in his eye,
And whom he saw most suiting to his mind
For joys of matrimonial rape designed.
Scarce could they wait the plaudits in their haste,
But ere the dances and the song were past
The monarch gave the signal from his throne
And rising, bade his merry men fall on.
The martial crew, like soldiers ready pressed,
Just at the word (the word too was the best)
With joyful cries each other animate.
Some choose, and some at hazard seize their mate.
As doves from eagles, or from wolves the lambs,
So from their lawless lovers fly the dames.
Their fear was one, but not one face of fear:
Some rend the lovely tresses of their hair,
Some shriek, and some are struck with dumb despair.
Her absent mother one invokes in vain;
One stands amazed, not daring to complain;
The nimbler trust their feet, the slow remain.
But naught availing, all are captives led
Trembling and blushing to the genial bed.
She who too long resisted or denied
The lusty lover made by force a bride,
And with superior strength compelled her to his side
Then soothed her thus: 'My soul's far better part
Cease weeping, nor afflict they tender heart,
For what thy father to thy mother was,
That faith to thee, that solemn vow I pass!'

Thus Romulus became so popular.
This was the way to thrive in peace and war,
To pay his army, and fresh whores to bring.
Who would not fight for such a gracious king!

[49]

Thus love in theatres did first improve,
And theatres are still the scene of love.
Nor shun the chariots' and the courser's race,
The circus is no inconvenient place.
No need is there of talking on the hand,
Nor nods, nor signs, which lovers understand,
But boldly next the fair your seat provide
Close as you can to hers; and side by side –
Pleased or unpleased, no matter – crowding sit,
For so the laws of public shows permit.
Then find occasion to begin discourse:
Enquire whose chariot this, and whose that horse?
To whatsoever side she is inclined,
Suit all your inclinations to her mind:
Like what she likes, from thence your court begin,
And whom she favours, wish that he may win.
But when the statues of the deities,
In chariots rolled, appear before the prize –
When Venus comes – with deep devotion rise.
If dust be on her lap, or grains of sand,
Brush both away with your officious hand.
If none be there, yet brush that nothing hence,
And still to touch her lap make some pretence.
Touch anything of hers, and if her train
Sweep on the ground, let it not sweep in vain
But gently take it up and wipe it clean –
And while you wipe it, with observing eyes
Who knows but you may see her naked thighs!
Observe who sits behind her, and beware
Lest his encroaching knee should press the fair.
Light service takes light minds, for some can tell
Of favours won by laying cushions well;
By fanning faces some their fortunes meet,
And some by laying footstools for their feet.
These overtures of love the circus gives.
Nor at the sword-play less the lover thrives,
For there the son of Venus fights his prize,

And deepest wounds are oft received from eyes.
One, while the crowd their acclamations make,
Or while he bets and puts his ring to stake
Is struck from far and feels the flying dart,
And of the spectacle is made a part.

(Book I, lines 111–197)

from *The Art of Love, Book Two*

First nature lay an undigested mass:
Heaven, Earth and Ocean wore one common face.
Then vaulted heaven was framed. Waves earth enclosed,
And Chaos was in beauteous forms disposed.
The beasts inhabit woods, the birds the air,
And to their floods the scaly fry repair.
Mankind alone enjoyed no certain place,
On rapine lived, a rude, unpolished race.
Caves were their houses, herbs their food and bed,
Whilst each a savage from the other fled.
Love first disarmed the fierceness of their mind,
And in one bed the men and women joined.
The youth was eager, but unskilled in joy,
Nor was the unexperienced virgin coy.
They knew no courtship, no instructor found,
Yet they enjoyed, and blessed the pleasing wound.
The birds with consorts propagate their kind,
And sporting fish their finny beauties find.
In amorous folds the wanton serpents twine,
And dogs with their salacious females join.
The lusty bull delights his frisking dames,
And more lascivious goat her male inflames.
Mares furious grow with love, their boundaries force,
Plunging through waves to meet the neighing horse.

[51]

Go on, brave youth, thy generous vigour try,
To the relenting maid this charm apply.
Love's softening pleasures every grief remove:
There's nothing that can make your peace like love.

(Book II, lines 514–541)

from *The Art of Love, Book Two*

The hours enjoy whilst youth and pleasures last.
Age hurries on, and death pursues too fast.
Or plough the seas, or cultivate the land,
Or wield the sword in thy adventurous hand,
Or much in love thy nervous strength employ –
Embrace the fair, the grateful maid enjoy.
Pleasure and wealth reward thy pleasing pains:
The labour's great, but greater far the gains.
Add their experience in affairs of love,
For years and practice do alike improve.
Their arts repair the injuries of time,
And still preserve them in their charming prime.
In varied ways they act the pleasure o'er –
Not pictured postures can instruct you more.
They want no courtship to provoke delight,
But meet your warmth with eager appetite.
Give 'em enjoyment, when the willing dame
Glows with desires, and burns with equal flame.
I love to hear the soft transporting joys,
The frequent sighs, the tender murmuring voice –
To see her eyes with varied pleasures move,
And all the nymphs confess the power of love.
Nature's not thus indulgent to the young.
These joys alone to riper years belong.
Who youth enjoys, drinks crude unready wine.

Let age your girl and sprightly juicy refine,
Mellow their sweets, and make the taste divine.
To Helen who'd Hermione prefer,
Or Gorge think beyond her mother fair?
But he that covets the experienced Dame
Shall crown his joys, and triumph in his flame.

One conscious bed receives the happy pair.
Retire, my muse; the door demands thy care.
What charming words, what tender things are said,
What language flows without thy useless aid!
There shall the roving hands employment find,
Inspire new flames, and make ev'n virgins kind.
Thus Hector did Andromache delight,
Hector in love victorious, as in fight.
When weary from the field Achilles came,
Thus with delays he raised Briseis' flame.
Ah, could those arms, those fatal hands delight!
Inspire kind thoughts, and raise thy appetite!
Couldst thou, fond maid, be charmed with his embrace
Stained with the blood of half thy royal race?

Nor yet with speed the fleeting pleasures waste,
Still moderate your love's impetuous haste!
The bashful virgin, though appearing coy,
Detains your hand and hugs the proffered joy.
Then view her eyes with humid lustre bright,
Sparkling with rage, and trembling with delight;
Her kind complaints, her melting accents hear,
The eye she charms, and wounds the listening ear.
Defer not then the clasping nymph's embrace,
But with her love maintain an equal pace.
Raise to her heights the transports of your soul,
And fly united to the happy goal.
Observe these precepts when with leisure blessed
No threatening fears your private hours molest;
When danger's near, your active force employ,

And urge with eager speed the hasty joy.
Then ply your oars, then practice this advice,
And strain, with whip and spur, to gain the prize.

(Book II, lines 740–802. tr John Dryden)

The Fifth Elegy (Book One)

In summer's heat, and mid-time of the day,
To rest my limbs upon a bed I lay;
One window shut, the other open stood,
Which gave such light as twinkles in a wood,
Like twilight glimpse at setting of the sun,
Or night being past, and yet not day begun.
Such light to shamefast maidens must be shown,
Where they may sport and seem to be unknown.
Then came Corinna in a long loose gown,
Her white neck hid with tresses hanging down,
Resembling fair Semiramis going to bed,
Or Lais of a thousand wooers sped.
I snatched her gown; being thin, the harm was small,
Yet strived she to be covered therewithal,
And striving thus as one that would be cast,
Betrayed herself, and yielded at the last.
Stark naked as she stood before mine eye,
Not one wen in her body could I spy.
What arms and shoulders did I touch and see,
How apt her breasts were to be pressed by me!
How smooth a belly under her waist saw I,
How large a leg, and what a lusty thigh!
To leave the rest, all liked me passing well;
I clinged her naked body, down she fell.
Judge you the rest: being tired she bade me kiss;
Jove send me more such afternoons as this.

(tr Christopher Marlowe)

from *The Sixth Elegy (Book Three)*

Either she was foul, or her attire was bad,
Or she was not the wench I wished t'have had.
Idly I lay with her, as if I loved not,
And like a burden grieved the bed that moved not.
Though both of us performed our true intent,
Yet could I not cast anchor where I meant.
She on my neck her ivory arms did throw,
Her arms far whiter than the Scythian snow,
And eagerly she kissed me with her tongue,
And under mine her wanton thigh she flung.
Yes, and she soothed me up, and called me 'Sir',
And used all speech that might provoke and stir.
Yet like as if cold hemlock I had drunk,
It mockéd me, hung down the head, and sunk.
Like a dull cipher or rude block I lay,
Or shade or body was I, who can say?
What will my age do, age I cannot shun,
When in my prime my force is spent and done?
I blush, that being youthful, hot and lusty,
I prove neither youth nor man, but old and rusty.
Pure rose she, like a nun to sacrifice,
Or one that with her tender brother lies.
Yet boarded I the golden Chie twice,
And Libas, and the white cheeked Pitho thrice.
Corinna craved it in a summer's night
And nine sweet bouts we had before daylight.
What, waste my limbs through some Thessalian
   charms?
May spells and drugs do silly souls such harms?
With virgin wax hath some imbased my joints,
And pierced my liver with sharp needles' points?
Charms change corn to grass and make it die;
By charms are running springs and fountains dry.
By charms masts drop from oaks, from vines grapes
   fall,

And fruit from trees when there's no wind at all.
Why might not then my sinews be enchanted,
And I grow faint as with some spirit haunted?
To this add shame: shame to perform it quailed me,
And was the second cause why vigour failed me.
My idle thoughts delighted her no more
Than did the robe or garment that she wore.
Yet might her touch make youthful Pylius fire,
And Tithon livelier than his years require.
Even her I had and she had me in vain,
What might I crave more, if I ask again?
I think the great gods grieved they had bestowed
The benefit which lewdly I forslowed.
I wished to be received in, in I get me;
To kiss, to kiss; to lie with her she let me.
Why was I blest? why made king to refuse it?
Chuff-like had I not gold and could not use it?
So in a spring thrives he that told so much,
And looks upon the fruits he cannot touch.
Hath any rose so from a fresh young maid,
As she might straight have gone to church and prayed?
Well, I believe she kissed not as she should,
Nor used the sleight and cunning which she could.
Huge oaks, hard adamants might she have moved,
And with sweet words cause deaf rocks to have loved.
Worthy she was to move both gods and men,
But neither was I man nor livéd then.
Can deaf ear take delight when Phaemius sings,
Or Thamyris in curious painted things?
What sweet thought is there but I had the same?
And one gave place still as another came.
Yet notwithstanding, like one dead it lay,
Drooping more than a rose pulled yesterday.
Now, when he should not jet, he bolts upright,
And craves his task, and seeks to be at fight.
Lie down with shame, and see thou stir no more,
Seeing thou wouldst deceive me as before.

Thou cozeneth me: by thee surprised am I,
And bide sore loss with endless infamy.
Nay more, the wench did not disdain a whit
To take it in her hand and play with it,
But when she saw it would by no means stand,
But still drooped down, regarding not her hand,
'Why mock'st thou me,' she cried, 'or being ill,
Who bade thee lie down here against thy will?
Either th'art witched with blood of frogs new dead,
Or jaded cam'st thou from some other's bed.'
With that, her gown loose on, from me she cast her;
In skipping out her naked feet much graced her.
And lest her maid should know of this disgrace,
To cover it, spilt water on the place.

(tr Christopher Marlowe)

To His Mistress

Your husband will be with us at the treat;
May that be the last supper he shall eat.
And am poor I, a guest invited there,
Only to see, while he may touch, the fair?
To see you kiss and hug your nauseous lord
While his lewd hand descends below the board?
Now wonder not that Hippodamia's charms,
At such a sight, the centaurs urged to arms –
That in a rage they threw their cups aside,
Assailed the bridegroom, and would force the bride.
I am not half a horse (I would I were),
Yet hardly can from you my hands forbear.
Take then my counsel, which observed may be
Of some importance both to you and me.
Be sure to come before your man be there.
There's nothing can be done: but come, howe'er.
Sit next him (that belongs to decency),

But tread upon my foot in passing by.
Read in my looks what silently they speak,
And slyly with your eyes your answer make.
My lifted eyebrow shall declare my pain,
My right hand to his fellow shall complain,
And on the back a letter shall design,
Besides a note that shall be writ in wine.
Whene'er you think upon our last embrace,
With your forefinger gently touch your face.
If you are pleased with what I do or say,
Handle your rings, or with your fingers play.
As suppliants use at altars, hold the board
Whene'er you wish the Devil may take your lord.
When he fills for you, never touch the cup,
But bid th'officious cuckold drink it up.
The waiter on those services employ.
Drink you, and I will snatch it from the boy,
Watching the part where your sweet mouth has been,
And thence with eager lips will suck it in.
If he, with clownish manners, thinks it fit
To taste, and offer you the nasty bit,
Reject his greasy kindness, and restore
Th'unsavory morsel he had chewed before.
Nor let his arms embrace your neck, nor rest
Your tender cheek upon his hairy breast.
Let not his hand within your bosom stray
And rudely with your pretty bubbies play.
But above all, let him no kiss receive:
That's an offence I never can forgive.
Do not, O do not that sweet mouth resign,
Lest I rise up in arms and cry ' 'Tis mine.'
I shall thrust in betwixt, and void of fear
The manifest adulterer will appear.
These things are plain to sight; but more I doubt
What you conceal beneath your petticoat.
Take not his leg between your tender thighs,
Nor with your hand provoke my foe to rise.

(How oft have I been forced the robe to lift
In company, to make a homely shift
For a bare bout, ill huddled o'er in haste,
While o'er my side the fair her mantle cast).
You to your husband shall not be so kind;
But lest you should, your mantle leave behind.
Encourage him to tope, but kiss him not,
Nor mix one drop of water in his pot.
If he be fuddled well, and snores apace,
Then we may take advice from time and place.
When all depart, when compliments are loud,
Be sure to mix among the thickest crowd.
There I will be, and there we cannot miss.
Alas, what length of labour I employ
Just to secure a short and transient joy! –
For night must part us, and when night is come
Tucked underneath his arm he leads you home.
He locks you in. I follow to the door,
His fortune envy, and my own deplore.
He kisses you – he more than kisses, too –
Th' outrageous cuckold thinks it all his due.
But add not to his joy by your consent,
And let it not be given, but only lent.
Return no kiss, nor move in any sort;
Make it a dull and a malignant sport.
Had I my wish, he should no pleasure take,
But slubber o'er your business for my sake –
And whate'er fortune shall this night befall,
Coax me tomorrow, by foreswearing all.

(tr John Dryden)

[59]

ANTIPATER OF THESSALONIKA
(c 40 BC–c AD 30?)

Euagoras

Phoebus was a herdsman,
    Poseidon was a horse,
Ammon was the famous snake,
    and Zeus a swan of course,
all of them after girls, or boys,
    and trying to keep it quiet,
not bedding by persuasion but
    rape without a riot.
But Euagoras is made of brass;
    he doesn't need disguises:
he does them with no change of shape,
    both sexes and all sizes.

(tr Alistair Elliott)

RUFINUS
(2–50 AD)

Generosity

a silvertoed virgin
    was washing her body
    drenching the golden
apples of her breasts
    their flesh like yogurt
the plump cheeks of her bum
    tossed against one another
as she swung about
    flesh as lithe as water
a hand spread down

                    to cover
                much swollen
            the fairflowing conduit
        not the whole thing but
            as much as she could

(tr Alan Marshfield)

MARCUS VALERIUS MARTIALIS
(c AD 40–c 104)

Epigram

Either get out of the house or conform to my tastes, woman.
I'm no strait-laced Roman.
I like prolonging the nights agreeably with wine: you, after one
                                          glass of water,
Rise and retire with an air of hauteur.
You prefer darkness: I enjoy love-making
With a witness – a lamp shining or the dawn breaking.
You wear bed-jackets, tunics, thick woollen stuff,
Whereas I think no woman on her back can ever be naked enough.
I love girls who kiss like doves and hang round my neck:
You give me the sort of peck
Due to your grandmother as a morning salute.
In bed, you're motionless, mute –
Not a wriggle,
Not a giggle –
As solemn as a priestess at a shrine
Proffering incense and pure wine.
Yet every time Andromache went for a ride
In Hector's room, the household slaves used to masturbate
                                          outside;
Even modest Penelope, when Ulysses snored,
Kept her hand on the sceptre of her lord.
You refuse to be buggered; but it's a known fact

That Gracchus', Pompey's and Brutus' wives were willing
                                        partners in the act,
And that before Ganymede mixed Jupiter his tasty bowl
Juno filled the dear boy's role.
If you want to be uptight – all right,
By all means play Lucretia by day. But I need a Lais at night.

(tr James Michie)

Epigrams

I – LVIII

'A thousand for the boy', the dealer said,
And Phoebus paid, and took him off to bed.
My poor cock droops, rebukes me for the shame:
Phoebus is praised, while I must take the blame.
I tell it, Phoebus' cock earned him a pile –
Earn me as much, and then I'll match his style.

III – LI

When I admire your body, all you say
Is 'You shall see me naked, one fine day.'
Yet when I ask you if you'll bath with me,
You dig up some excuse continually.
Surely it can't be, Galla, that you fear
My body's not as handsome as you hear?

III – LXXI

Poor Naevolus, you're uncomfy in your chair,
Shifting and fidgeting, wincing and then sighing.
You seem as sore as that boy over there.
Now, Naevolus, just what have you been trying?

III – LXXII

You want me, Saufeia, but you won't undress.
Is there some blemish that you won't confess?

Breasts like old bellows, stretchmarks in your skin?
Bones that stick out, or hollows that cave in?
I can't believe it: nude, you'd be divine.
But if that's so, you shoot a stupid line.

DECIMUS JUNIUS JUVENALIS
(AD 60–c 140)

The Vices of Women

You ask from whence proceed these monstrous crimes.
Once poor, and therefore chaste in former times
Our matrons were; no luxury found room
In low-roofed houses and bare walls of loam;
Their hands with labour hardened while 'twas light,
And frugal sleep supplied the quiet night.
While pinched with want, their hunger held 'em straight
When Hannibal was hovering at the gate.
But wanton now and lolling at our ease
We suffer all th'inveterate ills of peace
And wasteful riot, whose destructive charms
Revenge the vanquished world of our victorious arms.
No crime, no lustful postures are unknown
Since poverty, our guardian-god, is gone.
Pride, laziness and all luxurious arts
Pour like a deluge in from foreign parts
Since gold obscene and silver found the way
Strange fashions with strange bullion to convey
And our plain simple manners to betray.
What care our drunken dames to whom they spread?
(Wine no distinction makes of tail or head)
Who lewdly dancing at a midnight ball
For hot eringoes[1] and fat oysters call

[1] *eringoes* candied roots of sea holly, believed to be aphrodisiac

[63]

Full brimmers[1] to their fuddled noses thrust,
Brimmers the last provocatives of lust,
When vapours to their swimming brains advance
And double tapers on the tables dance.

    Now think what bawdy dialogues they have,
What Tullis talks to her confiding slave
At Modesty's old statue, when by night
They make a stand, and from their litters light;
The good man early to the levée goes
And treads the nasty puddle of his spouse.

    The Secrets of the goddess named the Good
Are even by boys and barbers understood,
Where the rank matrons dancing to the pipe
Gig with their bums and are for action ripe;
With music raised, they spread abroad their hair
And toss their heads like an enamoured mare.
Laufella lays her garland by, and proves
The mimick lechery of manly loves.
Ranked with the lady, the cheap sinner lies,
For here not blood but virtue gives the prize.
Nothing is feigned in this venereal strife –
'Tis downright lust, and acted to the life,
So full, so fierce, so vigorous and so strong
That, looking on would make old Nestor young.
Impatient of delay, a general sound,
An universal groan of lust goes round,
For then, and only then, the sex sincere is found.
'Now is the time of action; now begin,'
They cry, 'and let the lusty lovers in.
The whoresons are asleep – then bring the slaves
And watermen, a race of strong-backed knaves.'

(from the Sixth Satire)
(tr John Dryden)

[1]*brimmers* overflowing glasses

[64]

SKYTHINOS
(c AD 125?)

Retrospective

While she was here you hung limp
As a flag on a windless day.
Now you stand to attention, even weeping
In anticipation. Well don't ask *me* for a hand.

STRATO
(fl AD 125)

Graphicus

The sauna bench gave Graphicus' bum a pinch.
Even a bench has its fancies – and I'm a man!

Against Cleanliness

Fauntleroy curls faultlessly arranged by some Vidal
    Sassoon, more beautiful
Than nature intended, mean nothing to me.
I like my boy's body pink from jogging
In the Park, just a little grubby, and the skin
Shiny from a quick rub-down with oil.
No art, no pretence; certainly none of that
High romantic twaddle some men admire.

To Kyris

Why lean that ravishing backside
Against a wall? – The stone
Can do nothing, so why tempt it?

The Fatherly Eye

Giving a lesson to
A downy boy
The trainer took his chance.
He sat him on his knee,
And when his father turned up
The boy was impaled, and the trainer's hands
Were busily fumbling his balls.
The man tipped him off
And got him in a quick half-nelson.
But Dad was a grapple fan,
And just said: 'Watch it,
Or they'll come off in your hand.'

PAULUS
(c AD 560)

Making Love

Off with that wrap;
   lock naked thigh
with thigh;
   the lightest lawn
is like the walls of Babylon
   when we lie together.
Feel skin on skin
   and lip on lip
feel . . . but less talking:
   one thing I hate
is a still tongue.

ANON
(4th Century BC)

The Song of Songs

The Song of the Shulamite

My beloved is white and ruddy,
The chiefest among ten thousand.
His head is as the most fine gold,
His locks are bushy, and black as a raven.
His eyes are like doves beside the water brooks;
Washed with milk, and fitly set.
His cheeks are as a bed of spices, as banks of sweet herbs.

His lips are as lilies, dropping liquid myrrh.
His hands are as rings of gold set with beryl:
His body is as ivory work overlaid with sapphires.
His legs are as pillars of marble, set upon sockets of fine
    gold:
His aspect is like Lebanon, excellent as the cedars.
His mouth is most sweet: yea, he is altogether lovely.
This is my beloved, and this is my friend,
O daughters of Jerusalem.

The Song of King Solomon

How beautiful are thy feet in sandals, O prince's daughter!
The joints of thy thighs are like jewels,
The work of the hands of a cunning workman.
Thy navel is like a round goblet,
Wherein no mingled wine is wanting:
Thy belly is like a heap of wheat
Set about with lilies.

[67]

Thy two breasts are like two fawns
That are twins of a roe.
Thy neck is like the tower of ivory;
Thine eyes as the pools in Heshbon, by the gate of Bath-rabbim;
Thy nose is like the tower of Lebanon
Which looketh towards Damascus.

Thine head upon thee is like Carmel,
And the hair of thine head like purple;
The king is held captive in the tresses thereof.
How fair and how pleasant art thou,
O love, for delights!
This thy stature is like to a palm tree,
And thy breasts to clusters of grapes.

I said, 'I will climb up into the palm tree,
I will take hold of the branches thereof'.
Let thy breasts be as clusters of the vine,
And the smell of thy breath like apples;
And thy mouth like the best wine,
That goeth down smoothly for my beloved,
Gliding through the lips of those that are asleep.

ANON
(9th Century)

Surprise, Surprise

Nizam the pederast, whose delight in boys
Was known throughout Bagdad, one afternoon
In a secluded place saw in a clearing
The flash of limbs behind a nearby bush,
And looking closer came upon a youth
Who seemed more lovely than his dreams had promised,
Lying asleep in shade, his head pressed deep

[68]

Into crossed arms, his long slim body
Quite naked, the firm buttocks firmly offered.
Quick as a jackal pouncing, Nizam jumped
Upon the lad, his robe about his waist,
The startled boy pierced by his lusty cock
Before you could say knife. Not until later,
When boy lay panting on the flattened grass,
Did Nizam, pausing to embrace his love,
Discover him a her, surprised but pleased
At being given such pleasure at a source
No previous lover seemed to know about.

Nizam converted? Never. But the girl
Now gives her lovers strange instruction.

(Arabian: school of Ibn al-Mu'taz)

SIR THOMAS WYATT
(1503–1542)

The Forsaken Lover

They flee from me that sometime did me seek
With naked foot stalking in my chamber.
I have seen them gentle, tame and meek
That now are wild, and do not remember
That sometime they put themself in danger
To take bread[1] at my hand; and now they range,
Busily seeking with a continual change.

Thanked be fortune, it hath been otherwise
Twenty times better, but once in special:
In thin array after a pleasant guise
When her loose gown from her shoulders did fall

[1] *to take bread* receive sexual pleasure

And she me caught in her arms long and small[1]
Therewithal sweetly did me kiss,
And softly said, 'Dear heart, how like you this?'

It was no dream. I lay broad waking.
But all is turned through my gentleness
Into a strange fashion of forsaking,
And I have leave to go, of her goodness,
And she also to use newfangleness.
But since that I so kindly am served,
I would fain know what she hath deserved.

Desire

The furious gun in his raging ire,
When that the bowl[2] is rammed in too sore
And that the flame cannot part from the fire,
Cracketh in sunder, and in the air doth roar
The shivered pieces. Right so doth my desire,
Whose flame increaseth from more to more,
Which to let out I dare not look nor speak:
So now hard force my heart doth all to-break.[3]

BATTISTA GUARINI
(1538–1612)

The Shepherd Thirsis

The shepherd Thirsis longed to die,[4]
Gazing on the gracious eye
Of her whom he adored and loved,

[1]*small* slim [2]*bowl* ball [3]*to-break* break in pieces [4]*dying* Throughout the fifteenth and
sixteenth centuries death was a synonym for orgasm; this then is one of the earliest
poems about simultaneous orgasm.

When she whom no less passion moved
Thus said: 'O die not yet, I pray.
I'll die with thee if thou wilt stay.'
The shepherd then a while delays
The haste he had to end his days,
And while thus languishing he lies
Sucking sweet nectar from her eyes,
The lovely shepherdess, who found
The harvest of his love at hand,
With trembling eyes straight fell a-crying,
'Die, sweetheart, die, for I am dying.'
The shepherd then did straight reply,
'Behold, sweetheart, with thee I die.'
Thus did those lovers spend their breath
In such a sweet and deathless death
That they to life revived again,
Again to try death's pleasant pain.

(tr Sir Robert Aytoun)

EDMUND SPENSER
(1552–1599)

from *Amoretti*

Sonnet XXX

My love is like to ice, and I to fire;
How comes it then that this her cold so great
Is not dissolved through my so hot desire,
But harder grows the more I her entreat?
Or how comes it that my exceeding heat
Is not delayed by her heart frozen cold:
But that I burn much more in boiling sweat,
And feel my flames augmented manifold?
What more miraculous thing may be told

That fire which all thing melts, should harden ice?
And ice which is congealed with senseless cold
Should kindle fire by wonderful device?
Such is the power of love in gentle mind
That it can alter all the course of kind.

Sonnet LXIV

Coming to kiss her lips such grace I found
Me seemed I smelt a garden of sweet flowers:
That dainty odours from them threw around
For damsels fit to deck their lovers' bowers.
Her lips did smell like unto gillyflowers,
Her ruddy cheeks like unto roses red,
Her snowy brows like budded bellamours,
Her lovely eyes like pinks but newly spread,
Her goodly bosom like a strawberry bed,
Her neck like to a bunch of columbines,
Her breast like lilies, ere their leaves be shed,
Her nipples like young blossomed jessemines.
Such fragrant flowers do give most odorous smell,
But her sweet odour did them all excell.

FULKE GREVILLE
(1554–1628)

Sonnet L

Scoggin's[1] wife by chance mistook her bed;
Such chances oft befall poor womankind.
Alas, poor souls, for when they miss[2] their head,
What marvel it is, though the rest[3] be blind?

[1]*Scoggin* Fool to Edward IV [2]*miss* lose [3]*rest* of their bodies

This bed it was a lord's bed where she light,
Who nobly pitying this poor woman's hap¹
Gave alms both to relieve and to delight,
And made the golden shower² fall on her lap.

Then in a freedom asks her as they lay
Whose were her lips and breasts; and she sware, his
(For hearts are open when thoughts fall to play).
At last he asks her whose her backside is?
   She vowed that it was Scoggin's only part,
   Who never yet came nearer to her heart.

Scoggin o'erheard, but taught by common use
That he who sees all those which do him harm
Or will in marriage boast such small abuse
Shall never have his night-gown furred warm,
   And was content, since all was done in play,
   To know his luck, and bear his arms away.

Yet when his wife should to the market go
Her breast and belly he in canvas dressed,
And on her backside fine silk did bestow,
Joying to see it braver than the rest.

His neighbours asked him why? And Scoggin swore
That part of all his wife was only his.
The lord should deck the rest, to whom they are,
For he knew not what lordly-fashion is.
   If husbands now should only deck their own,
   Silk would make many by their backs be known.

Sonnet LVI

All my senses, like beacon's flame,
Gave alarm to desire
To take arms in Cynthia's name,

¹*hap* accident ²*golden shower* the way in which Jove came disguised to Danae

[73]

And set all my thoughts on fire.
Fury's wit persuaded me
Happy love was hazard's heir,
Cupid did best shoot and see
In the night, where smooth is fair.
Up I start, believing well,
To see if Cynthia is awake:
Wonders I saw, who can tell?
And thus unto myself I spake:
'Sweet god Cupid, where am I
That by pale Diana's light
Such rich beauties do espie
As harm our senses with delight?
Am I borne up to the skies?
See where Jove and Venus shine,
Showing in her heavenly eyes
That desire is divine.
Look where lies the Milky Way,
Way unto that dainty throne
Where while all the gods would play
Vulcan thinks to dwell alone.'
I gave rein to this conceit:
Hope went on the wheels of lust
(Fancy's scales are false of weight,
Thoughts take thought that go of trust).
I stepped forth to touch the sky –
I a god, by Cupid's dreams.
Cynthia, who did naked lie,
Runs away like silver streams,
Leaving hollow banks behind
Who can neither forward move
Nor if rivers be unkind
Turn away, or leave to love.
There stand I like Arctic pole
Where Sol[1] passeth o'er the line,
Mourning my benighted soul,

Which so loseth light divine.
There stand I like men that preach
From the execution place,
At their death content to teach
All the world with their disgrace.
He that lets his Cynthia lie
Naked on a bed of play
To say prayers e'er she die[1]
Teacheth time to run away.
Let no love-desiring heart
In the stars go seek his fate –
Love is only nature's art,
Wonder hinders love and hate.
   None can well behold with eyes
   But what underneath him lies

SIR ARTHUR GORGES
(1557–1625)

Carnation, White and Watchet

I saw of late a lady wear a shoe
That was as white as any driven snow;
Her soft silk hose was of carnation hue,
And this she wore because the world should know
She did desire a virgin's steps to tread.
This with those colours she her fancy fed.

The garter which did strain her tender knee
By special grace mine eyes did likewise view.
But more than that (O grief!) I might not see,
Whereof the colour was a watchet blue.
And labour lost, that garter's meaning was
To such as sought above the same to pass.

[1]*e'er she die* before the sexual climax

Yet some perhaps will deem this but a jest,
And say withal she never meant so much;
But you yourself, fair mistress, know it best
That in two colours I the truth did touch.
But if your watchet garter meant not so,
That fault I'll mend, if I the proof may know.

Ripe and Unripe

The unripe fruits of wanton youth's desire
   So different are to use from that they seem,
As when we do unto their height aspire
   Then most we loath that we most dear did dream,
To find ourselves so blinded in conceit
   Instead of food to fawn on flattering bait.

To hunters' sports these joys compared may be,
   Who with delight so long in chase do run
As they their game before their face do fly
   But lose their sport when they their prey have run.
Then reason would that we should toys neglect
   As are but shows and nothing in effect

Whose small above doth yield no more content
   Than licquorish meats, that do the palate please,
Whose pleasure fades when as their taste is spent
   And only serve to nourish one disease;
Whose count well made, lo, grief is all the gain,
   Where fading joys are bought with lasting pain.

Yet well I wote[1] that when these lines of mine
   Shall come before my mistress' carping eyes
She will me taunt, and say the fox is fine
   That loves no grapes because they hang too high,
And seem to make that dainty to be found
   Which all men see grow rife upon the ground.

[1]*wote* know

Full little knows my dear and sweetest friend
  What weary nights my restless fancy tries
When all men else to give their cares an end
  With slumbering hearts close up their waking eyes.
How oft have I laid in my quiet bed
  To think on her forborn my nightly ease,
And to myself how often have I said
  With deep-fot[1] sighs such trembling words as these:
'Ye stately limbs whom my desires pursue,
  Whereso ye lodge, receive your happy rest,
And for his sake that vows himself to you,
  Harbour one thought of me within that breast.'
Speaking such words sometimes asleep I fall,
And in sweet dreams embrace those limbs withal.

GEORGE CHAPMAN
(1559?–1634)

from *Ovid's Banquet of Sense*

In a loose robe of tinsel forth she came,
Nothing but it betwixt her nakedness
And envious light. The downward-burning flame
Of her rich hair did threaten new access
  Of venturous Phaeton to scorch the fields.
And thus to bathing came our poet's goddess,
  Her handmaids bearing all things pleasure yields
To such a service – odours most delighted
And purest linen which her looks had whited.

Then cast she off her robe, and stood upright,
As lightning breaks out of a labouring cloud,
Or as the morning heaven casts off the night,

[1] *fot* fetched

[77]

Or as that heaven cast off itself, and showed
  Heaven's upper light, to which the brightest day
Is but a black and melancholy shroud;
  Or as when Venus strived for sovereign sway
Of charmful beauty in young Troy's desire,
So stood Corinna vanishing her tire.[1]

And now she used the fount, where Niobe,
Tombed in herself, poured her lost soul in tears
Upon the bosom of this Roman Phoebe;
  Who, bathed and odoured, her bright limbs she rears
    And drying her on that disparent ground
Her lute she takes t'enamour heavenly ears
    And try if with her voice's vital sound
She could warm life through those cold states spread,
And cheer the dame that wept when she was dead.

So Ovid with his strong affections striving,
Masked in a friendly thicket near her bower,
Rubbing his temples, fainting and reviving,
Fitting his garments, praying to the hour,
Backwards and forwards went and durst not venture
To tempt the tempest of his mistress' lowre[2]
  Or let his eyes her beauties' ocean enter,
At last with prayer he pierceth Juno's ear:
'Great goddess of audacity and fear . . .

'Great goddess of audacity and fear,
Queen of Olympus, Saturn's eldest seed,
That dost the sceptre over Samos bear
And rulest all nuptial rites, with power and meed,[3]
  Since thou in nature art the means to mix
Still sulphure[4] humours, and canst therefore speed
  Such as in Cyprian sports their pleasures fix,
Venus herself, and Mars by thee embracing
Assist my hopes, me and my purpose gracing.'

[1]*tire* attire [2]*lowre* frown [3]*meed* excellence [4]*sulphure* sulphurous

This said, he charged the arbour with his eye,
Which pierced it through, and at her breasts reflected,
Striking him to the heart with ecstasy
As do the sunbeams 'gainst the earth prorected[1]
　　With their reverberate vigour mount in flames
And burn much more than where they were directed.
　　He saw th'extraction of all fairest dames –
The fair of beauty, as whole countries come
And show their riches in a little room.

Here Ovid sold his freedom for a look –
And with that look was ten times more enthralled.
He blushed, looked pale, and like a fever shook,
And as a burning vapour[2] being exhaled
　　(Promised by Phoebus' eye to be a star)
Heaven's walls denying to be further scald
　　The force dissolves that drew it up so far
And then it lightens gainst his death and falls,
So Ovid's power this powerful sight appals.

Now as she lay attired in nakedness
His eye did carve him on that feast of feasts:
Sweet fields of life[3] which death's foot dare not press
Flowered with th'unbroken waves of my love's breasts,
　　Unbroke by depth of those her beauty's floods;
See where with bent[4] of gold curled into nests
　　In her head's grove the spring-bird Lameate broods:
Her body doth present those fields of peace
Where souls are feasted with the soul of ease.

To prove which paradise that nurseth these,
See, see the golden rivers that renown[5] it:
Rich Gehon, Tigris, Phison, Euphrates,
Two from her bright Pelopian[6] shoulders crown it,

[1]*prorected* reflected　[2]*And as a burning vapour* . . . the comparison is with a comet
[3]*Sweet fields of life* . . . Corinna's body is compared to the fields of paradise　[4]*bent*
reeds　[5]*renown* make it famous　[6]*Pelopian* ivory

And two out of her snowy hills do glide
That with a deluge of delights do drown it;
The highest two their precious streams divide
To ten pure floods[1] that do the body duty
Bounding themselves in length, but not in beauty.

Herewith she rose like the autumnal star
Fresh burnished in the lofty ocean flood
That darts his glorious influence more far
Than any lamp of bright Olympus' brood.
    She lifts her lightning arms above her head
And stretcheth a meridian from her blood
    That slept awake in her Elysian bed;
Then knit she up, lest loose, her glowing hair
Should scorch the centre and incense the air.

With this, as she was looking in her glass
She saw therein a man's face looking on her:
Whereat she started from the frighted grass
As if some monstrous serpent had been shown her –
    Rising as when (the sun in Leo's sign)
Auriga[2] with the heavenly goat[3] upon her
    Shows her horned forehead with her kids divine
Whose rise kills vines, heaven's face with storms disguising;
No man is safe at sea, the Haedy[4] rising.

So straight wrapped she her body in a cloud,
And threatened tempests for her high disgrace;
Shame from a bower of roses did unshroud
And spread her crimson wings upon her face.
    When running out, poor Ovid humbly kneeling
Full in the arbour's mouth, did stay her race
    And said: 'Fair nymph, great goddess, have some feeling
Of Ovid's pains; but hear, and your dishonour
Vainly surmised shall vanish with my horror.'

[1]*ten pure floods* the fingers [2]*Auriga* the constellation of the Wagonner [3]*the heavenly goat* Capella [4]*Haedy* a small double star in the Wagonner

[80]

'Traitor to ladies' modesty' (said she)
'What savage boldness hardened thee to this?
Or what base reckoning of my modesty?
What should I think thy fact's proud reason is?'
    'Love, sacred Madam, love exhaling me,
Wrapped in his sulphur, to this cloud of his
    Made my affections his artillery,
Shot me at you, his proper citadel;
And losing all my forces, here I fell.'

[*Corinna allows Ovid a single kiss*]

Her moving towards him made Ovid's eye
Believe the firmament was coming down
To take him quick to immortality,
And that th'Ambrosian kiss set on the crown.
    She spake, in kissing, and her breath infused
Restoring syrup to his taste, in swoon,
    And he imagined Hebe's hands had bruised
A banquet of the gods into his sense,
Which filled him with this furious influence.

'The motion of the heavens that did beget
The golden age, and by whose harmony
Heaven is preserved, in me at work is set:
All instruments of deepest melody,
    Set sweet in my desires to my love's liking,
With this sweet kiss in me their tunes apply
    As if the best musicians' hands were striking.
This kiss in me hath endless music closed,
Like Phoebus' lute on Ninus' towers imposed.

'And as a pebble cast into a spring
We see a sort of trembling circles rise,
One forming other in their issuing
Till over all the fount they circulise,
    So this perpetual-motion-making kiss

[81]

Is propagate through all my faculties,
    And makes my breast an endless fount of bliss
Of which if gods could drink their matchless fare
Would make them much more blessed than they are.

'But as when sounds do hollow bodies beat
Air gathered there, compressed and thickened
The selfsame way she came doth make retreat
And so effects the sound re-echoed
    Only in part, because she weaker is
In that redition[1] than when first she fled,
    So I, alas, faint echo of this kiss
Only reiterate a slender part
Of that high joy it worketh in my heart.

'And thus with feasting, love is famished more.
Without my touch are all things turned to gold,
And till I touch, I cannot joy my store.
To purchase others, I myself have sold.
    Love is a wanton famine, rich in food,
But with a richer appetite controlled,
    An argument in figure and in mood,
Yet hates all arguments, disputing still
For sense gainst reason, with a senseless will.

'Then, sacred madam, since my other senses
Have in your graces tasted such content,
Let wealth not to be spent fear no expenses,
But give thy bounty true eternizement[2]
    Making my senses ground-work, which is feeling,
Effect the other, endless excellent,
    Their substance with flint-softening softness stealing,
Then let me feel, for know sweet beauty's queen
Dames may be felt, as well as heard or seen.'

---

[1]*redition* repetition [2]*eternizement* immortal fame

Herewith, even glad his arguments to hear,
Worthily willing to have lawful grounds
To make the wondrous power of heaven appear
In nothing more than her perfections found
   Close to her navel she her mantle wrests
Slacking it upwards, and the folds unwound,
    Showing Latona's twins, her plenteous breasts
The sun and Cynthia in their triumph-robes
Of lady-skin, more rich than both their globes

Whereto she bade blest Ovid put his hand.
He, well acknowledging it much too base
For such an action, did a little stand,
Ennobling it with titles full of grace,
   And conjures it with charge of reverend verse
To use with piety that sacred place,
   And through his feeling's organ to disperse
Worth to his spirits, amply to supply
The poorness of his flesh's faculty.

And thus he said: 'King of the king of senses,
Engines of all the engines under heaven,
To health and life defence of all defences,
Bounty by which our nourishment is given,
   Beauty's beautifier, kind acquaintance-maker,
Proportion's oddness that makes all things even,
   Wealth of the labourer, wrong's revengement-taker,
Pattern of concord, lord of exercise
And figure of that power the world did guise–[1]

'Dear hand, most duly honoured in this,
And therefore worthy to be well employed:
Yet know, that all that honour nothing is
Compared with that which now must be enjoyed.
   So think in all the pleasures these have shown

[1]*guise* make

[83]

(Likened to this) thou wert but mere annoyed,
   That all hands' merits in thyself alone
With this one touch have more than recompence,
And therefore feel, with fear and reverence.

'See Cupid's alps which now thou must go over,
Where snow that thaws the sun doth ever lie,
Where thou mayst plain and feelingly discover
The world's fore-past, that flowed with milk and honey;
   Where (like an empress seeing nothing wanting
That may her glorious childbed beautify)
   Pleasure herself lies big with issue panting –
Ever delivered, yet with child still growing;
Full of all blessings, yet all bliss bestowing.'

This said, he laid his hand upon her side,
Which made her start like sparkles from a fire
Or like Saturnia from th'Ambrosian pride
Of her morn's slumber, frighted with admire
   When Jove laid young Alcydes to her breast.
So startled she, not with a coy retire,
   But with the tender temper she was blessed,
Proving her sharp, undulled with handling yet,
Which keener edge on Ovid's longings set.

(Stanzas 7, 8, 11, 46, 47, 50, 58, 59, 69, 74–76, 97–102, 105–110)

from *The Amorous Zodiac*

Now past my month t'admire for built most pure
This marble pillar and her lineature,
   I come t'inhabit thy most gracious teats,
Teats that feed love upon the white riphees[1],
Teats where he hangs his glory and his trophies
   When victor from the gods' war he retreats.

[1]*riphees* a word coined from the Riphean mountains

Hid in the vale twixt those two hills confined,
This vale, the nest of loves and joys divined,
   Shall I enjoy mine ease, and fair be passed
Beneath those parching alps; and this sweet cold
Is first, this month, heaven doth to us unfold;
   But there shall I still grieve to be displaced.

To sort from this most brave and pompous sign
(Leaving a little my ecliptic line,
   Less superstitious than the other sun)
The rest of my autumnal race I'll end
To see thy hand (whence I the crown attend)
   Since in thy past parts I have slightly run.

Thy hand, a lily gendered[1] of a rose,
That makes the morning, hid in night's repose;
   And from Apollo's bed the vail doth twine
That each where doth th'Idalian minion guide,
That bends his bow, that ties and leaves untied
   The silver ribbons of his little ensign . . .

In fine (still drawing to th'antarctic pole)
The Tropic sign I'll run at for my goal,
   Which I can scarce express with chastity –
I know in heaven 'tis called Capricorn,
And with the sudden thought, my case takes horn.
   So, heaven-like, Capricorn the name shall be.

This (wondrous fit) the wintry solstice ceaseth,
Where darkness greater grows and day decreaseth;
   Where rather I would be in night than day.
But when I see my journeys do increase,
I'll straight dispatch me thence, and go in peace
   To my next house, where I may safer stay.

[1]*gendered* engendered

This house along thy naked thighs is found.
Naked of spot, made fleshy, firm and round,
  To entertain love's friends with feeling sport.
These, Cupid's secret mysteries unfurl,
And pillars are that Venus' fane[1] uphold,
  Of her dear joys the glory and support.

Sliding on thy smooth thighs to this month's end,
To thy well-fashioned calves I will descend,
  That soon the last house I may apprehend:
Thy slender feet – fine, slender feet that shame
Thetis' sheen[2] feet, which poets so much fame.
  And here my latest season I will end.

(Stanzas 21–28)

SIR JOHN HARINGTON
(1561–1612)

Against an Old Lecher

Since thy third curing of the French infection,
Priapus hath in thee found no erection,
Yet eat'st thou ringoes,[3] and potato roots,
And caviar, but it little boots.[4]
Besides the bed's head a bottle's lately found
Of liquor that a quart cost twenty pound:
For shame, if not more grace, yet shew more wit,
Surcease, now sin leaves thee, to follow it.
Some smile, I sigh, to see thy madness such
That that which stands not, stands thee in[5] so much.

---

[1]*fane* temple [2]*sheen* shining [3]*ringoes* eringoes [4]*it little boots* it has no effect [5]*stands thee in* costs

MICHAEL DRAYTON
(1563–1631)

To His Coy Love

I pray thee leave. Love me no more,
    Call home the heart you gave me.
I but in vain that saint adore
    That can, but will not, save me.
These poor half-kisses kill me quite:
    Was ever man thus served?
Amidst an ocean of delight
    For pleasure to be starved?

Show me no more those snowy breasts
    With azure riverets branched,
Where whilst mine eye with plenty feasts
    Yet is my thirst not stanched.
O Tantalus, thy pains n'er tell;
    By me thou art prevented;
'Tis nothing to be plagued in Hell,
    But thus in Heaven tormented.

Clip me no more in those dear arms,
    Nor thy live's comfort call me;
O, these are but too powerful charms,
    And do but more enthral me.
But see how patient I am grown
    In all this coil[1] about thee;
Come, nice thing, let thy heart alone:
I cannot live without thee.

[1] *coil* fuss

WILLIAM SHAKESPEARE
(1564–1616)

Sonnet CXXIX

The expense of spirit in a waste of shame
Is lust in action; and till action, lust
Is perjured, murderous, bloody, full of blame,
Savage, extreme, rude, cruel, not to trust;
Enjoyed no sooner but despised straight,
Past reason hunted, and no sooner had
Past reason hated, as a swallowed bait
On purpose laid to make the taker mad,
Mad in pursuit and in possession so,
Had, having, and in quest to have, extreme;
A bliss in proof, and proved, a very woe,
Before, a joy proposed, behind, a dream.
    All this the world well knows, yet none knows well
    To shun the heaven that leads men to this hell.

Sonnet CXLVII

My love is as a fever, longing still
For that which longer nurseth the disease;
Feeding on that which doth preserve the ill,
The uncertain sickly appetite to please.
My reason, the physician to my love,
Angry that his prescriptions are not kept,
Hath left me, and I desperate now approve
Desire is death, which physic did except.
Past cure am I, now reason is past care,
And frantic-mad with evermore unrest;
My thoughts and my discourse as madmen's are,
At random from the truth vainly expressed.
    For I have sworn thee fair, and thought thee bright,
    Who art as black as hell, as dark as night.

[88]

from *Venus and Adonis*

And now Adonis, with a lazy spite,
And with a heavy, dark, disliking eye,
His lowering brows o'erwhelming his fair sight
Like misty vapours when they plot the sky,
    Souring his cheeks, cries, 'Fie, no more of love!
    The sun doth burn my face – I must remove.'

'Aye, me', quoth Venus, 'young, and so unkind?
What bare excuses makest thou to be gone?
I'll sigh celestial breath, whose gentle wind
Shall cool the heat of this descending sun.
    I'll make a shadow for thee of my hairs;
    If they burn too, I'll quench them with my tears.

'The sun that shines from heaven shines but warm;
And lo, I lie between that sun and thee.
The heat I have from thence doth little harm;
Thine eye darts forth the fire that burneth me,
    And were I not immortal, life were done
    Between this heavenly and earthly sun.

'Art thou obdurate, flinty, hard as steel?
Nay, more than flint, for stone at rain relenteth.
Art thou a woman's son, and canst not feel
What 'tis to love? how want of love tormenteth?
    O, had thy mother borne so hard a mind
    She had not brought forth thee, but died unkind.

'What am I that thou shouldst condemn me thus?
Or what great danger dwells upon my suit?
What were thy lips the worse for one poor kiss?
Speak, fair, but speak fair words or else be mute.
    Give me one kiss, I'll give it thee again,
    And one for interest, if thou wilt have twain.

[89]

'Fie, lifeless picture, cold and senseless stone,
Well-painted idol, image cold and dead,
Statue contenting but the eye alone,
Thing like a man, but of no woman bred!
   Thou art no man, though of a man's complexion,
   For men will kiss even by their own direction.'

This said, impatience chokes her pleading tongue,
And swelling passion doth provoke a pause;
Red cheeks and fiery eyes blaze forth her wrong.
Being judge in love, she cannot right her cause.
   And now she weeps, and now she fain would speak,
   And now her sobs do her intendments break.

Sometimes she shakes her head, and then his hand;
Now gazeth she on him, now on the ground;
Sometimes her arms enfold him like a band –
She would, he will not, in her arms be bound.
   And when from whence he struggles to be gone
   She locks her lily fingers one in one.

'Fondling', she saith, 'since I have hemmed thee here
Within the boundary of this ivory pale,
I'll be a park, and thou shalt be my deer:
Feed where thou wilt, on mountains or in dale.
   Graze on my lips – and if those hills be dry
   Stray lower, where the pleasant fountains lie.

'Within this limit is relief enough –
Sweet bottom-grass and high delightful plain,
Round rising hillocks, brakes obscure and rough,
To shelter thee from tempest and from rain.
   Then be my deer, since I am such a park.
   No dog shall rouse thee, though a thousand bark.'

At this Adonis smiles as in disdain,
That in each cheek appears a pretty dimple.
Love made these hollows, if himself were slain,

He might be buried in a tomb so simple,
  Foreknowing well, if there he came to lie,
  Why there Love lived, and there he could not die.

These lovely caves, these round enchanting pits
Opened their mouths to swallow Venus' liking.
Being mad before, how doth she now for wits?
Struck dead at first, what needs a second striking?
  Poor queen of love, in thine own law forlorn,
  To love a cheek that smiles at thee in scorn!

Now which way shall she turn? what shall she say?
Her words are done, her woes the more increasing;
The time is spent, her object will away,
And from her twining arms doth urge releasing.
  'Pity', she cries, 'Some favour, some remorse!'
  Away he springs and hasteth to his horse.

(lines 181–258)

'Fair queen', quoth he, 'if any love you owe me,
Measure my strangeness with my unripe years.
Before I know myself, seek not to know me.
No fisher but the ungrown fry forbears.
  The mellow plum doth fall, the green sticks fast,
  Or being early plucked is sour to taste.

'Look, the world's comforter, with weary gait
His day's hot task hath ended in the west.
The owl, night's herald, shrieks; 'tis very late.
The sheep are gone to fold, birds to their nest,
  And coal-black clouds, that shadow heaven's light
  Do summon us to part and bid goodnight.

'Now let me say "Goodnight", and so say you.
If you will say so, you shall have a kiss.'
'Goodnight', quoth she; and ere he says 'Adieu'

[91]

The honey fee of parting tendered is.
　Her arms do lend his neck a sweet embrace;
　Encorporate then they seem; face grows to face;

Till breathless he disjoined, and backward drew
The heavenly moisture, that sweet coral mouth
Whose precious taste her thirsty lips well knew,
Whereon they surfeit, yet complain on drouth.
　He with her plenty pressed, she faint with dearth,
　Their lips together glued, fall to the earth.

Now quick desire hath caught the yielding prey,
And glutton-like she feeds, yet never filleth.
Her lips are conquerors, his lips obey,
Paying what ransom the insulter willeth;
　Whose vulture thought doth pitch the price so high
　That she will draw his lips' rich treasure dry.

And having felt the sweetness of the spoil,
With blindfold fury she begins to forage.
Her face doth reek and smoke, her blood doth boil,
And careless lust stirs up a desperate courage,
　Planting oblivion, beating reason back,
　Forgetting shame's pure blush and honour's wrack.

Hot, faint and weary with her hard embracing,
Like a wild bird being tamed with too much handling,
Or as the fleet-foot roe that's tired with chasing,
Or like the froward infant stilled with dandling,
　He now obeys and now no more resisteth,
　While she takes all she can, not all she listeth.

What wax so frozen but dissolves with tempering
And yields at last to every light impression?
Things out of hope are compassed oft with venturing,
Chiefly in love, whose leave exceeds commission.
　Affection faints not like a pale-faced coward,
　But then woos best when most his choice is froward.

When he did frown, O, had she then gave over,
Such nectar from his lips she had not sucked.
Foul words and frowns must not repel a lover.
What though the rose have prickles, yet 'tis plucked.
    Were beauty under twenty locks kept fast
    Yet love breaks through and picks them all at last.

For pity now she can no more detain him;
The poor fool prays her that he may depart.
She is resolved no longer to restrain him,
Bids him farewell, and look well to her heart.
    The which, by Cupid's bow she doth protest,
    He carries thence incagéd in his breast.

'Sweet boy', she says, 'this night I'll waste in sorrow,
For my sick heart commands mine eyes to watch.
Tell me, love's master, shall we meet tomorrow?
Say, shall we? shall we? wilt thou make the match?'
    He tells her, no; tomorrow he intends
    To hunt the boar with certain of his friends.

'The boar!' quoth she; whereat a sudden pale,
Like lawn being spread upon the blushing rose,
Usurps her cheek; she trembles at his tale,
And on his neck her yoking arms she throws;
    She sinketh down, still hanging by his neck,
    He on her belly falls, she on her back.

Now is she in the very lists of love,
Her champion mounted for the hot encounter.
All is imaginary she doth prove,
He will not manage her, although he mount her.
    That worse than Tantalus' is her annoy,
    To clip Elysium and to lack her joy.

Even so poor birds, deceived with painted grapes,
Do surfeit by the eye and pine the maw;
Even so she languisheth in her mishaps

As those poor birds that helpless berries saw.
  The warm effects which she in him finds missing
  She seeks to kindle with continual kissing.

But all in vain. Good Queen, it will not be!
She hath assayed as much as may be proved.
Her pleading hath deserved a greater fee:
She's Love, she loves, and yet she is not loved.
  'Fie, fie!' he says, 'You crush me; let me go!
  You have no reason to withhold me so.'

(lines 523–612)

from *The Rape of Lucrece*

Her lily hand her rosy cheek lies under,
Cozening the pillow of a lawful kiss;
Who, therefore angry, seems to part in sunder,
Swelling on either side to want his bliss;
Between whose hills her head entombed is;
  Where like a virtuous monument she lies,
  To be admired of lewd unhallowed eyes.

Without the bed her other fair hand was,
On the green coverlet, whose perfect white
Showed like an April daisy on the grass,
With pearly sweat resembling dew of night.
Her eyes, like marigolds, had sheathed their light,
  And canopied in darkness sweetly lay
  Till they might open to adorn the day.

Her hair like golden threads played with her breath –
O modest wantons, wanton modesty!
Showing life's triumph in the map of death,

And death's dim look in life's mortality.
Each in her sleep themselves so beautify
  As if between them twain there were no strife,
  But that life lived in death, and death in life.

Her breasts like ivory globes circled with blue,
A pair of maiden worlds unconquerèd,
Save of their lord no bearing yoke they knew,
And him by oath they truly honourèd.
These worlds in Tarquin new ambition bred,
  Who like a foul usurper went about
  From this fair throne to heave the owner out.

What could he see but mightily he noted?
What did he note but strongly he desired?
What he beheld, on that he firmly doted,
And in his will his willful eye he tired.
With more than admiration he admired
  Her azure veins, her alabaster skin,
  Her coral lips, her snow-white dimpled chin.

As the grim lion fawneth o'er his prey
Sharp hunger by the conquest satisfied,
So o'er this sleeping soul doth Tarquin stay,
His rage of lust by gazing qualified;
Slacked, not suppressed; for, standing by her side,
  His eye, which late this mutiny restrains,
  Unto a greater uproar tempts his veins.

And they, like straggling slaves for pillage fighting,
Obdurate vassals fell exploits effecting,
In bloody death and ravishment delighting,
Nor children's tears nor mothers' groans respecting,
Swell in their pride, the onset still expecting.
  Anon his beating heart, alarum striking,
  Gives the hot charge and bids them do their liking.

His drumming heart cheers up his burning eye,
His eye commends the leading to his hand;
His hand, as proud of such a dignity,
Smoking with pride, marched on to make his stand
On her bare breast, the heart of all her land,
    Whose ranks of blue veins, as his hand did scale,
    Left their round turrets destitute and pale.

They, mustering to the quiet cabinet
Where their dear governess and lady lies,
Do tell her she is dreadfully beset
And fright her with confusion of their cries.
She, much amazed, breaks ope her locked-up eyes,
    Who, peeping forth this tumult to behold,
    Are by his flaming torch dimmed and controlled.

Imagine her as one in dead of night
From forth dull sleep by dreadful fancy waking,
That thinks she hath beheld some ghastly sprite,
Whose grim aspect sets every joint a-shaking.
What terror 'tis! but she, in worser taking,
    From sleep disturbèd, heedfully doth view
    The sight which makes supposèd terror true.

Wrapped and confounded in a thousand fears,
Like to a new-killed bird she trembling lies.
She dares not look; yet, winking, there appears
Quick-shifting antics ugly in her eyes.
Such shadows are the weak brain's forgeries,
    Who, angry that the eyes fly from their lights,
    In darkness daunts them with more dreadful sights.

His hand, that yet remains upon her breast
(Rude ram, to batter such an ivory wall!)
May feel her heart (poor citizen) distressed,
Wounding itself to death, rise up and fall,

Beating her bulk, that his hand shakes withal.
  This moves in him more rage and lesser pity,
  To make the breach and enter this sweet city.

(lines 386–468)

CHRISTOPHER MARLOWE
(1564–1593)

from *Hero and Leander*

Leander

Amorous Leander, beautiful and young
(Whose tragedy divine Musaeus sung)
Dwelt at Abydos; since him dwelt there none
For whom succeeding times make greater moan.
His dangling tresses that were never shorn,
Had they been cut, and unto Colchos borne,
Would have allured the venturous youth of Greece
To hazard more than for the Golden Fleece.
Fair Cynthia wished his arms might be her sphere;
Grief makes her pale because she moves not there.
His body was as straight as Circe's wand;
Jove might have sipped out nectar from his hand.
Even as delicious meat is to the taste,
So was his neck in touching, and surpassed
The white of Pelops' shoulder. I could tell ye
How smooth his breast was, and how white his belly,
And whose immortal fingers did imprint
That heavenly path with many a curious dint
That runs along his back, but my rude pen
Can hardly blazon forth the loves of men,
Much less of powerful gods: let it suffice
That my slack muse sings of Leander's eyes,

Those orient cheeks and lips, exceeding his
That leapt into the water for a kiss
Of his own shadow, and despising many,
Died ere he could enjoy the love of any.
Had wild Hippolytus Leander seen,
Enamoured of his beauty had he been;
His presence made the rudest peasant melt,
That in the vast uplandish country dwelt.
The barbarous Thracian soldier, moved with nought,
Was moved with him, and for his favour sought.
Some swore he was a maid in man's attire,
For in his looks were all that men desire,
A pleasant, smiling cheek, a speaking eye,
A brow for love to banquet royally;
And such as knew he was a man would say,
'Leander, thou art made for amorous play:
Why art thou not in love, and loved of all?
Though thou be fair, yet be not thine own thrall.'

(First Sestiad, lines 51–90)

Leander swims to Hero

'O Hero, Hero!' thus he cried full oft,
And then he got him to a rock aloft,
Where having spied her tower, long stared he on't,
And prayed the narrow toiling Hellespont
To part in twain, that he might come and go,
But still the rising billows answered 'No.'
With that he stripped him to the ivory skin,
And crying, 'Love, I come,' leapt lively in.
Whereat the sapphire-visaged god grew proud,
And made his capering Triton sound aloud,
Imagining that Ganymede, displeased,

Had left the heavens; therefore on him he seized.
Leander strived, the waves about him wound,
And pulled him to the bottom, where the ground
Was strewed with pearl, and in low coral groves
Sweet singing mermaids sported with their loves
On heaps of heavy gold, and took great pleasure
To spurn in careless sort the shipwrack treasure.
For here the stately azure palace stood
Where kingly Neptune and his train abode.
The lusty god embraced him, called him love,
And swore he never should return to Jove.
But when he knew it was not Ganymede,
For under water he was almost dead,
He heaved him up, and looking on his face,
Beat down the bold waves with his triple mace,
Which mounted up, intending to have kissed him,
And fell in drops like tears because they missed him.
Leander, being up, began to swim,
And, looking back, saw Neptune follow him;
Whereat aghast the poor soul 'gan to cry,
'O let me visit Hero ere I die.'
The god put Helle's bracelet on his arm,
And swore the sea should never do him harm.
He clapped his plump cheeks, with his tresses played,
And smiling wantonly, his love bewrayed.
He watched his arms, and as they opened wide
At every stroke, betwixt them would he slide
And steal a kiss, and then run out and dance,
And as he turned, cast many a lustful glance,
And threw him gaudy toys to please his eye,
And dive into the water, and there pry
Upon his breast, his thighs, and every limb,
And up again, and close beside him swim,
And talk of love. Leander made reply,
'You are deceived, I am no woman, I.'

(Second Sestiad, lines 147–192)

BARTHOLOMEW GRIFFIN
(d 1602)

Cytherea and Adonis

Scarce had the sun dried up the dewy morn,
And scarce the herd gone to the hedge for shade,
When Cytherea, all in love forlorn,
A longing tarriance for Adonis made
Under an osier growing by a brook –
A brook where Adon used to cool his spleen.
Hot was the day; she hotter that did look
For his approach that often there had been.
Anon he comes, and throws his mantle by,
And stood stark naked on the brook's green brim.
The sun looked on the world with glorious eye,
Yet not so wistfully as this queen on him.
    He spying her bounced in whereas he stood.
    'O Jove!' quoth she, 'Why was not I a flood?'

Venus and Adonis

Venus, with young Adonis sitting by her
Under a myrtle shade, began to woo him.
She told the youngling how god Mars did try her,
And as he fell to her, she fell to him.
'Even thus', quoth she, 'the warlike god embraced me.'
And then she clipped Adonis in her arms.
'Even thus', quoth she, 'the warlike god unlaced me,'
As if the boy should use like loving charms.
'Even thus', quoth she, 'he seized on my lips',
And with her lips on his did act the seizure;
And as she fetchèd breath, away he skips,
And would not take her meaning nor her pleasure.
    Ah, that I had my lady at this bay,
    To kiss and clip me till I run away!

ANON
(c 1600)

Look Merrily

Come, pretty one, shall I love thee?
Say, little one, shall I prove thee?
Gently moving, be not cruel,
Wish lovingly, O my jewel;
Talk coyly, move affection;
Toy prettily, cause erection;
Look merrily while I woo thee,
Blush cheerfully whilst I do thee.
Look prettily, O that's meetest!
Do feelingly, O that's sweetest!
Fall willingly and lie flatly,
Keep close to me whilst thou'rt at me,
Move sprightfully and lie panting,
Show rightly nothing be wanting.
Speak faintly – fairly languish –
Die daintily in sweet anguish.
Swear evermore I shall woo thee,
And evermore pluck me to thee.

ANON
(c 1600)

Dainty Darling

Dainty darling, kind and free,
Fairest maid I ever see,
Dear, vouchsafe to look on me –
Listen when I sing to thee
    What I will do
    With a dildo[1]:
    Sing, do with a dildo.

[1]*dildo* in the 17th century, still a penis; only later, an artificial one

Sweet, now go not yet, I pray;
Let no doubt thy mind dismay.
Here with me thou shalt but stay –
Only till I can display
  What I will do
  With a dildo:
  Sing, do with a dildo.

Quickly, prithee, now be still:
'Nay, you shall not have your will.
Trow, you men will maidens kill!'
Tarry but to learn the skill
  What I will do
  With a dildo:
  Sing, do with a dildo.

Pretty, witty, sit me by;
Fear no cast of any eye.
We will pray so privily
None shall see but you and I
  What I will do
  With a dildo:
  Sing, do with a dildo.

ANON
(c 1600)

The Lonely Maid

Can anyone tell what I ail
That I look so lean, so wan, so pale?
Unto that plight, alas, I'm grown
That can, nor will, no longer lie alone.

Was ever woman's case like mine?
At fifteen I began to pine;
So now unto this plight I'm grown
That can, nor will, no longer lie alone.

If dreams be true, then ride I can –
I lack nothing but a man,
For only he can ease my moan
That can, nor will, no longer lie alone.

When day is come, I wish for night;
When night is come, I wish for light;
Thus all my time I sit and moan
That can, nor will, no longer lie alone.

To woo him first, ashamed am I;
But if he ask, I'll not deny –
Such is my case, I must have one
That can, nor will, no longer lie alone.

Therefore my prayer, it shall be still
I may have one to work my will,
For only he can ease me anon,
That can, nor will, no longer lie alone.

ANON
(c 1600)

A Riddle

Come, pretty nymph, fain would I know
What thing it is that breeds delight,
That strives to stand, and cannot go,
And feeds the mouth that cannot bite.

It is a kind of pleasing thing,
A pricking and a piercing sting.
It is Venus' wanton wand.
It hath no legs, and yet can stand.
A bachelor's button thoroughly ripe,
The kindest new tobacco-pipe.

It is the pen that Helen took
To write in her two-leavéd book.
It's a prick-shaft of Cupid's cut,
Yet some do shoot it at a butt.
And every wench by her good will
Would keep it in her quiver still.
The fairest yet that e'er had life
For love of this became a wife.

ANON
(c 1600?)

Have at a Venture

A country lad and bonny lass
   they did together meet,
And as they did together pass,
   thus he began to greet:
'What I do say I may mind well,
   and thus I do begin:
If you would have your belly swell,
   hold up, and I'll put in.'

'Oh, sir,' quoth she, 'I love the sport,
   yet am afraid to try,
And for your love, I thank you for't,
   find but conveniency.
My mind I'll tell you by and by,
   your love my heart doth win,
And presently I down will lie –
   Oh, then, boy, push it in.'

He clasped this damsel round the waist
   and softly laid her down,
Yea, wantonly he her embraced,
   and her delights did crown.

'Thrust home!' quoth she, 'My brisk young lad,
  'Tis but a venial sin,
For I should soon have run quite mad
  had you not put it in.'

The sport he did so close pursue
  that he was quickly tired,
But when her beauty he did view
  his heart again was fired:
He came on with such fresh supplies
  he did her favour win,
And finding babies in her eyes
  he bravely thrust it in.

'What pleasure is there like to this!'
  this damsel then did cry;
'I've heard them talk of lovers' bliss,
  Oh what a fool was I
So long to live a maid, ere I
  did this same sport begin.
This death I now could freely die –
  I prithee thrust it in!'

She held this youngster to his task
  till he began to blow,
Then at the last he leave did ask
  and so she let him go.
Then down he panting lay awhile,
  and rousing up again
She charmed him with a lovely smile
  again to put it in.

To work he went most earnestly
  his fancy to fulfil,
Till at the last she loud did cry
  'I do't with such good will –

I pleasure feel in every vein,
   My joys do now begin:
Oh, dearest, quickly to't again
   and stoutly thrust it in!'

She seemed at last to be content,
   and glad at heart was he:
His youthful strength was almost spent,
   so brisk a lass was she.
He vowed he never was so matched,
   nor ne'er shall be again:
And for that time they both dispatched
   though he had put it in.

But when she from him parted was,
   thus she began to cry:
'Was ever any wanton lass
   in such a case as I?
He that hath got my maidenhead
   I ne'er shall see again,
And now my heart is almost dead
   to think he put it in.

'But yet it had the sweetest taste
   that ever mortal knew,
Our time we did not vainly waste –
   believe me, this is true.
Should I e'er see my bonny lad
   I'd venture once again,
And let the world account me mad
   again I'll put it in.'

ANON
(1602)

Beauty's Self

My love in her attire doth show her wit,
   It doth so well become her;
For every season she has dressings fit,
   For winter, spring and summer.
No beauty she doth miss
   When all her robes are on:
But Beauty's self she is
   When all her robes are gone.

(from *A Poetical Rhapsody*)

HENRY PARROT
(c 1606)

Oculus Adulter

Of all the pleasures that our London yields
Calvus commends the walks about Moorfields.[1]
There's many reasons that provoke him to it:
He must be looking, though he cannot do it.

JOHN HOSKYNS
(1566–1638)

On a Whore

One stone sufficeth (lo what death can do)
Her that in life was not content with two.

[1] *Moorfields* an open space notable for promiscuity

THOMAS CAMPION
(1567–1620)

Song from *Astrophel and Stella*

My love bound me with a kiss
That I should no longer stay.
When I felt so sweet a bliss,
I had less power to pass away.
Alas that women do not know
Kisses make men loath to go.

Song

I care not for these ladies
That must be wooed and prayed;
Give me kind Amarillis,
The wanton country maid.[1]
Nature art disdaineth,
Her beauty is her own.
   Who when we court and kiss
   She cries 'Forsooth, let go!'
   But when we come where comfort is,
   She never will say no.

If I love Amarillis
She gives me fruit and flowers,
But if we love these ladies
We must give golden showers.
Give them gold that sell love;
Give me the nutbrown lass
   Who when we court and kiss
   She cries 'Forsooth, let go!'
   But when we come where comfort is
   She never will say no.

[1]*country maid* an obscene pun, repeated in Shakespeare and elsewhere, is intended

These ladies must have pillows
And beds by stranger wrought;
Give me a bower of willows
Of moss and leaves unbought
And fresh Amarillis
With milk and honey fed,
    Who when we court and kiss
    She cries 'Forsooth, let go!'
    But when we come where comfort is
    She never will say no.

The Forsaken Mistress

My love hath vowed he will forsake me,
And I am already sped.
Far other promise he did make me
When he had my maidenhead.
If such danger be in playing
And sport must to earnest turn,
I will go no more a-maying.

Had I forseen what is ensued
And what now with pain I prove
Unhappy then I had eschewed
This unkind event of love.
Maids foreknow their own undoing,
But fear naught till all is done
When a man alone is wooing.

Dissembling wretch, to gain thy pleasure
What didst thou not vow and swear?
So didst rob me of my treasure
Which so long I held so dear.
Now thou provest to me a stranger.
Such is the vile guise of men
When a woman is in danger.

[109]

That heart is nearest to misfortune
That will trust a fained tongue.
When flattering men our loves importune,
They intend us deepest wrong.
If this shame of love's betraying
But this once I cleanly shun,
I will go no more a–maying.

It Fell on a Summer's Day

It fell on a summer's day
While sweet Bessie sleeping lay
In her bower, on her bed,
Light with curtains shadowed,
Jamy came, she him spies
Opening half her heavy eyes.

Jamy stole in through the door.
She lay slumbering as before.
Softly to her he drew near.
She heard him, yet would not hear.
Bessie vowed not to speak.
He resolved that dump[1] to break.

First a soft kiss he doth take.
She lay still and would not wake.
Then his hands learned to woo.
She dreamed not what he would do
But still slept, while he smiled
To see love by sleep beguiled.

Jamy then began to play.
Bessie as one buried lay,
Gladly still through this slight
Deceived in her own deceit.
And since this trance began
She sleeps every afternoon.

[1]*dump* dream

Thou Art Not Fair

Thou art not fair, for all thy red and white,
For all those rosy ornaments in thee.
Thou art not sweet, though made of mere delight,
Nor fair nor sweet, unless thou pity me.
I will not sooth thy fancies; thou shalt prove
That beauty is no beauty without love.

Yet love not me, nor seek thou to allure
My thoughts with beauty, were it more divine.
Thy smiles and kisses I cannot endure –
I'll not be wrapped up in those arms of thine.
Now show it, if thou be a woman right:
Embrace and kiss and love me, in despite.

Pined Am I

Pined am I, and like to die,
And all for lack of that which I
   Do every day refuse.
If I musing sit or stand
Some puts it daily in my hand
   To interrupt my muse.
The same thing I seek, and fly,
And want that which none would deny.

In my bed, when I should rest,
It breeds such trouble in my breast
   That scarce mine eyes will close.
If I sleep, it seems to be
Oft playing in the bed with me,
   But waked, away it goes.
'Tis some spirit, sure, I ween
And yet it may be felt and seen.

Would I had the heart and wit
To make it stand, to conjure it,
    That haunts me thus with fear.
Doubtless 'tis some harmless sprite,
For it by day as well as night
    Is ready to appear.
Be it friend or be it foe,
Ere long I'll try what it will do.

Fire! Fire! Fire!

Fire, fire, fire, fire!
Lo, here I burn in such desire
That all the tears that I can strain
Out of mine idle empty brain
Cannot allay my scorching pain.
    Come Trent and Humber and fair Thames,
    Dread ocean, haste with all thy streams,
    And if you cannot quench my fire
    O, drown both me and my desire.

Fire, fire, fire, fire!
There is no hell[1] to my desire.
See, all the rivers backward fly
And th'ocean doth his waves deny
For fear my heat should drink them dry.
    Come heavenly showers, then, pouring down!
    Come you that once the world did drown!
    Some then you spared, but now save all
    That else must burn, and with me fall.

[1]*hell* as in Boccaccio's story of 'putting the devil in hell', the vagina

SIR JOHN DAVIES
(1569–1626)

In Librum

Liber doth vaunt how chastely he hath lived
Since he hath been seven years in town and more,
For that he swears he hath four only swived –
A maid, a wife, a widow and a whore.
   Then, Liber, thou hast swived all women kind,
   For a fifth sort I know thou can'st not find.

In Katam

Kate being pleased, wished that her pleasure could
Endure as long as a buff jerkin would.
Content thee, Kate, although thy pleasure wasteth,
Thy pleasure's place like a buff jerkin lasteth.
   For no buff jerkin hath been oftener worn,
   Nor hath more scrapings, or more dressings born.

In Francum

When Francus comes to solace with his whore,
He sends for rod and strips himself stark naked:
For his lust sleeps, and will not rise before,
By whipping of the wench, it be awaked.
   I envy him not, but wish I had the power
   To make myself his wench but one half hour.

In Neream

Sweet mistress Nerea, let it not thee grieve
That I did take a pin from off thy headgear,
For I to thee a greater pin will give

Which shall do better service to thy bedgear,
So that thou'lt grant that I shall choose the pin
And stick it where I will, and where it will run in.

To a Woman Fallen from Horseback

Madam, what needs this care to make it known
You caught a bruise from horseback lately thrown?
That cast you were is clearer than the skies –
Had you not fallen, your belly could not rise.
The only scruple is, that men do scan,
Whether your gelding threw you, or your man.

In Gellam

Gella of late is grown a puritan:
Unless she jape,[1] she will not kiss a man.

A Lover out of Fashion

Faith, wench, I cannot court thy sprightly eyes
With the base viol placed between my thighs;
I cannot lisp, nor to some fiddle sing,
Nor run upon a high stretched minikin.[2]

I cannot whine in puling elegies
Entombing Cupid with sad obsequies.
I am not fashioned for these amorous times
To court thy beauty with lascivious rhymes.

[1]*jape* joke, but also have intercourse [2]*minikin* treble string of a lute

I cannot dally, caper, dance and sing,
Oiling[1] my saint with supple sonneting.
I cannot cross my arms, or sigh 'Ah, me –
Ah, me, forlorn!' – egregious foppery.

I cannot buss thy fist, play with thy hair,
Swearing by Jove thou art most debonaire.
   Not I, by cock; but shall I tell thee roundly,
    Hark in thine ear: zounds, I can swive thee soundly.

To his Mistress

Sweet, what doth he deserve that loves you so?
At least some little favour he deserves,
Which you in justice and in kindness owe
To him which with such true devotion serves.
Yet know you this, that he contents him not
With a sweet glove, or an enamelled ring,
A feather of a fan, a true love's knot,
A Cypress scarf, or such a light vain thing.
As for such tokens of true love as this
Children and fools perhaps they may content;
But that which my aspiring thoughts would please
Is far more rare and far more excellent –
Yet which with lesser cost may granted be:
For all is but a little lechery.

SIR ROBERT AYTOUN
(1570–1638)

To his Forsaken Mistress

I do confess th'art smooth and fair,
And I might ha' gone near to love thee
Had I not found the slightest prayer

---

[1]*oiling* flattering

[115]

That lip could move, had power to move thee.
But I can let thee now alone
As worthy to be loved by none.

I do confess th'art sweet; yet find
Thee such an unthrift of thy sweets –
Thy favours are but like the wind,
Which kisseth everything it meets.
And since thou canst[1] with more than one,
Th'art worthy to be kissed by none.

The morning rose that untouched stands
Armed with her briars, how sweet she smells!
But plucked, and strained through ruder hands,
Her sweets no longer with her dwells,
But scent and beauty both are gone,
And leaves fall from her one by one.

Such fate ere long will thee betide,
When thou hast handled been a while,
With sere flowers to be thrown aside;
And I shall sigh when some will smile
To see thy love to everyone
Hath brought thee to be loved by none.

BEN JONSON
(?1572–1637)

On the New Hot-House

Where lately harboured many a famous whore,
A purging bill now fixed upon the door
Tells you it is a hot-house.[2] So it may:
And still be a whore-house. They're *synonima*.

[1]*canst* 'can' used as meaning 'to know', in the sexual sense
[2]*hot-house* a bagnio or baths with hot water supplied; but 'bagnio' was often a
synonym for brothel.

To Pertinax Cob

Cob, thou nor soldier, thief nor fencer art,
Yet by thy weapon liv'st: thou hast one good part.

from *A Celebration of Charis*

For his mind, I do not care,
That's a toy that I could spare;
Let his title be but great,
His clothes rich, and band sit neat,
Himself young, and face be good,
All I wish is understood.
What you please you parts may call,
'Tis one good part I'd die withal.

A Fragment from Petronius

Doing, a filthy pleasure is, and short –
And done, we straight repent us of the sport.
Let us not then rush blindly in unto it
Like lustful beasts, that only know to do it,
For lust will languish, and that heat decay.
But thus, thus, keeping endless holy-day
Let us together closely lie, and kiss;
There is no labour, nor no shame in this.
This hath pleased, doth please, and long will please; never
Can this decay, but is beginning ever.

Song: to Celia

Come, my Celia, let us prove
While we may, the sports of love.
Time will not be ours for ever:

He at length our good will sever.
Spend not then his gifts in vain.
Suns that set may rise again,
But if once we lose this light
'Tis with us perpetual night.
Why should we defer our joys?
Fame and rumour are but toys.
Cannot we delude the eyes
Of a few poor household spies?
Or his easier ears beguile
So removed by our wile?
'Tis no sin love's fruit to steal,
But the sweet theft to reveal –
To be taken, to be seen –
These have crimes accounted been.

JOHN DONNE
(1572–1631)

Elegy 19 – To his Mistress Going to Bed

Come, Madam, come, all rest my powers defy,
Until I labour, I in labour lie.
The foe oft-times having the foe in sight
Is tired with standing though they never fight.
Off with that girdle, like heaven's zone glistering,
But a far fairer world encompassing.
Unpin that spangled breastplate which you wear,
That th'eyes of busy fools may be stopped there.
Unlace yourself, for that harmonious chime
Tells me from you, that now 'tis your bed time.
Off with that happy busk,[1] which I envy,
That still can be, and still can stand so nigh.
Your gown going off, such beauteous state reveals
As when from flowery meads th'hill's shadow steals.

[1]*busk* corset

Off with that wiry coronet and show
The hairy diadem which on you doth grow;
Now off with those shoes, and then safely tread
In this love's hallowed temple, this soft bed.
In such white robes heaven's angels used to be
Received by men; thou angel bring'st with thee
A heaven like Mahomet's paradise; and though
Ill spirits walk in white, we easily know
By this these angels from an evil sprite,
Those set our hairs, but these our flesh upright.
    Licence my roving hands, and let them go
Before, behind, between, above, below.
O my America, my new found land,
My kingdom, safeliest when with one man manned,
My mine of precious stones, my empery,
How blessed am I in this discovering thee!
To enter in these bonds is to be free;
Then where my hand is set, my seal shall be.
    Full nakedness, all joys are due to thee.
As souls unbodied, bodies unclothed must be,
To taste whole joys. Gems which you women use
Are like Atlanta's balls, cast in men's views,
That when a fool's eye lighteth on a gem,
His earthly soul may covet theirs, not them.
Like pictures, or like books' gay coverings made
For laymen, are all women thus arrayed;
Themselves are mystic books, which only we
Whom their imputed grace will dignify
Must see revealed. Then since I may know,
As liberally, as to a midwife, show
Thyself: cast all, yea, this white linen hence,
Here is no penance, much less innocence.
    To teach thee, I am naked first, why then
What needst thou have more covering than a man.

THOMAS HEYWOOD
(1575-1641)

She that Denies Me

She that denies me, I would have;
    Who craves me, I despise:
Venus hath power to rule mine heart,
    But not to please mine eyes.
Temptations offered, I still scorn,
    Denied, I cling them still;
I'll neither glut mine appetite
    Nor seek to starve my will.

Diana, double-clothed, offends –
    So Venus, naked quite.
The last begets a surfeit, and
    The other no delight.
That crafty girl shall please me best
    That 'no' for 'yea' can say,
And every wanton willing kiss
    Can season with a 'nay'.

ROBERT HERRICK
(1591-1674)

The Good-Night or Blessing

Blessings in abundance come
To the bride and to her groom;
May the bed, and this short night,
Know the fulness of delight!
Pleasures many here attend ye,
And ere long a boy love send ye
Curled and comely, and so trim
Maids (in time) may ravish him.
Thus a dew of graces fall
On ye both; goodnight to all.

The Poet Loves a Mistress, but not to Marry

I do not love to wed,
Though I do like to woo;
And for a maidenhead
I'll beg, and buy it too.

I'll praise and I'll approve
Those maids that never vary,
And fervently I'll love –
But yet I would not marry.

I'll hug, I'll kiss, I'll play,
And, cock-like, hens I'll tread,
And sport it any way
But in the bridal-bed.

For why? That man is poor
Who hath but one of many;
But crowned is he with store
That single may have any.

Why then, say what is he
To freedom so unknown
Who having two or three
Will be content with one?

Upon the Nipples of Julia's Breast

Have ye beheld (with much delight)
A red rose peeping through a white?
Or else a cherry, double graced,
Within a lily-centre placed?
Or even marked the pretty beam
A strawberry shows half drowned in cream?

[121]

Or seen rich rubies blushing through
A pure, smooth pearl, and orient too?
So like to this, nay all the rest,
Is each sweet niplet of her breast.

Fresh Cheese and Cream

Would ye have fresh cheese and cream?
Julia's breast can give you them –
And if more, each nipple cries:
To your cream, here's strawberries.

The Eye

A wanton and lascivious eye
Betrays the heart's adultery.

To Anthea

Let's call for Hymen if agreed thou art –
Delays in love but crucify the heart.
Love's thorny tapers yet neglected lie;
Speak thou the word, they'll kindle by and by.
The nimble hours woo us on to wed,
And Genius waits to have us both to bed.
Behold, for us the naked Graces stay
With maunds¹ of roses for to strew the way.
Besides, the most religious prophet stands
Ready to join as well our hearts as hands.
June yet smiles; but if she chance to chide,
Ill luck 'twill bode to th'bridegroom and the bride.
Tell me Anthea, dost thou fondly dread
The loss of that we call a maidenhead?
Come, I'll instruct thee. Know, the vestal fire
Is not by marriage quenched, but flames the higher.

¹*maunds* baskets

To Oenone

Thou sayest Love's dart
Hath pricked thy heart;
And thou dost languish too:
If one poor prick
Can make thee sick,
Say, what would many do?

The Vine

I dreamed this mortal part of mine
Was metamorphosed to a vine,
Which crawling one and every way
Enthralled my dainty Lucia.
Methought her long, small legs and thighs
I with my tendrils did surprise;
Her belly, buttocks and her waist
By my soft nervelets were embraced;
About her head I writhing hung,
And with rich clusters (hid among
The leaves) her temples I behung,
So that my Lucia seemed to me
Young Bacchus ravished by his tree.
My curls about her neck did crawl,
And arms and hands they did enthrall
So that she could not freely stir
(All parts there made one prisoner).
But when I crept with leaves to hide
Those parts which maids keep unespyed,
Such fleeting pleasures there I took
That with the fancy I awoke,
And found (ah, me!) this flesh of mine
More like a stock than like a vine.

Clothes do but Cheat and Cozen us

Away with silks, away with lawn,
I'll have no scenes or curtains drawn;
Give me my mistress as she is,
Dressed in her naked simplicities –
For as my heart, e'en so my eye
Is won with flesh, not drapery.

ANON
(c 1620)

Drooping and Whopping

A man and a young maid that loved a long time
Were ta'en in a frenzy i' the midsummer prime.
    The maid she lay drooping, hye,
    The man he lay whopping, hey.

Thus talking and walking they came to a place
Environed about with trees and with grass.
    The maid she lay drooping, hye,
    The man he lay whopping, hey.

He shifted his hand whereas he had placed,
He handled her legs instead of her waist.
    The maid she lay drooping, hye,
    The man he lay whopping, hey.

He shifted his hand till he came to her knees,
He tickled her and she opened her thighs.
    The maid she lay drooping, hye,
    The man he lay whopping, hey.

He hottered and tottered, and there was a lane
That drew him on forward – he went on amain.
    The maid she lay drooping, hye,
    The man he lay whopping, hey.

The lane it was strait – he had not gone far
He lit in a hole ere he was aware.
    But she fell a-kissing, hye,
    And he lay drooping, ho.

'My Billy, my pilly, how now?' quoth she.
'Get up again, Billy, if thou lovest me.'
    Yet still he lay drooping, hye,
    And still she was whopping, hey.

He thought mickle[1] shame to lie so long:
He got up again and grew very strong.
    The maid she lay drooping, hye,
    The man he lay whopping, hey.

The trees and the woods did ring about
And every leaf began to shout –
    And there was such whopping, hye,
    And there was such whopping, hey!

ANON
(c 1660)

Walking in a Meadow Green

Walking in a meadow green,
    Fair flowers for to gather,
Where primrose ranks did stand on banks
    To welcome comers thither,
I heard a voice which made a noise
    Which caused me to attend it,
I heard a lass say to a lad
    'Once more, and none can mend it.'

They lay so close together
    They made me much to wonder;
I know not which was whether
    Until I saw her under.

[1]*mickle* much

[125]

Then off he came and blushed for shame
  So soon that he had ended;
Yet still she lies, and to him cries
  'Once more, and none can mend it.'

His looks were dull and very sad,
  His courage she had tamed;
She made him play the lusty lad
  Or else he quite was shamed.
'Then stiffly thrust, he hit me just,
  Fear not, but freely spend it,
And play about at in and out;
  Once more, and none can mend it.'

And then he thought to venture her
  Thinking the fit was on him;
But when he came to enter her,
  The point turned back upon him.
Yet she said, 'Stay! Go not away,
  Although the point be bended!
But to't again, and hit the vein!
  Once more, and none can mend it.'

Then in her arms she did him fold,
  And oftentimes she kissed him;
And yet his courage still was cold
  For all the good she wished him.
Yet with her hand she made it stand
  So stiff she could not bend it,
And then anon she cries 'Come on,
  Once more, and none can mend it!'

'Adieu, adieu, sweetheart,' quoth he,
  'For in faith I must be gone.'
'Nay, then you do me wrong,' quoth she,
  'To leave me thus alone.'

Away he went when all was spent,
Whereat she was offended;
Like a Trojan true she made a vow
She would have one should mend it.

THOMAS CAREW
(1594–1640)

A Rapture

I will enjoy thee now, my Celia, come,
And fly with me to Love's Elysium.
The giant, Honour, that keeps cowards out
Is but a masquer, and the service rout
Of baser subjects only bend in vain
To the vast idol; whilst the nobler train
Of valiant lovers daily sail between
The huge Colosse's legs, and pass unseen
Unto the blissful shore. Be bold and wise,
And we shall enter: the grim Swiss denies
Only to tame fools a passage, that not know
He is but form, and only frights in show
The duller eyes that look from far; draw near,
And thou shalt scorn what we were wont to fear.
We shall see how the stalking pageant goes
With borrowed legs, a heavy load to those
That made and bear him: not, as we once thought,
The seed of gods, but a weak model wrought
By greedy men, that seek to enclose the common,
And within private arms impale free woman.
   Come, then, and mounted on the wings of Love
We'll cut the flitting air, and soar above
The monster's head, and in the noblest seats
Of those blest shades quench and renew our heats.
There shall the Queens of Love and Innocence,
Beauty and Nature, banish all offence

From our close ivy-twines; there I'll behold
Thy bared snow and thy unbraided gold;
There my enfranchised hand on every side
Shall o'er thy naked polished ivory slide.
No curtain there, though of transparent lawn
Shall be before thy virgin-treasure drawn;
But the rich mine, to the enquiring eye
Exposed, shall ready still for mintage lie,
And we will coin young Cupids. There a bed
Of roses and fresh myrtles shall be spread
Under the cooler shade of cypress groves;
Our pillows of the down of Venus' doves,
Whereon our panting limbs we'll gently lay,
In the faint respites of our active play:
That so our slumbers may in dreams have leisure
To tell the nimble fancy our past pleasure,
And so our souls that cannot be embraced
Shall the embraces of our bodies taste.
Meanwhile the bubbling stream shall court the shore,
Th'enamoured chirping wood-choir shall adore
In varied tunes the Deity of Love;
The gentle blasts of western winds shall move
The trembling leaves, and through their close boughs breathe
Still music, whilst we rest ourselves beneath
Their dancing shade; till a soft murmur, sent
From souls entranced in amorous languishment,
Rouse us, and shoot into our veins fresh fire,
Till we in their sweet ecstasy expire.
    Then, as the empty bee, that lately bore
Into the common treasure all her store,
Flies 'bout the painted field with nimble wing,
Deflowering the fresh virgins of the Spring,
So will I rifle all the sweets that dwell
In my delicious paradise, and swell
My bag with honey, drawn forth by the power
Of fervent kisses from each spicy flower.
I'll seize the rose-buds in their perfumed bed,

The violet knots, like curious mazes spread
O'er all the garden, taste the ripened cherry,
The warm firm apple, tipped with coral berry;
Then will I visit with a wandering kiss
The vale of lilies, and the bower of bliss;
And where the beauteous region doth divide
Into two milky ways, my lips shall slide
Down those smooth alleys, wearing as I go
A tract for lovers on the printed snow;
Thence climbing o'er the swelling Apennine,
Retire into thy grove of eglantine,
Where I will all those ravished sweets distil
Through Love's alembic,[1] and with chemic skill
From the mixed mass one sovereign balm derive,
Then bring that great elixir to thy hive.
　　Now in more subtle wreaths I will entwine
My sinewy thighs, my legs and arms with thine;
Thou like a sea of milk shalt lie displayed,
Whilst I the smooth calm ocean invade
With such a tempest, as when Jove of old
Fell down on Danaë in a storm of gold;
Yet my tall pine shall in the Cyprian strait
Ride safe at anchor, and unlade her freight:
My rudder with thy bold hand, like a tried
And skilful pilot, thou shalt steer, and guide
My bark into love's channel, where it shall
Dance, as the bounding waves do rise or fall.
Then shall thy circling arms embrace and clip
My willing body, and thy balmy lip
Bathe me in juice of kisses, whose perfume
Like a religious incense shall consume,
And send up holy vapours to those powers
That bless our loves and crown our sportful hours,
That with such halcyon calmness fix our souls
In steadfast peace, as no affright controls.
　　There no rude sounds shake us with sudden starts;

[1]*alembic* an apparatus used in distilling

No jealous ears, when we unrip our hearts,
Suck our discourse in; no observing spies
This blush, that glance traduce; no envious eyes
Watch our close meetings; nor are we betrayed
To rivals by the bribed chambermaid.
No wedlock bonds unwreathe our twisted loves;
We seek no midnight arbour, no dark groves
To hide our kisses: there the hated name
Of husband, wife, lust, modest, chaste or shame,
Are vain and empty words, whose very sound
Was never heard in the Elysian ground.
All things are lawful there that may delight
Nature or unrestrained appetite;
Like and enjoy, to will and act is one:
We only sin when Love's rites are not done.
    The Roman Lucrece there reads the divine
Lectures of love's great master, Aretine,
And knows as well as Lais how to move
Her pliant body in the act of love.
To quench the burning ravisher, she hurls
Her limbs into a thousand winding curls,
And studies artful postures, such as be
Carved on the bark of every neighbouring tree
By learned hands, that so adorned the rind
Of those fair plants, which, as they lay entwined,
Have fanned their glowing fires. The Grecian dame,
That in her endless web toiled for a name
As fruitless as her work, doth there display
Herself before the youth of Ithaca,
And th'amorous sport of gamesome nights prefer
Before dull dreams of the lost traveller.
Daphne hath broke her bark, and that swift foot
Which th'angry gods had fastened with a root
To the fixed earth, doth now unfettered run
To meet th'embraces of the youthful Sun.
She hangs upon him like his Delphic lyre;
Her kisses blow the old, and breathe new fire;

Full of her god, she sings inspired lays,
Sweet odes of love, such as deserve the bays,
Which she herself was. Next her, Laura lies
In Petrarch's learned arms, drying those eyes
That did in such sweet smooth-paced numbers flow
As made the world enamoured of his woe.
These, and ten thousand beauties more, that died
Slave to the tyrant, now enlarged deride
His cancelled laws, and for their time mis-spent
Pay into Love's exchequer double rent.
    Come then, my Celia, we'll no more forbear
To taste our joys, struck with a panic fear,
But will depose from his imperious sway
This proud usurper, and walk free as they,
With necks unyoked; nor is it just that he
Should fetter your soft sex with chastity,
Which Nature made unapt for abstinence;
When yet this false imposter can dispense
With human justice and with sacred right,
And, maugre[1] both their laws, command me fight
With rivals or with emulous loves that dare
Equal with thine their mistress' eyes or hair.
If thou complain of wrong, and call my sword
To carve out thy revenge, upon that word
He bids me fight and kill; or else he brands
With marks of infamy my coward hands.
And yet religion bids from bloodshed fly,
And damns me for that act. Then tell me why
    This goblin Honour, which the world adores,
    Should make men atheists, and not women whores.

Upon a Mole in Celia's Bosom

That lovely spot which thou dost see
In Celia's bosom was a bee,

---

[1] *maugre* in spite of

Who built her amorous spicy nest
I'th'Hyblas of her either breast.
But from close ivory hives she flew
To suck the aromatic dew
Which from the neighbour vale distils,
Which parts those two twin-sister hills,
There feasting on ambrosial meat,
A rolling file of balmy sweat
(As in soft murmurs before death
Swan-like she sung) choked up her breath:
So she in water did expire,
More precious than the phoenix' fire.
   Yet still her shadow there remains
Confined to those Elysian plains,
With this strict law, that who shall lay
His bold lips on that milky way,
The sweet and smart from thence shall bring
Of the bee's honey and her sting.

The Compliment

My dearest, I shall grieve thee
When I swear, yet sweet believe me,
By thine eyes – the tempting book
On which even crabbed old men look –
I swear to thee (though none abhor them)
Yet I do not love thee for them.

I do not love thee for that fair
Rich fan of thy most curious hair,
Though the wires thereof be drawn
Finer than the threads of lawn
And are softer than the leaves
On which the subtle spinner weaves.

I do not love thee for those flowers
Growing on thy cheeks (love's bowers),
Though such cunning them hath spread
None can part their white and red;
Love's golden arrows thence are shot,
Yet for them I love thee not.

I do not love thee for those soft
Red coral lips I've kissed so oft,
Nor teeth of pearl, the double guard
To speech, whence music still is heard –
Though from those lips a kiss being taken
Might tyrants melt and death awaken.

I do not love thee (O my fairest)
For that richest, for that rarest
Silver pillar which stands under
Thy round head, that globe of wonder,
Though that neck be whiter far
Than towers of polished ivory are.

I do not love thee for those mountains
Hilled with snow, whence milky fountains
(Sugared sweet, as syrup'd berries)
Must one day run through pipes of cherries;
O how much those breasts do move me –
Yet for them I do not love thee.

I do not love thee for that belly,
Sleek as satin, soft as jelly,
Though within that crystal round
Heaps of treasure might be found
So rich that for the least of them
A king might leave his diadem.

I do not love thee for those thighs
Whose alabaster rocks do rise
So high and even that they stand

[133]

Like sea-marks to some happy land.
Happy are those eyes have seen them;
More happy they that sail between them.

I love thee not for thy moist palm
Though the dew thereof be balm,
Nor for thy pretty leg and foot,
Although it be the precious root
On which this goodly cedar grows;
Sweet, I love thee not for those,

Nor for thy wit, though pure and quick,
Whose substance no arithmetic
Can number down; nor for those charms
Masked in thy embracing arms –
Though in them one night to lie,
Dearest, I would gladly die.

I love not for those eyes, nor hair,
Nor cheeks, nor lips, nor teeth so rare,
Nor for thy speech, thy neck, or breast,
Nor for thy belly, nor the rest,
Nor for thy hand nor foot so small –
But, wouldst thou know, dear sweet – for all.

The Second Rapture

No, worldling, no, 'tis not thy gold
Which thou dost use but to behold,
Nor fortune, honour, nor long life,
Children or friends, nor a good wife
That makes thee happy: these things be
But shadows of felicity.
Give me a wench about thirteen,
Already voted to the queen
Of lust and lovers; whose soft hair
Fanned with the breath of gentle air

O'erspreads her shoulders like a tent
And is her veil and ornament;
Whose tender touch will make the blood
Wild in the aged and the good;
Whose kisses, fastened to the mouth
Of threescore years and longer slouth,
Renew the age; and whose bright eye
Obscures those lesser lights of sky;
Whose snowy breasts (if we may call
That snow that never melts at all)
Makes Jove invent a new disguise
In spite of Juno's jealousies;
Whose every part doth reinvite
The old, decayed appetite;
And in whose sweet embraces I
May melt myself to lust, and die.
   This is true bliss, and I confess
   There is no other happiness.

JAMES SHIRLEY
(1596–1666)

Ho! Cupid Calls

Ho! Cupid calls: come, lovers, come,
Bring his wanton harvest home.
The west-wind blows, the birds do sing,
The earth's enamelled, 'tis high spring.
   Let hinds whose soul is corn and hay
   Expect their crop another day.

Into love's spring-garden walk.
Virgins dangle on their stalk,
Full-blown, and playing at fifteen.
Come, bring your amorous sickles then! –
   See, they are pointing to their beds,–
   And call to reap their maidenheads.

Hark, how in yonder shady grove
Sweet Philomel is warbling love,
And with her voice is courting kings;
For since she was a bird, she sings.
   'There is no pleasure but in men:
   Oh, come and ravish me again.'

Virgins that are young and fair
May kiss, and grow into a pair.
Then warm and active use your blood:
No sad thought congeal the flood.
   Nature no medicine can impart
   When age once snows upon your heart.

EDWARD FAIRFAX
(d 1635)

Armida Entertains Rinaldo
from *Tasso's Godfrey of Bulloigne*

Her breasts were naked, for the day was hot,
Her locks unbound waved in the wanton wind,
Somedeal she sweat (tired with the game you wot),
Her sweat drops bright, white, round, like pearls of Ind,
Her humid eyes a fiery smile forth shot,
That like sun-beams in silver fountains shined,
   O'er him her looks she hung, and her soft breast
   The pillow was, here he and love took rest.

His hungry eyes upon her face he fed,
And feeding them so pined himself away;
And she, declining often down her head,
His lips, his cheeks, his eyes kissed, as he lay,
Wherewith he sighed, as if his soul had fled
From his frail breast to hers, and there would stay
   With her beloved sprite: the armed pair
   These follies all behold, and this hot fare.

Down by the lovers' side there pendant was
A crystal mirror, bright, pure, smooth and neat;
He rose and to his mistress held the glass
(A noble page, graced with that service great);
She with glad looks, he with inflamed (alas!)
Beauty and love beheld, both in one seat;
    Yet them in sundry objects each espies,
    She, in the glass; he saw them in her eyes.

Her, to command; to serve, it pleased the knight;
He proud of bondage; of her empire, she;
'My dear', she said, 'that blessest with thy sight
Even blessed angels, turn thine eyes to me,
For painted in my heart and portrayed right
Thy worth, thy beauties, and perfections be,
    Of which the form, the shape, and fashion best,
    Not in this glass is seen, but in my breast.

'And if thou me disdain, yet be content
At least so to behold thy lovely hue,
That while thereon thy looks are fixed and bent,
Thy happy eyes themselves may see and view;
So rare a shape, no crystal can present,
No glass contain that heaven of beauties true;
    Oh let the skies thy worthy mirror be,
    And in clear stars thy shape and image see!

And with that word she smiled, and ne'ertheless
Her love-toys still she used, and pleasures bold:
Her hair that done she twisted up in tress,
And looser locks in silken laces rolled,
Her curlés garland-wise she did updress,
Wherein (like rich enamel laid on gold)
    The twisted flowerets smiled, and her white breast
    The lilies (there that spring) and roses dressed.

SIR JOHN SUCKLING
(1609–1642)

The Candle

There is a thing which in the light
Is seldom used; but in the night
It serves the maiden female crew,
The ladies, and the good-wives too:
They use to take it in their hand,
And then it will uprightly stand;
And to a hole they it apply,
Where by its goodwill it would die;
It spends, goes out, and still within
It leaves its moisture thick and thin.

ANON
(1641)

Arithmetic of the Lips

Give me a kiss from those sweet lips of thine
And make it double by enjoining mine,
Another yet, nay yet and yet another,
And let the first kiss be the second's brother.
Give me a thousand kisses and yet more;
And then repeat those that have gone before.
Let us begin while daylight springs in heaven
And kiss till night descends into the even,
And when that modest secretary, night,
Discolours all but thy heaven beaming bright,
We will begin revels of hidden love
In that sweet orb where silent pleasures move.
In high new strains, unspeakable delight,
We'll vent the dull hours of the silent night.

Were the bright day no more to visit us,
Oh, then for ever would I hold thee thus,
Naked, enchained, empty of idle fear,
As the first lovers in the garden were.
I'll die betwixt thy breasts that are so white,
For to die there would do a man delight.
Embrace me still, for time runs on before,
And being dead we shall embrace no more.
Let us kiss faster than the hours do fly,
Long live each kiss and never know to die . . .
Let us vie kisses, till our eyelids cover,
And if I sleep, count me an idle lover;
Admit I sleep, I'll still pursue the theme,
And eagerly I'll kiss thee in a dream. . . .

(from *Wit's Recreations*)

SAMUEL BUTLER
(1612–1680)

Lust

One under millstone will wear out
Six upper ones that turn about.

Susanna

The two wicked elders Susanna would grope
While she sent out her maid to fetch her some soap;
But when they could not make her a whore
They swore she had swived with another before.

Marriage

A married man comes nearest to the dead,
And to be buried, 's but to go to bed.

[139]

from *Love*

When a surfeit of delight
Has dulled the lover's appetite,
He must have time, till new desire
Restore again his amorous fire.

O! 'tis a happy and heavenly death
When a man dies above, and a woman beneath.

JOHN CLEVELAND
(1613–1658)

A Fair Nymph Scorning a Black Boy Courting her

NYMPH   Stand off, and let me take the air.
             Why should the smoke pursue the fair?
BOY   My face is smoke, thence may be guessed
             What flames within have scorched my breast.
NYMPH   The flame of love I cannot view
             For the dark lantern of thy hue.
BOY   And let this lantern keeps love's taper
             Surer than yours, that's of white paper.
             Whatever midnight hath been here
             The moonshine of your face can clear.
NYMPH   My moon of an eclipse is 'fraid
             If thou should'st interpose thy shade.
BOY   Yet one thing, sweetheart, I will ask:
             Take me for a new-fashioned mask.
NYMPH   Done! But my bargain shall be this:
             I'll throw my mask off when I kiss.
BOY   Our curled embraces shall delight
             To chequer limbs with black and white.
NYMPH   Thy ink, my paper, make me guess
             Our nuptial bed will prove a press;
             And in our sports, if any come,
             They'll read a wanton epigram.

BOY Why should my black thy love impair?
     Let the dark shop commend the ware.
     Or if thy love from black forbears
     I'll strive to wash it off with tears.
NYMPH Spare fruitless tears, since thou must needs
       Still wear about thee mourning weeds;
       Tears can no more affection win
       Than wash thy Ethiopian skin.

A Song of Mark Antony

When as the nightingale chanted her vesper
And the wild forester couched on the ground,
Venus invited me in th'evening whisper
Unto a fragrant bed with roses crowned:
    Where she before had sent
    My wishes complement
    Who to my soul's content
Played with me on the green.
    Never Mark Antony
    Dallied more wantonly
With the fair Egyptian queen.

First on her cherry cheeks I mine eyes feasted,
Thence fear of surfeiting made me retire
Unto her warmer lips, which, when I tasted,
My spirits dull were made active as fire.
    This heat again to calm
    Her moist hand yielded balm
    While we joined palm to palm
As if they one had been.
    Never Mark Antony
    Dallied more wantonly
With the fair Egyptian queen.

[141]

Then in her golden hair I my arms twined
She her hands in my locks twisted again
As if our hair had been fetters assigned
Great little Cupid's loose captives to chain.
  Then we did often dart
  Each at the other's heart
  Arrows that knew no smart,
  Sweet looks and smiles between.
    Never Mark Antony
    Dallied more wantonly
  With the fair Egyptian queen.

Wanting a glass to plait those amber tresses
Which like a bracelet decked richly my arm
(Gaudier than Juno wears when as she blesses
Jove with embraces more stately than warm)
  Then did she peep in mine
  Eyes' humour crystalline
  And by reflexive shine
  I in her eye was seen.
    Never Mark Antony
    Dallied more wantonly
  With the fair Egyptian queen.

Mystical grammar of amorous glances,
Feeling of pulses, the physic of love,
Rhetorical courtings and musical dances,
Numbering of kisses arithmetic prove.
  Eyes like astronomy,
  Straight limbs' geometry,
  In her art's ingeny[1]
  Our wits were sharp and keen.
    Never Mark Antony
    Dallied more wantonly
  With the fair Egyptian queen.

[1]*ingeny* ingenuity

To the State of Love, or, the Senses' Festival

I saw a vision yesternight
Enough to sate a Seeker's[1] sight;
I wished myself a Shaker[2] there
And her quick pants my trembling sphere.
It was a she so glittering bright
You'd think her soul an Adamite;[3]
A person of so rare a frame
Her body might be lined with th'same.
Beauty's chiefest Maid of Honour,
You may break Lent with looking on her.
   Not the fair Abbess of the skies
   With all her nunnery of eyes
   Can show me such a glorious prize.

And yet, because 'tis more renown
To make a shadow shine, she's brown;
A brown for which Heaven would disband
The galaxy, and stars be tanned;
Brown by reflection, as her eye
Deals out the summer's livery.
Old dormer windows must confess
Her beams; their glimmering spectacles,
Struck with the splendour of her face,
Do th'office of a burning-glass.
   Now where such radiant lights have shown
   No wonder if her cheeks be grown
   Sun-burnt with lustres of her own.

My sight took pay, but (thank my charms)
I now empale her in my arms
(Love's compasses), confining you,
Good angels, to a circle, too.
Is not the universe strait-laced

[1]*Seekers* religious sect [2]*Shaker* member of religious sect who quivered while praying
[3]*Adamite* member of a religious sect which worshipped naked

[143]

When I can clasp it in the waist?
My amorous folds about thee hurled,
With Drake I girdle in the world.
I hoop the firmament, and make
This my embrace the Zodiac.
  How would thy centre take my sense
  When admiration doth commence
  At the extreme circumference?

Now to the melting kiss that sips
The jellied philtre of her lips;
So sweet, there is no tongue can phrase't
Till transubstantiate with a taste.
Inspired like Mahomet from above
By th'billing of my heavenly dove,
Love prints his signets in her smacks,
Those ruddy drops of squeezing wax,
Which, wheresoever she imparts
They're Privy Seals to take up hearts.
  Our mouths encountering at the sport
  My slippery soul had quit the fort,
  But that she stopped the sally-port.[1]

Next to those sweets her lips dispense
As twin-conserves of eloquence
The sweet perfume her breath affords,
Incorporating with her words.
No rosary this votress needs,
Her very syllables are beads.
No sooner twixt those rubies born
But jewels are in ear-rings worn.
With what delight her speech doth enter:
It is a kiss o'th'second venture.
  And I dissolve at what I hear
  As if another Rosamund were
  Couched in the labyrinth of my ear.

[1]*sally-port* a way through a fortified wall

[144]

Yet that's but a preludious[1] bliss;
Two souls pickearing[2] in a kiss.
Embraces do but draw the line –
'Tis storming that must take her in.
When bodies join, and victory hovers
'Twixt the equal fluttering lovers:
This is the game. Make stakes, my dear,
Hark how the sprightly chanticleer,
That Baron Tell-clock of the night,
Sounds boot-esel[3] to Cupid's knight.
    Then have at all, the pass is got,
    For coming off, oh name it not:
    Who would not die[4] upon the spot?

ABRAHAM COWLEY
(1618–1667)

Maidenhead

Thou worst estate even of the sex that's **worst;**
  Therefore by Nature made at first
  T'attend the weakness of our birth!
Slight, outward curtain to the nuptial bed!
Thou case to buildings not yet finished!
  Who like the centre of the earth
  Dost heavier things attract to thee,
Though thou a point imaginary be.

A thing God thought for mankind so unfit
  That his first blessing ruined it.
  Cold frozen nurse of fiercest fires!
Who, like the parched plains of Africk's sand

[1]*preludious* by way of prelude [2]*pickearing* skirmishing [3]*boot-esel* trumpet call to cavalry to saddle up [4]*die* in the sense of orgasm

(A sterile and a wild, unlovely land)
   Art always scorched with hot desires,
   Yet barren quite, didst thou not bring
Monsters and serpents forth thy self to sting!

Thou that bewitchest men, whilst thou dost dwell
   Like a close conjurer in his cell
   And fearest the day's discovering eye!
No wonder 'tis at all that thou shouldst be
Such tedious and unpleasant company
   Who livest so melancholily!
   Thou thing of subtle, slippery kind,
Which women lose, and yet no man can find.

Although I think thou never found wilt be
   Yet I'm resolved to search for thee;
   The search itself rewards the pains.
So, though the chemist his great secret miss
(For neither it in art nor nature is)
   Yet things well worth his toil he gains
   And does his charge and labour pay
With good unsought experiments by the way.
Say what thou wilt, Chastity is no more
   Thee, than a porter is his door.
   In vain to honour they pretend
Who guard themselves with ramparts and with walls.
Them only fame the truly valiant calls
   Who can an open breach defend.
   Of thy quick loss can be no doubt,
Within so hated, and so loved without.

ALEX BROME
(1620–1666)

Though Oxford be Yielded

Though Oxford be yielded[1] and Reading be taken,
I'll put in for quarter at thy Maidenhead.
There while I'm esconced, my standard unshaken,
Lie thou in my arms, and I in thy bed.
Let the young zealots march with their wenches
Mounting their tools to edify trenches,
While thou and I do make it our pleasure
To dig in thy mine for the purest treasure,
    Where nobody else shall plunder but I.

And when we together in battles do join
We scorn to wear arms but what are our own.
Strike thou at my body, and I'll thrust at thine.
By nakedness best the truth is made known.
Cannons may roar and bullets keep flying;
While we are in battle we never fear dying.
Isaac[2] and's wenches are busy a-digging
But all our delight is in japing[3] and jigging,
    And nobody else shall plunder but I.

And when at the last our bodies are weary,
We'll straight to the tavern our strength to recruit,
Where when we've refreshed our hearts with canary
We shall be the fitter again to go to't.
We'll tipple and drink until we do stagger,
For then is the time for soldiers to swagger.
Thus night and day we'll thump it and knock it,
And when we've no money, then look to your pocket,
    For nobody else shall plunder but I.

[1]*Oxford be yielded* In 1646 the King's forces at Oxford surrendered to Cromwell's
[2]*Isaac* Isaac Pennington, Lord Mayor of London [3]*japing* copulating

ANDREW MARVELL
(1621–1678)

To his Coy Mistress

Had we but world enough, and time,
This coyness, lady, were no crime –
We would sit down and think which way
To walk, and pass our long love's day.
Thou by the Indian Ganges' side
Should'st rubies find; I by the tide
Of Humber would complain. I would
Love you ten years before the Flood,
And you should if you please refuse
Till the Conversion of the Jews.
My vegetable love should grow
Vaster than empires, and more slow.
An hundred years should go to praise
Thine eyes, and on thy forehead gaze;
Two hundred to adore each breast,
But thirty thousand to the rest;
An age at least to every part,
And the last age should show your heart.
For, lady, you deserve this state,
Nor would I love at lower rate.

But at my back I always hear
Time's winged chariot hurrying near;
And yonder all before us lie
Deserts of vast eternity.
Thy beauty shall no more be found,
Nor in thy marble vault shall sound
My echoing song; then worms shall try
That long-preserved virginity,
And your quaint honour turn to dust,
And into ashes all my lust.
The grave's a fine and private place,
But none, I think, do there embrace.

Now, therefore, while the youthful hue
Sits on thy skin like morning dew,
And while thy willing soul transpires
At every pore with instant fires,
Now let us sport us while we may,
And now, like amorous birds of prey
Rather at once our time devour
Than languish in his slow-chapped power.
Let us roll all our strength, and all
Our sweetness, up into one ball
And tear our pleasures with rough strife
Thorough the iron gates of life.
Thus, though we cannot make our sun
Stand still, yet we will make him run.

CHARLES COTTON
(1630–1687)

A Paraphrase

The beauty that must me delight,
Must have a skin and teeth snow white:
Black arched brows, black sprightly eyes,
And a black beauty twixt her thighs;
Soft blushing cheeks, a person tall,
Long hair, long hands, and fingers small;
Short teeth; and feet that little are,
Dilated brows, and haunches fair:
Fine silken hair, lips full and red,
Small nose, with little breast and head:
All these in one, and that one kind
Would make a mistress to my mind.

An Epitaph on M.H.

In this cold monument lies one
That I knew who has lain upon
The happier He: her sight would charm
And touch have kept King David warm.
Lovely as is the dawning east
Was this marble's frozen guest;
As soft and snowy as that down
Adorns the blow-ball's frizzled crown;
As straight and slender as the crest
Or antler of the one-beamed beast;
Pleasant as th'odorous month of May
As glorious and as light as day.

    Whom I admired as soon as knew,
And now her memory pursue
With such a superstitious lust
That I could fumble with her dust.

    She all perfections had, and more,
Tempting, as if designed a whore –
For so she was; and since there are
Such, I could wish them all as fair.

    Pretty she was, and young, and wise,
And in her calling so precise
That industry had made her prove
The sucking schoolmistress of love;
And death, ambitious to become
Her pupil, left his ghastly home
And seeing how we used her here
The rawboned rascal ravished her.

    Who, pretty soul, reigned her breath
To seek new lechery in death.

ANON
(c 1650)

John Anderson, My Jo

John Anderson, my jo, John,
   I wonder what ye mean,
To lie sae lang i' the mornin',
   And sit sae late at e'en?
Ye'll bleer[1] a' your een, John,
   And why do ye so?
Come sooner to your bed at een,
   John Anderson, my jo.

John Anderson, my jo, John,
   When first that ye began,
Ye had as good a tail-tree
   As any ither man;
But now it's waxen wan, John,
   And wrinkles to and fro;
I've twa gae-ups for ae gae-down,
   John Anderson, my jo.

I'm backit like a salmon,
   I'm breastit like a swan;
My wame[2] it is a down-cod,[3]
   My middle ye may span:
Frae my tap-knot to my tae, John,
   I'm like the new-fa'n snow;
And it's a' for your convenience,
   John Anderson, my jo.

O it is a fine thing
   To keep out[4] o'er the dyke;
But it's a meikle[5] finer thing
   To see your hurdies fyke;[6]

[1]*bleer* ruin [2]*wame* belly [3]*down-cod* feather pillow [4]*keep out* watch out [5]*meikle* much
[6]*hurdies fyke* buttocks bounce

To see your hurdies fyke, John,
   And hit the rising blow;
   It's then I like your chanter-pipe,
   John Anderson, my jo.

When ye come on before, John,
   See that ye do your best;
When ye begin to haud[1] me,
   See that ye grip me fast;
See that ye grip me fast, John,
   Until that I cry 'Oh!'
You back shall crack or I do that,
   John Anderson, my jo.

John Anderson, my jo, John,
   Ye're welcome when ye please;
It's either in the warm bed
   Or else aboon the claes:[2]
Or ye shall hae the horns, John,
   Upon your head to grow;
An' that's the cuckold's mallison,
   John Anderson, my jo.

JOHN DRYDEN
(1631–1700)

Song: from An Evening's Love

Calm was the Even, and clear was the sky
   And the new budding flowers did spring,
When all alone went Amyntas and I
   To hear the sweet Nightingale sing;
I sat, and he laid him down by me;
   But scarcely his breath he could draw;
For when with a fear he began to draw near,
   He was dash'd with A ha ha ha ha!

[1]*haud* hold [2]*aboon the claes* outside the bedclothes

He blush'd to himself, and lay still for a while,
  And his modesty curb'd his desire;
But straight I convinc'd all his fear with a smile,
  Which added new flames to his fire.
'O Sylvia', he said, 'you are cruel,
  To keep your poor Lover in awe';
Then once more he pressed with his hand to my breast,
But was dash'd with A ha ha ha ha

I knew 'twas his passion that caus'd all his fear;
  And therefore I pitied his case:
I whisper'd him softly 'There's no body near',
  And laid my cheek close to his face:
But as he grew bolder and bolder,
  A Shepherd came by us and saw;
And just as our bliss we began with a kiss,
  He laughed out with A ha ha ha ha.

Song: from Marriage-à-la-Mode

Whilst Alexis lay pressed
In her Arms he loved best
With his hands round her neck
And his head on her breast,
He found the fierce pleasure too hasty to stay,
And his soul in the tempest just flying away.

When Celia saw this,
With a sigh, and a kiss,
She cry'd, 'Oh my dear, I am robbed of my bliss;
'Tis unkind to your Love, and unfaithfully done,
To leave me behind you, and die all alone.'

The Youth, though in haste,
And breathing his last,
In pity died slowly, while she died more fast;
Till at length she cried, 'Now, my dear, now let us go,
Now die, my Alexis, and I will die too.'

[153]

Thus entranced they did lie,
Till Alexis did try
To recover new breath, that again he might die:
Then often they died; but the more they did so,
The Nymph died more quick, and the Shepherd more slow.

A New Song

Sylvia the fair, in the bloom of fifteen,
Felt an innocent warmth as she lay on the green;
She had heard of a pleasure, and something she guessed
By the towzing and tumbling and touching her breast;
She saw the men eager, but was at a loss
What they meant by their sighing, and kissing so close.
By their praying and whining
And clasping and twining,
And panting and wishing,
And sighing and kissing
And sighing and kissing so close.

'Ah!' she cried, 'Ah for a languishing maid
In a country of Christians to die without aid!
Not a Whig, or a Tory, or Trimmer at least,
Or a Protestant Parson, or Catholic Priest
To instruct a young virgin, that is at a loss
What they meant by their sighing, and kissing so close!
By their praying and whining
And clasping and twining,
And panting and wishing,
And sighing and kissing
And sighing and kissing so close.'

Cupid in shape of a swain did appear,
He saw the sad wound, and in pity drew near,
Then showed her his arrow, and bid her not fear
For the pain was no more than a maiden might bear;

When the balm was infused she was not at a loss
What they meant by their sighing and kissing so close;
    By their praying and whining,
    And clasping and twining,
    And panting and wishing,
    And sighing and kissing,
    And sighing and kissing so close.

Pygmalion and The Statue
Out of the Tenth Book of Ovid's Metamorphoses

Pygmalion loathing their lascivious life
Abhorred all womankind, but most a wife;
So single chose to live, and shunned to wed,
Well pleased to want a consort of his bed.
Yet fearing idleness, the nurse of ill,
In sculpture exercised his happy skill,
And carved in ivory such a maid, so fair,
As nature could not with his art compare
Were she to work – but in her own defence
Must take her pattern here, and copy hence.
Pleased with his idol, he commends, admires,
Adores; and last, the thing adored desires.
A very virgin in her face was seen,
And had she moved, a living maid had been.
One would have thought she could have stirred, but
    strove
With modesty, and was ashamed to move.
Art hid with art, so well performed the cheat
It caught the carver with his own deceit:
He knows 'tis madness, yet he must adore,
And still the more he knows it, loves the more.
The flesh, or what so seems, he touches oft,
Which feels so smooth that he believes it soft.
Fired with this thought at once he strained the breast

And on the lips a burning kiss impressed.
'Tis true the hardened breasts resist the gripe
And the cold lips return a kiss unripe –
But when retiring back he looked again
To think it ivory was a thought too mean,
So would believe she kissed, and courting more
Again embraced her naked body o'er
And straining hard the statue, was afraid
His hands had made a dint and hurt his maid,
Explored her limb by limb, and feared to find
So rude a gripe had left a livid mark behind.
With flattery now he seeks her mind to move,
And now with gifts (the powerful bribes of love).
He furnishes her closet first, and fills
The crowded shelves with rarities of shells,
Adds orient pearls which from the conches he drew
And all the sparkling stones of various hue,
And parrots imitating human tongue
And singing-birds in silver cages hung,
And every fragrant flower and odorous green
Were sorted well, with lumps of amber laid between.
Rich, fashionable robes her person deck,
Pendants her ears and pearls adorn her neck;
Her tapered fingers too with rings are graced
And an embroidered zone surrounds her slender waist.
Thus like a queen arrayed, so richly dressed,
Beauteous she showed, but naked showed the best.
Then from the floor he raised a royal bed
With coverings of Sydonian purple spread.
The solemn rites performed, he calls her bride,
With blandishments invites her to his side,
And as she were with vital sense possessed
Her head did on a plumy pillow rest.
    The feast of Venus came, a solemn day
To which the Cypriots due devotion pay.
With gilded horns the milk-white heifers led,
Slaughtered before the sacred altars, bled.

Pygmalion offering first approached the shrine
And then with prayers implored the powers divine:
'Almighty gods, if all we mortals want,
If all we can require, be yours to grant,
Make this fair statue mine', he would have said –
But changed his words for shame, and only prayed
'Give me the likeness of my ivory maid.'
   The golden goddess, present at the prayer,
Well knew he meant the animated fair,
And gave the sign of granting his desire –
For thrice in cheerful flames ascends the fire.
The youth, returning to his mistress, hies,
And impudent in hope, with ardent eyes
And beating breast by the dear statue lies.
He kisses her white lips, renews the bliss,
And looks, and thinks they redden at the kiss
(He thought them warm before), nor longer stays
But next his hand on her hard bosom lays –
Hard as it was, beginning to relent –
It seemed the breast beneath his fingers bent.
He felt again – his fingers made a print –
'Twas flesh, but flesh so firm it rose against the dint.
The pleasing task he fails not to renew.
Soft and more soft at every touch it grew,
Like pliant wax when chafing hands reduce
The former mass to form, and frame for use.
He would believe, but yet is still in pain
And tries his argument of sense again,
Presses the pulse, and feels the leaping vein.
Convinced, o'erjoyed, his studied thanks and praise
To her who made the miracle, he pays,
Then lips to lips he joined; now freed from fear
He found the savour of the kiss sincere.
At this, the wakened image op'd her eyes
And viewed at once the light and lover with surprise.
The goddess, present at the match she made,
So blessed the bed, such fruitfulness conveyed,

That e'er ten moons had sharpened either horn,
To crown their bliss a lovely boy was born,
Paphos his name, who grown to manhood, walled
The city Paphos, from the founder called.

Young I Am

Young I am, and yet unskilled
How to make a lover yield,
How to keep or how to gain,
When to love and when to feign.

Take me, take me, some of you,
While I yet am young and true,
Ere I can my soul disguise,
Heave my breast and roll my eyes.

Stay not till I learn the way
How to lie and to betray;
He that has me first is blessed,
For I may deceive the rest.

Could I find a blooming youth
Full of love and full of truth,
Brisk and of a jaunty mien,
I should long to be fifteen.

Love's Fancy

After the pangs of a desperate lover,
When day and night I have sighed all in vain,
Ah what a pleasure it is to discover
In her eyes pity, who causes my pain!

When with unkindness our love at a stand is,
And both have punished ourselves with the pain,
Ah what a pleasure the touch of her hand is!
Ah what a pleasure to press it again!

When the denial comes fainter and fainter,
And her eyes give what her tongue does deny,
Ah what a trembling I feel when I venture!
Ah what a trembling does utter my joy!

When with a sigh she accords me the blessing,
And her eyes twinkle 'twixt pleasure and pain,
Ah what a joy 'tis, beyond all expressing,
Ah what a joy to hear, 'Shall we again?'

SIR GEORGE ETHEREGE
(1635?-1691)

The Imperfect Enjoyment

After a pretty amorous discourse,
She does resist my love with pleasing force,
Moved not with anger but with modesty:
Against her will she is my enemy.
Her eyes the rudeness of her arms excuse,
Those do accept what these seem to refuse;
To ease my passion and to make me blest,
The linen of itself falls from her breast;
Then with her lovely hands she does conceal
Those wonders chance so kindly did reveal.
In vain, alas, her nimble fingers strove
To keep her beauties from my greedy love;
Guarding her breasts, they do her lips expose,
To save a lily she must lose a rose.
What charms are here in every part? what grace?

A hundred hands can't shield each beauteous place.
Now she consents, her force she does recall,
And since I must have part she'll give me all.
Her arms, which did repulse me, now embrace
And seem to guide me to the fought-for place.
Her love is in her sparkling eyes expressed,
She falls on the bed for pleasure more than rest.
But oh, strange passions! oh, abortive joy!
My zeal does my devotion quite destroy:
Come to the temple where I should implore
My saint, I worship at the sacred door.
Oh cruel chance! the town which did oppose
My strength so long now yields to my dispose
When, overjoyed with victory, I fall
Dead at the foot of the surrendered wall.
Without the usual ceremony, we
Have both fulfilled the amorous mystery;
The action which we should have jointly done,
Each has unluckily performed alone;
The union which our bodies should enjoy,
The union of our eager souls destroy.
Our flames are punished by their own excess –
We'd had more pleasure had our love been less.
She blushed and frowned, perceiving we had done
The sport she thought we had not yet begun.
Alas, said I, condemn yourself, not me;
This is the effect of too much modesty.
Hence with that harmful virtue, the delight
Of both our victories was lost in the fight;
From my defeat your glory does arise,
My weakness proves the vigour of your eyes;
They did consume the victim, ere it came
Unto the altar, with a purer flame.
Phillis, let this same comfort ease your care,
You'd been more happy had you been less fair.

So soft and amorously you write
Of cunt and prick, the cunt's delight,
That were I still in lantern sweating,
Swallowing of bolus or a-spitting,[1]
I should forgive each injury
The pocky whores have offered me,
And only of my fate complain
Because I must from cunt abstain.
The powerful cunt! whose very name
Kindles in me an amorous flame!
Begins to make my pintle rise,
And long again to fight Love's prize!
Forgetful of those many scars
Which he has gotten in those wars.
This shows Love's chiefest magic lies
In women's cunts, not in their eyes:
There Cupid does his revels keep,
There lovers all their sorrows steep;
For having once but tasted that,
Their mysteries are quite forgot.
This may suffice to let you know
That I to cunt am not a foe,
Though you are pleased to think me so;
'Tis strange his zeal should be in suspicion
Who dies a martyr for's religion.
    But now to give you an account
Of Cuffley, that whore paramount!
Cuffley! whose beauty warms the age,
And fills our youth with love and rage,
Who like fierce wolves pursue the game,
While secretly the lecherous dame
With some choice gallant takes her flight
And in a corner fucks all night.
Then the next morning we all hunt

[1]cures for venereal disease

To find whose fingers smell of cunt,
With jealousy and envy moved
Against the man that was beloved.
Whilst you to Echo teach her name,
Thus it becomes the voice of fame
In every corner of the Town.
We here proclaim her high renown
Whilst you within some neighbouring grove
Indite the story of your love,
And with your penknife keen and bright,
On stately trees your passion write,
So that each nymph that passes through
Must envy her and pity you.
We at the Fleece or at the Bear,
With good case knife, well whet on stair
(A gentle weapon, made to feed
Mankind and not to let him bleed)
A thousand amorous fancies scrape.
There's not a pewter dish can scape
Without her name or arms which are
The same that Love himself does bear.

   Here one, to show you love's no glutton,
In the midst of supper leaves his mutton,
And on his greasy plate, with care,
Carves the bright image of the fair.

   Another, though a drunken sot,
Neglects his wine and on the pot
A band of naked Cupids draws,
With pricks no bigger than wheat straws.
Then on a nasty candlestick
One figures Love's hieroglyphic,
A couchant cunt and rampant prick.
And that the sight may more inflame,
The lookers-on subscribe her name:
Cuffley! – her sex's pride and shame.
There's not a man but does discover
By some such action he's her lover.

But now 'tis time to give her over,
And let your Lordship know you are
The mistress that employs our care.
Your absence makes us melancholy,
Nor drink nor cunt can make us jolly,
Unless we've you within our arms,
In whom there dwells diviner charms.
Then quit with speed your pensive grove
And here in Town pursue your love;
Where at your coming you shall find
Your servants glad, your mistress kind,
All things devoted to your mind.

THOMAS SCOTT
(c 1695)

A Roundelay

Man, that is for woman made
And the woman made for man.
As the spur is for the jade,
As the scabbard for the blade,
As for liquor is the can,
So man is for the woman made,
And the woman made for man.

Man, that is for woman made,
And the woman made for man.
As the sceptre to be swayed,
As to night the serenade,
As for pudding is the pan,
As to cool us is the fan,
So man is for the woman made,
And the woman made for man.

[163]

Man is for the woman made,
And the woman made for man.
As the widow, wife, or maid,
Be she wanton, be she staid,
Be she well or ill arrayed,
Whore, bawd or harridan,
So man is for the woman made,
And the woman made for man.

(from *The Mock Marriage* 1695)

ANON
(c 1670)

Stand, Stately Tavie

Stand, stately Tavie, out of the codpiece rise,
And dig a grave between thy mistress' thighs;
Swift stand, then stab 'till she replies,
Then gently weep, and after weeping, die.
Stand, Tavie, and gain thy credit lost;
Or by this hand I'll never draw thee, but against a post.

ANON
(c 1671)

Against Platonic Love

'Tis true, fair Celia, that by thee I live;
That every kiss, and every fond embrace
Forms a new soul within me, and doth give
A balsam to the wound made by thy face.

Yet still methinks I miss
　That bliss
Which lovers dare not name,
And only then described is
When flame doth meet with flame.

Those favours which do bless me every day
Are yet but empty and platonical.
Think not to please your servants with half pay.
Good gamesters never stick to throw at all.
　Who can endure to miss
　　That bliss
　Which lovers dare not name,
　And only then described is
　When flame doth meet with flame?

If all those sweets within you must remain,
Unknown and ne'er enjoyed, like hidden treasure,
Nature, as well as I, will lose her name,
And you as well as I lose youthful pleasure.
　We wrong ourselves to miss
　　That bliss
　Which lovers dare not name,
　And only then described is
　When flame doth meet with flame.

Our souls which long have peeped at one another
Out of the narrow casements of our eyes
Shall now by love conducted meet together
In secret caverns, where all pleasure lies.
　There, there we shall not miss
　　That bliss
　Which lovers dare not name,
　And only then described is
　When flame doth meet with flame.

SIR CHARLES SEDLEY
(1639–1701)

Young Coridon and Phillis

Young Coridon and Phillis
   Sat in a lovely grove
Contriving crowns of lilies,
   Repeating tales of love:
And something else, but what I dare not name.

But as they were a-playing
   She ogled so the swain
It saved her plainly saying
   'Let's kiss to ease our pain:
And something else, but what I dare not name.'

A thousand times he kissed her,
   Laying her on the green,
But as he further pressed her,
   Her pretty leg was seen:
And something else, but what I dare not name.

So many beauties removing
   His ardour still increased,
And greater joys pursuing
   He wandered o'er her breast:
And something else, but what I dare not name.

A last effort she trying
   His passion to withstand,
Cried (but it was faintly crying)
   'Pray take away your hand,
And something else, but what I dare not name.'

Young Coridon grown bolder
   The minute would improve;
'This is the time', he told her,
   'To show you how I love –
And something else, but what I dare not name.'

The nymph seemed almost dying,
   Dissolved in amorous heat;
She kissed and told him sighing
   'My dear, your love is great:
And something else, but what I dare not name.'

But Phillis did recover
   Much sooner than the swain;
She blushing asked her lover
   'Shall we not kiss again,
And something else, but what I dare not name?'

Thus love his revels keeping
   Till nature at a stand
From talk they fell to sleeping,
   Holding each other's hand:
And something else, but what I dare not name.

Tush! Never Tell Me

Tush! never tell me I'm too young
   For loving, or too green;
She stays at least seven years too long
   That's wedded at eighteen.
Lambs bring forth lambs and doves bring doves
   As soon as they're begotten,
Then why should ladies linger loves
   As if not ripe till rotten?

Grey hairs are fitter for the grave
  Than for the bridal bed;
What pleasure can a lover have
  In a withered maidenhead?
Nature's exalted in our time
  And what our grandams then
At four and twenty scarce could climb
  We can arrive at ten.

Phillis

Phillis, this early zeal assuage;
  You over-act your part.
The martyrs at your tender age
  Gave Heaven but half their heart.

Old men till past the pleasure ne'er
  Declaim against the sin;
'Tis early to begin to fear
  The Devil at fifteen.

The world to youth is too severe
  And, like a treacherous light,
Beauty, the actions of the fair,
  Exposes to their sight.

And yet the world, as old as 'tis,
  Is oft deceived by't too;
Kind combinations seldom miss –
  Let's try what we can do.

On Fruition

None but a muse in love can tell
The sweet, tumultuous joys I feel
When on Celia's breast I lie,
When I tremble, faint and die,

Mingling kisses with embraces,
Darting tongues and joining faces,
Panting, stretching, sweating, cooing
All in the ecstasy of doing.

APHRA BEHN
(1640–1689)

Song: Love Arm'd

Love in fantastic triumph sat
  Whilst bleeding hearts around him flowed,
For whom fresh pains he did create,
  And strange, tyrannic power he showed.

From thy bright eyes he took his fire,
  Which round about in sport he hurled;
But 'twas from mine he took desire,
  Enough to undo the amorous world.

From me he took his sighs and tears,
  From thee his pride and cruelty,
From me his languishments and fears,
  And every killing dart from thee.

Thus thou and I the god have armed
  And set him up a deity;
But my poor heart alone is harmed,
  Whilst thine the victor is, and free.

The Disappointment

One day the amorous Lysander,
By an impatient passion swayed,
Surprised fair Cloris, that loved maid,

Who could defend herself no longer.
All things did with his love conspire:
The gilded planet of the day
In his gay chariot drawn by fire
Was now descending to the sea,
And left no light to guide the world
But what from Cloris' brighter eyes was hurled.

In a lone thicket made for love,
Silent as yielding maid's consent,
She with a charming languishment
Permits his force, yet gently strove.
Her hands his bosom softly meet,
But not to put him back designed –
Rather to draw 'em on inclined.
Whilst he lay trembling at her feet
Resistance 'tis in vain to show:
She wants the power to say, 'Ah, what d'ye do?'

Her bright eyes sweet, and yet severe,
Where love and shame confusedly strive,
Fresh vigour to Lysander give;
And breathing faintly in his ear
She cried: 'Cease, cease your vain desire
Or I'll call out! What would you do?
My dearer honour even to you
I cannot, must not give! Retire!
Or take this life, whose chiefest part
I gave you with the conquest of my heart.'

But he as much unused to fear
As he was capable of love
The blessed minutes to improve
Kisses her mouth, her neck, her hair.
Each touch her new desire alarms,
His burning, trembling hand he pressed

Upon her swelling, snowy breast,
While she lay panting in his arms.
All her unguarded beauties lie
The spoils and trophies of the enemy.

And now without respect or fear
He seeks the object of his vows
(His love no modesty allows),
By swift degrees advancing – where
His daring hand that altar seized
Where gods of love do sacrifice:
That awful throne, that paradise
Where rage is calmed and anger pleased,
That fountain where delight still flows
And gives the universal world repose.

Her balmy lips encountering his,
Their bodies, as their souls, are joined
Where both in transports unconfined
Extend themselves upon the moss.
Cloris half dead and breathless lay,
Her soft eyes cast a humid light
Such as divides the day and night,
Or falling stars whose fires decay;
And now no signs of life she shows
But what in short-breathed sighs returns and goes.

He saw how at her length she lay.
He saw her rising bosom bare,
Her loose, thin robes, through which appear
A shape designed for love and play,
Abandoned by her pride and shame.
She does her softest joys dispense,
Offering her virgin-innocence
A victim to love's sacred flame,
While the o'er-ravished shepherd lies
Unable to perform the sacrifice.

Ready to taste a thousand joys
The too transported, hapless swain
Found the vast pleasure turned to pain –
Pleasure which too much love destroys.
The willing garments by he laid,
And heaven all opened to his view.
Mad to possess, himself he threw
On the defenceless, lovely maid.
But oh, what envying god conspires
To snatch his power, yet leave him the desire!

Nature's support (without whose aid
She can no human being give)
Itself now wants the art to live;
Faintness its slackened nerves invade.
In vain th'enraged youth essayed
To call its fleeting vigour back,
No motion 'twill from motion take.
Excess of love is Love betrayed.
In vain he toils, in vain commands –
Insensible falls weeping in his hands.

In this so amorous, cruel strife
Where love and fate were too severe
The poor Lysander in despair
Renounced his reason with his life.
Now all the brisk and active fire
That should the nobler part inflame
Served to increase his rage and shame
And left no spark for new desire.
Not all her naked charms could move
Or calm that rage that had debauched his love.

Cloris returning from the trance
Which love and soft desire had bred,
Her timorous hand she gently laid

(Or guided by desire or chance)
Upon that fabulous priapus,
That potent god, as poets feign –
But never did young shepherdess
Gathering of fern upon the plain
More nimbly draw her fingers back
Finding beneath the verdant leaves a snake

Than Cloris her fair hand withdrew,
Finding that god of her desires
Disarmed of all his awful fires
And cold as flowers bathed in the morning dew.
Who can the nymph's confusion guess?
The blood forsook the hinder place
And strewed with blushes all her face,
Which both disdain and shame expressed;
And from Lysander's arms she fled,
Leaving him fainting on the gloomy bed.

Like lightning through the groves she hies,
Or Daphne from the Delphic god;
No print upon the grassy road
She leaves, t'instruct pursuing eyes.
The wind that wantoned in her hair
And with her ruffled garments played
Discovered in the flying maid
All that the gods e'er made, if fair.
So Venus, when her love was slain,
With fear and haste flew o'er the fatal plain.

The nymph's resentments none but I
Can well imagine or condole.
But none can guess Lysander's soul
But those who swayed his destiny.
His silent griefs swell up to storms,
And not one god his fury spares;

He cursed his birth, his fate, his stars –
But more the shepherdess's charms,
Whose soft, bewitching influence
Had damned him to the hell of impotence.

ROBERT GOULD
(c 1695)

Song

Take not a woman's anger ill,
But let this be your comfort still,
That if one won't, another will;

Though she that's foolish does deny,
She that is wiser will comply,
And if 'tis but a woman, what care I?

Then who'd be damned to swear untrue,
And sigh and weep and whine and woo,
As all our supple coxcombs do?

All women love it, and though this
Does sullenly forbid the bliss,
Try the next – you cannot miss.

(from *The Rival Sisters* 1695)

ANON
(c 1671)

The Pretty, Drowsy Rogue

Last night I dreamed of my love
When sleep did overtake her.
It was a pretty, drowsy rogue;
She slept; I durst not wake her.

Her lips were like to coral red;
A thousand times I kissed 'um,
And a thousand more I might have stolen,
For she had never missed 'um.

Her crisped locks, like threads of gold,
Hung dangling o'er the pillows;
Great pity 'twas that one so fair
Should wear the rainbow-willow.

I folded down the holland sheet
A little below her belly,
But what I did you ne'er shall know,
Nor is it meet to tell ye.

Her belly's like to yonder hill –
Some call it Mount of Pleasure –
And underneath there springs a well
Which no man's depth can measure.

ANON
(c 1671)

The Tenement

If any man do want a house,
Be he prince, baronet or squire,
Or peasant, hardly worth a louse,
    I can fit his desire.

I have a tenement the which
I'm sure can fit them all;
'Tis seated near a stinking ditch,
    Some call it Cunny Hall.

[175]

It stands close by Cunny Alley
At foot of Belly Hill.
This house is freely to be let
      To whom soever will.

For term of life or years or days
I'll let this pleasant bower,
Nay, rather than a tenant want,
      I'll let it for an hour.

About it grows a lofty wood
Will save you from the sun;
Well watered 'tis, for throughout
      A pleasant stream doth run.

If hot, you there may cool yourself,
If cool, you'll there find heat;
For greatest 'tis not too little
      For least 'tis not too great.

I must confess my house is dark,
Be it by night or day,
But when you're once but got therein
      You'll never lose your way.

And when you're in go boldly on
As fast as e'er you can,
For if you go to the end thereof
      You go where ne'er did man.

But though my house be deep and dark,
'T has many a man made merry,
And in't much liquor has been spent
      More precious than the sherry.

Thus if you like my Cunny Hall
Your house-room shall be good,
For such a temper as you find
      Burns neither cole nor wood,

For if it rain or freeze or snow –
To speak I dare be bold –
If you keep your nose within the door
        You ne'er shall feel the cold.

But I must covenant with him
That takes this house of mine,
Whether it be for term of life
        Or else for shorter time.

See that you dress it twice a day
And rub it round about,
And if you do dislike of this
        I'll seek a new tenant out.

ANON
(c 1680)

One Writing Against his Prick

Base metal hanger by your master's thigh!
Eternal shame to all Prick's heraldry,
Hide thy despiséd head and do not dare
To peep, no not so much as take the air
But through a button hole, but pine and die
Confined within the codpiece monastery.
The little childish boy that hardly knows
The way through which his urine flows
Touched by my mistress her magnetic hand
His little needle presently will stand.
Did she not raise thy drooping head on high
As it lay nodding on her wanton thigh?
Did she not clap her legs about my back
Her port-hole open? Damned Prick what is't you lack?
Henceforth stand stiff and gain your credit lost
Or I'll ne'er draw thee but against a post.

[177]

ANON
(c 1682)

The Bell to the Bed

See how charming Celia lies upon her bridal bed.
  There's no such beauty at Court –
  She's fit for the sport
And she looks so lovely, white and red.
After the first and second time
The bridegroom 'gins to slack his pace,
But she cries: 'Come, come, come, come to me
And lay thy cheek close to my face.'
Tinkle, tinkle, ting goes the bell to the bed
Whilst common time they keep;
  With a parting kiss
  They end their bliss
And so retire to sleep.

ANON
(c 1686)

The Lady of Pleasure: A Satire

The Life of Nelly,[1] *truly shown,*
From Coal-yard and Cellar to the Throne,
Till into the Grave she tumbled down.

I sing the Story of a Scoundrel Lass
Raised from a Dunghill to a King's embrace:
I trace her from her birth and infant years;
To Venus none so like as she appears.
To Madam Venus the sea-froth gave birth:

[1] *Nelly* Nell Gwyn

To Madam Nell, the scum of all the earth.
No man alive could ever call her daughter,
For a battalion of armed men begot her.
The pious mother of this flaming whore
Maid, punk and bawd full sixty years and more
Died drunk with brandy in a common-shore.
No matter that, not what we are must shame us,
'Tis what we last arrive to, that must fame us.
Famed be the cellar, then, wherein the babe
Was first brought forth to be a Monarch's drab.
In a low cellar under ground, this trull –
Heavens! what can Fortune do, if Fortune will? –
In a low cellar this same trull was kindled
That hast so oft old Rowley's[1] sceptre dwindled.
How far did the famed Amazonian come to woo
Great Alexander for a touch and go?
But thee, thy Sovereign courted for thy fame,
Enjoyed thee, 'cause 'twas thou hadst got the name –
Thou didst not come to him with gold and spice,
And nothing introduced thee but thy vice.
Oh may that cellar never be forgot
Wherein was hatched such a Prince-pleasing trot.
He that had seen her muddling in the street
Her face all pot-lid black, unshod her feet,
And in a cloud of dust her cinders shaking –
Could he have thought her fit for Monarch's taking?
Even then she had her charms of brisk and witty
Which first enslaved a cully of the city.
He had her breech washed clean, and smocked her white
That she might be his darling and delight.
Then in her wine began this dialogue:
'My little deity, my pretty rogue
That hast redeemed me from my slitten milk
To worsted hose and petticoat of silk:
Be kind, my dear, and flowing joy impart.
Apply love's sovereign balsam to my heart.'

[1]*Rowley* Charles II

[179]

Thus for some time each other they enjoyed,
Until the merchant, not the girl, was cloyed –
For either with th'expense of purse or love
At length the fool did wondrous Nell-sick prove.
Howe'er, he would not leave her as he found her:
That had been base, since he had got the plunder.
Besides, he knew she had both wit and sense,
Beauty, and such a stock of impudence
As to the playhouse well might recommend her;
And therefore thither was resolved to send her.
Where soon she grew, being in her proper sphere,
The pride and envy of the theatre.
Then entered Nelly on the public stage,
Harlot of harlots, Lais of the age.
But there what Lacy's fumbling age abused
Hart's[1] sprightly vigour more robustly used –
Yet Hart more manners had than not to tender
When noble Buckhurst[2] begged him to surrender.
He saw her roll the stage from side to side
And through her drawers the powerful charm descried.
'Take her, my lord', quoth Hart, 'since you're so mean
To take a player's leavings for your queen.
For though I love her well, yet as she's poor,
I'm well contented to prefer the whore.'
To Buckhurst thus resigned in friendly wise
Our glaring lass begins apace to rise,
Distributing her favours very thick
(And sometimes witty Wilmot[3] had a lick)
And thus she traded on in noble ware
Serving the rest with what her lord could spare.
Buckhurst was lord of all her hairy manor,
The rest was only tenants to his honour.
By these degrees the ranting whore crept up
Until she mounted to the Sovereign top.
'Dread Sir', quoth Buckingham, in duty bound,

[1]*Hart* Charles Hart, the popular actor   [2]*Buckhurst* Lawyer and minor poet, who
exchanged verse-letters with Etherege (see p. 161)   [3]*Wilmot* 1st Earl of Rochester

'I come to give your Kingship counsel sound.
I wonder you should dote so like a fop
On Cleveland,[1] whom her very footmen grope.
D'ye think you don't your Parliament offend
That all they give you on a beggar spend?
Permit me, Sir, to recommend a whore:
Kiss her but once, you'll ne'er kiss Cleveland more.
She'll fit you to a hair – all wit, all fire
And impudence – to your own heart's desire –
And more than this, Sir, you'll save money by her.
She's Buckhurst's whore at present, but you know
When Sovereign wants a whore, that subjects must forego.'
This put old Rowley's codpiece in a heat.
'Go, Mrs Knight', quoth he, 'and fetch her straight.'
'Soft', quoth Lord Buckhurst, 'But first pay my score –
She's cost me many a pound – then take the whore.'
Rowley assented, and to lay his itch
Gave him an earldom to resign his bitch.
And now behold a common drab become
The glorious mate for English monarch's bum.
Nor was it long before the artful slut
Had got the length of her great Master's foot;
She knew so well to wield his Royal Thing
That none had such a knack to please the King.
When he was dumpish, she would still be jocund,
And chuck the Royal Chin of Charles the Second;
Then with her heels lock in the sceptred cull,[2]
Whom finding somewhat phlegmatic and dull
'My Liege', she'd say, 'come let's be frank and merry,
And in love's cave our melancholy bury.'
Thrice happy Nell, that hadst a King so gracious
To raise up Princes to thy dust and ashes,
Whose great humility would stoop so low
On thee and thine his favours to bestow.
Sure, there are hidden charms about thy middle,
And sure, experienced females have a fiddle.

[1]*Cleveland* Duchess of Cleveland   [2]*cull* man

For this old Rowley gave 'em coach and horses,
Furnished them palaces, and stuffed their purses,
Called parliaments, pretending war with France,
And all his harlots' grandeur to advance.
His shut up 'chequer[1] did his passion prove,
As well as crown lands sold for humble love.
How will succeeding story blush to tell
What this, Great Britain's Monarch, e'er did well?
Who would not wonder, while he takes such pains,
And on both old and young his vigour drains?
Nor would his Nelly long be his survivor.
Alas, who now was good enough to drive her?
So she gave way to her consuming grief
Which brought her past all gallipot[2] relief.
How'er it were, as the old women say,
Her time was come, and then there's no delay –
So down into the Stygian Lake she dropped
To meet the Prince she had so often topped.

ANON
(c 1691)

The Dream

She lay all naked in her bed
    And I myself lay by;
No veil nor curtain there was spread,
    No covering but I.
Her head upon one shoulder seeks
    To hang in careless wise;
All full of blushes were her cheeks
    And wishes were her eyes.

---

[1]*'chequer* Exchequer   [2]*gallipot* chemist's pot for medicines

Her blood lay flushing in her face
　　As on a message came
To say that in some other place
　　It meant some other game;
Her nether lip, moist, plump and fair,
　　Millions of kisses crowned,
Which ripe and uncropped dangled there
　　And weighed the branches down.

Her breasts, that lay swelled full and high,
　　Bred pleasant pangs in me,
And all the world I did deny
　　For that felicity;
Her thighs and belly, soft and plump,
　　To me were only shown –
To have seen such meat and not to eat
　　Would have angered anyone.

Her knees lay up, but stoutly bent,
　　And all was hollow under,
As if on easy terms they meant
　　To fall unforced asunder;
Just so the Cyprian Queen did lie
　　Expecting in her bower,
When too long stay had kept the boy
　　Beyond his promised hour.

'Dull clown', quoth she, 'why dost delay
　　Such proffered bliss to take?
Canst thou not find another way
　　Similitudes to make?'
Mad with delight, I thundered in
　　And threw my arms about her.
But pox on it, 'twas but a dream,
　　And so I lay without her.

ANON
(c 1691)

Love's Physiognomy

If thou wilt know how to choose a shrew,
    Come listen unto me:
I'll tell you the signs and the very, very lines
    Of love's physiognomy.

If her hair be brown, with a flaxen crown,
    And graced with a nutmeg hue,
Both day and night she's best for delight
    And her colour everlasting true.

If her forehead be high, with a rolling eye,
    And lips that will sweetly melt,
The thing below is better, you know,
    Although it be oftener felt.

If her hair be red she'll sport in bed,
    But take heed of the danger, though,
For if she carry fire in her upper attire,
    What a devil doth she carry below?

If her hair be yellow, she'll tempt each fellow
    In the Emmanuel College;
For she that doth follow the colour of Apollo
    May be like him in zeal of knowledge.

If she be pale and a virgin stale,
    Inclined to the sickness green,
Some raw fruit give her to open her liver,
    Her stomach and the thing between.

If her nose be long and sharp as her tongue,
    Take heed of a desperate maid;
For she that will swagger with an incurable dagger
    With a stab and a killing betrayed.

[184]

If her face and neck have here and there a speck,
　　　Ne'er stick, but straight you go stride her;
For it hath been tried, and never denied,
　　　Such flesh ne'er fails the rider.

If none of these thy fancy will please,
　　　Go seek thy complexion store,
And take for thy saint a lady that will paint:
　　　Such beauties thou may'st adore.

If beauty do write in her face red and white
　　　And Cupid his flowers there breed,
It pleaseth the eye, but the rose will die
　　　As soon as it runs to seed.

ANON
(c 1691)

The Lusty Old Woman

Walking abroad in a morning
Where Venus herself was adorning,
I heard a bird sing to welcome the spring,
Its music so sweetly according.

I listened unto him –
Methought a voice did summon.
I spied an old whore and a lusty young rogue
Together as they sat a-wooing.

She tickled him under the sides
To make their courage coming,
She hoisted her thigh and she twinkled her eye:
'Twas a dainty, fine, curious old woman.

[185]

If Venus and Mars so stout
Had joined together in battle
There could not have been more claps and more bangs,
For he made her old buttocks rattle.

She gave him a lift for his thrust
And catched him as he was a-coming.
She gave him five shillings to make a recruit –
And was not this a fine, lusty old woman?

ANON
(c 1698)

The Women's Complaint to Venus

How happy were good English faces
    Till Monsieur from France
    Taught pego[1] a dance
To the tune of old Sodom's embraces.

But now we are quite out of fashion:
    Poor whores may be nuns
    Since men turn their guns
And vent on each other their passion.

In the reign of good Charles the Second
    Full many a jade
    A lady was made
And the issue right noble was reckoned,

But now we find to our sorrow
    We are overrun
    By sparks of the bum
And peers of the land of Gomorrah.

[1] *pego* penis

The beaux too, whom most we relied on,
    At night make a punk[1]
    Of him that's first drunk
Though unfit for the sport as John Dryden.

The soldiers, whom next we put trust in,
    No widow can tame
    Or virgin reclaim
But at the wrong place will be thrusting.

Fair Venus, thou goddess of beauty,
    Receive our complaint,
    Make Rigby[2] recant
And the soldiers henceforth do their duty.

ANON
(c 1699)

Pleasure and Innocence

I gently touched her hand: she gave
A look that did my soul enslave.
I pressed her rebel lips in vain:
They rose up to be pressed again.
    Thus happy, I no further meant
    Than to be pleased and innocent.

On her soft breasts my hand I laid,
And a quick, light impression made:
They with a kindly warmth did glow,
And swelled, and seemed to overflow.
    Yet trust me, I no further meant
    Than to be pleased and innocent.

[1]*punk* prostitute [2]*Rigby* A naval captain convicted in 1698 of sodomy

On her eyes my eyes did stay,
O'er her smooth limbs my hands did stray:
Each sense was ravished with delight,
And my soul stood prepared for flight.
  Blame me not if at last I meant
  More to be pleased than innocent.

ANON
(c 1700)

The Bathing Lady

The four and twentieth day of May –
  Of all days in the year –
A virgin lady, fresh and gay,
  Did privately appear.
Hard by a river side got she
  And did sing loud the rather,
'Cause she was sure she was secure
  And had an intent to bath her.

With glittering, glancing, jealous eyes
  She slily looks about
To see if any lurking spies
  Were hid to find her out;
And being well resolved that none
  Could see her nakedness,
She pulled her robes off one by one
  And did herself undress.

Her purple mantle, fringed with gold,
  Her ivory hands unpinned –
It would have made a coward bold,
  Or tempted a saint to 'a sinned.

She turned about and looked around.
   Quoth she: 'I hope I'm safe.'
Then her rosy petticoat
   She presently put off.

The snow-white smock which she had on,
   Transparently to deck her,
Looked like cambric or like lawn
   Upon an alabaster picture,
Through which array I did faintly spy
   Her belly and her back;
Her limbs were straight and all was white
   But that which should be black.

The part which she's ashamed to see
   Without a bashful blush
Appeared like curious tiffany
   Displayed upon a bush;
But that posterior extreme limb
   She cannot look upon
Did like a twisted cherry seem
   Before the white was gone.

As when a masqueing scene is drawn
   And new lights do appear,
When she put off her smock of lawn
   Just such a sight was there:
The bright reflection of her eyes
   In every limb was strowed,
As when the radiant sun doth rise
   And gild each neighbouring cloud.

Into a fluent stream she leapt.
   She looked like Venus' glass.
The fishes from each quarter crept
   To see what angel 'twas.

She did so like a vision look
　　Or fairy in a dream
'Twas thought the sun the skies forsook
　　And dropped into the stream.

Each fish did wish himself a man –
　　About her all was drawn –
And at the sight of her began
　　To spread abroad his spawn.
She turned to swim upon her back,
　　And so displayed her banner;
If Jove had then in Heaven been
　　He would have dropped upon her.

Thus was the river's diamond head
　　With pearl and sapphire crowned;
Her legs did shove, her arms did move,
　　Her body did rebound –
She that did quaff the juice of joy
　　(Fair Venus, queen of Love)
With Mars did never in more ways
　　Of melting motion move.

A lad that long her love had been
　　And could obtain no grace,
For all her prying lay unseen
　　Hid in a secret place,
Who often being repulsed when he
　　Came shyly in to woo her,
Pulled off his clothes and furiously
　　Did run and leap in to her.

She squeaked, she cried, and down she dived,
　　He brought her up again.
He brought her o'er upon the shore
　　And then – and then – and then –

As Adam did old Eve enjoy
   (You may guess what I mean)
Because she all uncovered lay
   He covered her again.

With watered eyes she pants and cries
   'I'm utterly undone
If you will not be wed to me
   E'er the next morning sun!'
He answered her he ne'er would stir
   Out of her sight till then.
'We'll both clap hands in wedlock's bands,
   Marry – and to't again!'

JOHN HOPKINS
(c 1700)

To Amasia, Tickling a Gentleman

Methinks I see how the blessed swain was laid
While round his sides your nimble fingers played.
With pleasing softness did they swiftly rove,
Raising the sweet, delicious pangs of love,
While at each touch they made his heart-strings move.
As round his breast, his ravished breast, they crowd,
We hear their music, when he laughs aloud.
You ply him still, and as he melting lies
Act your soft triumphs while your captive dies.
Thus he perceives, thou, dearest, charming fair
Without your eyes you can o'ercome him there.
Thus too he shows what's your unbounded skill,
You please and charm us, though at once you kill.
Lodged in your arms he does in transport lie,
While through his veins the fancied lightnings fly
And, gushed with vast delights, I see him haste to die.

ANON
(c 1700)

Riding Paces

When for air
   I take my mare
And mount her, first
   She walks just thus:
Her head held low
   And motion slow,
With nodding, plodding,
   Wagging, jogging,
Dashing, plashing,
   Snorting, starting
Whimsically she goes,
Then whip stirs up,
   Trot, trot, trot.
Ambling then with easy flight
She wriggles like a bird at night;
   Her shifting hitch
   Regales my britch,
Whilst trot, trot, trot, trot,
   Brings on the gallop,
The gallop, the gallop,
The gallop, and then a short
   Trot, trot, trot, trot
Straight again up and down
   Up and down, up and down,
Till she comes home with a trot,
When night dark grows.

Just so Phillis
   Fair as lilies
As her face is
   Has her paces;
And in bed too
   Like my pad too

Nodding, plodding,
  Wagging, jogging,
Dashing, plashing,
  Flirting, spurting;
Artful are all her ways –
  Hearts thump, pit pat,
  Trot, trot, trot, trot.
Ambling then her tongue gets loose
Whilst wriggling near I press more close.
  'Ye devil!' she cries,
  'I'll tear your eyes!'
When, mane seized,
  Bum squeezed,
I gallop, I gallop, I gallop, I gallop,
  And trot, trot, trot, trot,
Straight again up and down,
Up and down, up and down,
Till the last jerk, with a trot,
Ends our love chase.

ANON
(1700)

My Longing Desire

Hey boy, hey boy,
Come, come away boy,
And bring me my longing desire:
A lass that is neat and can well do the feat
When lusty young blood is on fire.

Let her body be tall
And her waist be small,
And her age not above eighteen;
Let her care for no bed, but here let her spread
Her mantle upon the green.

Let her face be fair
And her breasts be bare,
And a voice let her have that can warble;
Let her belly be soft, but to mount me aloft
Let her bounding buttocks be marble.

Let her have a cherry lip
Where I nectar my sip,
Let her eyes be as black as the sloe.
Dangling locks I do love, so that those hung above
Are the same with what grows below.

Oh, such a bonny lass
May bring wonders to pass
And make me grow younger and younger;
And whene'er we do part she'll be mad at the heart
That I am able to tarry no longer.

ANON
(c 1700)

The Sound Country Lass

These London wenches are so stout
   They care not what they do;
They will not let you have a bout
   Without a crown or two.

They double their chops, and curl their locks,
   Their breaths perfume they do;
Their tails are peppered with the pox,
   And that you're welcome to.

But give me the buxom country lass,
   Hot piping from the cow,
That will take a touch upon the grass,
   Ay, marry, and thank you too!

[194]

Her colour's fresh as a rose in June,
  Her temper as kind as a dove;
She'll please the swain with a wholesome tune,
  And freely give her love.

ANON
(c 1700)

The Maid's Conjuring Book

A young man lately in our town
  He went to bed one night;
He had no sooner laid him down
  But was troubled with a sprite.
So vigorously the spirit stood
  Let him do what he can,
Sure then he said it must be laid
  By woman, not by man.

A handsome maid did undertake,
  And into bed she lept,
And to allay the spirit's power
  Full close to him she crept.
She having such a guardian care
  Her office to discharge,
She opened wide her conjuring book
  And laid the leaves at large.

Her office she did well perform
  Within a little space;
Then up she rose, and down he lay,
  And durst not show his face.
She took her leave and away she went
  When she had done the deed,
Saying 'If't chance to come again,
  Then send for me with speed.'

[195]

ANON
(c 1700)

The Blushing Nymph

Pretty nymph, why always blushing?
　　If thou lov'st why art thou so coy?
In thy cheeks these roses flushing
　　Show thee fearful of thy joy.
What is man, that thou should'st dread
To change with him a maidenhead?

At first all virgins fear to do it
　　And but trifle away their time,
And still unwilling to come to it,
　　In foolish whining spend their time;
But when they once have found the way,
Then they are for it night and day.

ANON
(c 1700)

As Oyster Nan Stood by her Tub

As Oyster Nan stood by her tub,
　　To show her vicious inclination,
She gave her noblest parts a scrub
　　And sighed for want of copulation.
A vintner of no little fame
　　Who excellent red and white can sell ye
Beheld the little dirty dame
　　As she stood scratching of her belly.

'Come in', says he, 'you silly slut,
　　'Tis now a rare convenient minute;
I'll lay the itching of your scut
　　Except some greedy devil be in it.'

[196]

With that the flat-capped fubsy smiled,
   And would have blushed, but that she could not;
'Alas!' says she, 'we're soon beguiled
   By men to do those things we should not.'

From door they went behind the bar
   As it's by common fame reported,
And there upon a turkey chair
   Unseen the loving couple sported.
But being called by company
   As he was taking pains to please her,
'I'm coming, coming sir,' says he,
   'My dear, and so am I!' says she, sir.

Her mole-hill belly swelled about
   Into a mountain quickly after,
And when the pretty mouse crept out
   The creature caused a mighty laughter.
And now she's learned the pleasing game
   Although much pain and shame it cost her,
She daily ventures at the same
   And shuts and opens like an oyster.

ANON
(c 1700)

As I Cam O'er the Cairney Mount

As I cam o'er the Cairney mount,
   And down amang the blooming heather,
The Highland laddie drew his durk[1]
   And sheath'd it in my wanton leather.

       O my bonnie, bonnie Highland lad,
       My handsome, charming Highland laddie;
       When I am sick and like to die,
       He'll row me in his Highland plaiddie.

[1]*durk* dagger

[197]

With me he play'd his warlike pranks,
  And on me boldly did adventure,
He did attack me on both flanks,
  And pushed me fiercely in the centre.

A furious battle then began,
  Wi' equal courage and desire,
Altho' he struck me three to one,
  I stood my ground and receiv'd his fire.

But our ammunition being spent,
  And we quite out o' breath an' sweating,
We did agree with ae consent
  To fight it out at the next meeting.

ANON
(c 1709)

The Enjoyment

Ye gods! the raptures of that night!
What fierce convulsions of delight!
How in each other's arms involved
We lay confounded and dissolved!
Bodies mingling, sexes blending,
Which should be most lost contending,
Darting fierce and flaming kisses,
Plunging into boundless blisses,
Our bodies and our souls on fire,
Tossed by a tempest of desire
Till with utmost fury driven
Down, at once, we sunk to heaven.

[198]

CHARLES SACKVILLE, EARL OF DORSET
(1643-1706)

From the Latin

Enflamed with love and led by blind desires,
  The man pursues, the blushful maid retires.
He hopes for pleasures, but she fears the pain,
  His love but ignorance is, her fears more vain.
When e'er he tastes those joys so prized before
  He'll love no longer and she'll fear no more.

The Advice

Would you in love succeed, be brisk, be gay,
Cast all dull thoughts and serious looks away;
Think not with downcast eyes, and mournful air
To move to pity the relentless Fair,
Or draw from her bright eyes a crystal tear.
This method foreign is to your affair,
Too formal for the frolic you prepare:
Thus, when you think she yields to love's advance,
You'll find 'tis no consent, but complaisance.
Whilst he who boldly rifles all her charms,
Kisses and ravishes her in his arms,
Seizes the favour, stays not for a grant,
Alarms her blood and makes her sigh and pant,
Gives her no time to speak, or think't a crime,
Enjoys his wish, and well employs his time.

ALEXANDER RADCLIFFE
(c 1645–1696)

Upon Mr Bennet, Procurer Extraordinary

Reader beneath this marble stone
St Valentine's adopted son,
Bennet the bawd now lies alone.

Here lies alone the amorous spark
Who was used to lead them in the dark
Like beasts by pairs into the ark.

If maid of honour would begin,
He'd never stick out at any sin,
For he was still for sticking't in.

If Justice chiefest of the bench
Had an occasion for a wench,
His revered flames 'twas he could quench.

And for his son and heir apparant
He could perform as good an errand
Without a tipstaff or a warrant.

Over the clergy he'd such a lock
That he could make a spiritual frock
Fly off at sight of temporal smock.

Like Will-o'-the-Wisp still up and down
He led the wives of London town
To lodge with squires of high renown

While they (poor fools) being unaware
Did find themselves in mansion fair
Near Leicester Fields or James's Square.

Thus worthy Bennet was employed.
At last he held the door so wide
He caught a cold, so coughed, and died.

JOHN WILMOT, EARL OF ROCHESTER
(1647–80)

To a Lady in a Letter

Such perfect bliss, fair Cloris, we
   In our enjoyment prove,
'Tis pity restless jealousy
   Should mingle with our love.

Let us, since wit has taught us how,
   Raise pleasure to the top:
You rival bottle must allow,
   I'll suffer rival fop.

Think not in this that I design
   A treason 'gainst love's charms,
When following the god of wine
   I leave my Cloris' arms,

Since you have that, for all your haste,
   At which I'll ne'er repine,
Will take its liquor off as fast
   As I can take off mine.

There's not a brisk insipid spark
   That flutters in the town
But with your wanton eyes you mark
   Him out to be your own;

Nor do you think it worth your care
   How empty, and how dull,
The heads of your admirers are
   So that their cods[1] be full.

All this you freely may confess,
   Yet we ne'er disagree,
For did you love your pleasure less
   You were no match for me,

[1] *cods* testicles

[201]

Whilst I, my pleasure to pursue,
  Whole nights am taking in
The lusty juice of grapes, take you
  The juice of lusty men.

A Song of a Young Lady to her
*   Ancient Lover*

Ancient person, for whom I
All the flattering youth defy,
Long be it e'er thou grow old,
Aching, shaking, crazy, cold –
But still continue as thou art,
Ancient person of my heart.

On thy withered lips and dry,
Which like barren furrows lie,
Brooding kisses I will pour
Shall thy youthful heart restore.
Such kind showers in autumn fall
And a second spring recall,
Nor from thee will ever part,
Ancient person of my heart.

Thy nobler part, which but to name
In our sex would be counted shame,
By age's frozen grasp possessed
From their ice shall be released
And soothed by my reviving hand
In former warmth and vigour stand.
All a lover's wish can reach
For thy joy my love shall teach
And for thy pleasure shall improve
All that art can add to love.
Yet still I love thee without art,
Ancient person of my heart.

The Imperfect Enjoyment

Naked she lay, clasped in my longing arms,
I filled with love, and she all over charms;
Both equally inspired with eager fire,
Melting through kindness, flaming in desire.
With arms, legs, lips, close clinging to embrace,
She clips me to her breast and sucks me to her face.
Her nimble tongue, Love's lesser lightning, played
Within my mouth, and to my thoughts conveyed
Swift orders that I should prepare to throw
The all-dissolving thunderbolt below.
My fluttering soul, sprung with the pointed kiss,
Hangs hovering o'er her balmy brinks of bliss.
But whilst her busy hand would guide that part
Which should convey my soul up to her heart,
In liquid raptures I dissolve all o'er,
Melt into sperm, and spend at every pore.
A touch from any part of her had done't –
Her hand, her foot, her very look's a cunt.

Smiling, she chides in a kind murmuring noise
And from her body wipes the clammy joys,
When with a thousand kisses wandering o'er
My panting bosom, 'Is there then no more?'
She cries. 'All this to love and rapture's due;
Must we not pay a debt to pleasure, too?'

But I, the most forlorn, lost man alive
To show my wished obedience vainly strive.
I sigh, alas!, and kiss – but cannot swive.
Eager desires confound my first intent,
Succeeding shame does more success prevent,
And rage at last confirms me impotent.
Even her fair hand, which might bid heat return
To frozen age, and make cold hermits burn,
Applied to my dead cinder warms no more

Than fire to ashes could past flames restore.
Trembling, confused, despairing, limber, dry,
A wishing, weak, unmoving lump I lie.
This dart of love whose piercing point, oft tried,
With virgin blood ten thousand maids has dyed,
Which nature still directed with such art
That it through every cunt reached every heart
(Stiffly resolved, 'twould carelessly invade
Woman or man, nor aught its fury stayed –
Where'er it pierced, a cunt it found or made)
Now languid lies in this unhappy hour
Shrunk up and sapless like a withered flower.

    Thou treacherous, base deserter of my flame,
False to my passion, fatal to my fame,
Through what mistaken magic dost thou prove
So true to lewdness, so untrue to love?
What oyster- cinder- beggar- common whore
Didst thou e'er fail in all thy life before?
When vice, disease and scandal lead the way
With what officious haste dost thou obey!
Like a rude, roaring hector in the streets
Who scuffles, cuffs and jostles all he meets,
But if his King or country claim his aid
The rake-hell villain shrinks and hides his head;
Even so thy brutal valour is displayed,
Breaks every stew,[1] does each small whore invade,
But when great Love the onset does command,
Base recreant to thy prince, thou darest not stand.
Worse part of me, and henceforth hated most,
Through all the town a common fucking post
On whom each whore relieves her tingling cunt
As hogs on gates do rub themselves and grunt:
Mayst thou to ravenous cankers be a prey,
Or in consuming weepings waste away;
May stranguary and stone thy days attend,

[1]*stew* brothel

Mayst thou ne'er piss who didst refuse to spend
When all my joys did on false thee depend.
And may ten thousand abler pricks agree
To do the wronged Corinna right for thee.

A Ramble in St James's Park

Much wine had passed, with grave discourse
Of who fucks who and who does worse
(Such as you usually do hear
From those who diet at the Bear),
When I, who still take care to see
Drunkenness relieved by lechery,
Went out into St James's Park
To cool my head and fire my heart.
But though St James has th'honour on't
'Tis consecrate to prick and cunt.
There by a most incestuous birth
Strange woods spring from the teeming earth,
For they relate how heretofore
When ancient Pict began to whore,
Deluded of his assignation
(Jilting it seems was then in fashion)
Poor pensive lover in this place
Would frig¹ upon his mother's face
Where rows of mandrakes tall did rise
Whose lewd tops fucked the very skies.
Each imitative branch does twine
In some loved fold of Aretine,²
And nightly now beneath their shade
Are buggeries, rapes and incests made.
Unto this all-sin-sheltering grove
Whores of the bulk³ and the alcove,

¹*frig* masturbate ²*Aretine* Aretino, whose erotic sonnets (now lost) were illustrated by drawings few of which survive ³*bulk* a public bench

Great ladies, chambermaids and drudges,
The ragpicker and heiress trudges.
Car-men, divines, great lords and tailors,
Prentices, poets, pimps and jailers,
Footmen, fine fops, do here arrive
And here promiscuously they swive.

Along these hallowed walks it was
That I beheld Corinna pass.
Whoever had been by to see
The proud disdain she cast on me
Through charming eyes, he would have swore
She dropped from heaven that very hour,
Forsaking the divine abode
In scorn of some despairing god.
But mark what creatures women are,
How infinitely vile when fair!

Three knights o'th'elbow[1] and the slur
With wriggling tails made up to her.

The first was of your Whitehall blades
Near kin t'th'mother of the Maids,[2]
Graces by whose favour he was able
To bring a friend t'th'waiters' table,
Where he had heard Sir Edward Sutton
Say how the king loved Banstead mutton;
Since when he'd ne'er be brought to eat
By's good will any other meat.
In this, as well as all the rest,
He ventures to do like the best,
But wanting common sense, th'ingredient
In choosing well not least expedient,
Converts abortive imitation
To universal affection.

Thus he not only eats and talks
But feels and smells, sits down and walks,
Nay, looks and lives and loves by rote,
In an old tawdry birthday coat.

The second was a Gray's Inn wit
A great inhabiter of the pit,
Where critic-like he sits and squints,
Steals pocket-handkerchiefs and hints
From neighbour, and the comedy,
To court and pay his landlady.

The third, a lady's eldest son
Within a few years of twenty-one,
Who hopes from his propitious fate
Against he comes to his estate
By these two worthies to be made
A most accomplished tearing blade.

One in a strain 'twixt tune and nonsense
Cries, 'Madam, I have loved you long since.
Permit me your fair hand to kiss' –
When at her mouth her cunt cries 'Yes!'
In short, without much more ado,
Joyful and pleased away she flew
And with these three confounded asses
From park to hackney coach she passes.

So a proud bitch does lead about
Of humble curs the amorous rout
Who most obsequiously do hunt
The savoury scent of salt-swoln cunt.
Some power more patient now relate
The sense of this surprising fate:
Gods that a thing admired by me
Should fall to so much infamy!
Had she picked out to rub her arse on

Some stiff-pricked clown or well-hung parson
Each jet of whose spermatic sluice
Had filled her cunt with wholesome juice,
I the proceeding should have praised
In hope she's quenched a fire I raised.
Such natural freedoms are but just –
There's something generous in mere lust.
But to turn damned abandoned jade
When neither head nor tail persuade –
To be a whore in understanding
A passive pot for fools to spend in!
The devil played booty,[1] sure, with thee
To bring a blot on infamy.

    But why am I, of all mankind,
To so severe a fate designed?
Ungrateful! Why this treachery
To humble, fond, believing me,
Who gave you privilege above
The nice allowances of love?
Did ever I refuse to bear
The meanest part your lust could spare?
When your lewd cunt came spewing home
Drenched with the seed of half the town,
My dram of sperm was supped up after
For the digestive surfeit water.[2]

    Full gorgéd at another time
With a vast meal of nasty slime
Which your devouring cunt had drawn
From porters' backs and footmen's brawn,
I was content to serve you up
My bollock-full for your grace cup,
Nor ever thought it an abuse
While you had pleasure for excuse –
You that could make my heart away

[1]*played booty* conspired   [2]*surfeit water* a cure for indigestion

For noise and colour, and betray
The secrets of my tender hours
To such knight-errant paramours,
When leaning on your faithless breast
Wrapped in security and rest
Soft kindness all my powers did move
And reason lay dissolved in love!

   May stinking vapours choke your womb
Such as the men you dote upon!
May your depraved appetite
That could in whiffling foots delight
Beget such frenzies in your mind
You may go mad for the north wind
And fixing all your hopes upon't
To have him bluster in your cunt,
Turn up your longing arse in th'air
And perish in a wild despair!
But cowards shall forget to rant,
Schoolboys to frig, old whores to paint;
The Jesuits' fraternity
Shall leave the use of buggery;
Crab-louse, inspired with grace divine,
From earthly cod to heaven shall climb;
Physicians shall believe in Jesus
And disobedience cease to please us
Ere I desist with all my power
To plague this woman and undo her.
But my revenge will best be timed
When she is married that is limed.
In that most lamentable state
I'll make her feel my scorn and hate,
Pelt her with scandals, truth or lies,
And her poor cur with jealousies
Till I have torn him from her breech
While she whines like a dog-drawn bitch,
Loathed and despised, kicked out o'th'town

Into some dirty hole alone
To chew the cud of misery
And know she owes it all to me.

And may no woman better thrive
That dares profane the cunt I swive!

A Whore

She was so exquisite a whore
  That in the belly of her mother
She turned her cunt so right before
  Her father fucked them both together.

Quartet

NELL GWYN   When to the king I bid good morrow,
              With tongue in mouth and hand on tarse,[1]
            Portsmouth may rend her cunt for sorrow
              And Mazarin may kiss my arse.

DUCHESS OF PORTSMOUTH
            When England's monarch's on my belly
              With prick in cunt, though double crammed,
            Fart of mine arse for small whore Nelly,
              And great whore Mazarin be damned.

Song

Love a woman? You're an ass!
'Tis a most insipid passion
To choose out for happiness
The idlest part of God's creation.

[1] *tarse* penis

Let the porter and the groom
Things designed for dirty slaves
Drudge in fair Amanda's womb
To get supplies for age and graves.

Farewell, women! I intend
Henceforth every night to sit
With my lewd, well-natured friends
Drinking to engender wit.

Then give me health, wealth, mirth and wine
And if busy love entrenches,
There's a sweet, soft page of mine
Does the trick worth forty wenches!

HENRY HALL
(–1713)

Song

Lucinda has the devil and all
Of that bright thing we beauty call;
But if she won't come to my arms
What care I for all her charms?
Beauty's the sauce to love's high meat –
But who minds sauce that must not eat?
It is indeed a mighty treasure,
But in *using* lies the pleasure.
Bullies thus, that only see't
Damn all the gold in Lombard Street!

THOMAS DOGGETT
(-1721)

Mr Doggett's Song

I'll sing you a song of my mistress that's pretty,
   A lady so frolic and gay;
It tickles my fancy to tune her sweet ditty,
   For love was all her play.

She's witty and pretty and tunes like a fiddle,
   The lady so frolic and gay;
She begins at both ends, and ends in the middle,
   For love was all her play.

She hugs and she kisses without a word speaking,
   The lady so frolic and gay;
She falls on her back without flinching or squealing,
   For love was all her play.

She's laden in graces of virtue and honour,
   The lady so frolic and gay;
'Twixt a pair of sheets with warm love upon her,
   For love was all her play.

MATTHEW PRIOR
(1664-1721)

A Lover's Anger

As Cloe came into the room t'other day,
I peevish began, 'Where so long could you stay?
In your life-time you never regarded your hour:
You promised at two, and pray look, child, 'tis four.
A lady's watch needs neither figures nor wheels,
'Tis enough that 'tis loaded with baubles and seals.

A temper so heedless no mortal can bear – '
Thus far I went on with a resolute air.
'Lord bless me!' said she; 'Let a body but speak:
Here's an ugly hard rose-bud fallen into my neck . . .
It has hurt me, and vexed me, to such a degree –
See here, for you never believe me – pray, see –
On the left side my breast what a mark it has made.'
On saying, her bosom she careless displayed.
That seat of delight I with wonder surveyed,
And forgot every word I designed to have said.

A Song

For God's sake – nay, dear Sir,
Lord, what do you mean?
I protest and I vow, Sir,
Your ways are obscene.

Pray give o'er; O, fie,
Pish, leave off your fooling,
Forbear, or I'll cry –
I hate this rude doing.

Let me die if I stay –
Does the Devil possess you?
Your hand take away,
Then perhaps I may bless you.

Since We Your Husband Daily See

Since we your husband daily see
  So jealous out of season,
Phyllis, let you and I agree
  To make him so with reason.

[213]

I'm vexed to think that every night
   A sot within thy arms
Tasting the most divine delight
   Should sully all your charms

While fretting I must lie alone
   Cursing the powers divine
That undeservedly have thrown
   A pearl unto a swine.

Then, Phyllis, heal my wounded heart,
   My burning passion cool;
Let me at least in thee have part
   With thy insipid fool.

Let him by night his joys pursue
   And blunder in the dark,
While I by day enjoying you
   Can see to hit the mark.

A True Maid

'No, no – for my virginity!
   When I lose that', says Rose, 'I'll die.'
'Behind the elms last night,' cried Dick,
   'Rose, were you not extremely sick?'

Celia

Were Celia absent and remembrance brought
Her and past raptures thick upon my thought,
The next kind She might meet my raised desire,
And beastly lust quench love's disabled fire.
But when I want my friend, when my vexed heart
Beats short, and pants, and seeks its nobler part,
For the said ill no medicine can be found:
'Tis you that made, 'tis you must cure the wound.

JONATHAN SWIFT
(1667–1745)

from *Strephon and Chloe*

Of Chloe all the town has rung –
By every size of poets sung.
So beautiful a nymph appears
But once in twenty thousand years.
By nature formed with nicest care,
And faultless to a single hair.
Her graceful mein, her shape and face
Confessed her of no mortal race:
And then, so nice, and so genteel,
Such cleanliness from head to heel.
No humours gross, or frowsy steams,
No noisome whiffs, or sweaty streams
Before, behind, above, below
Could from her taintless body flow . . .

You'd swear that so divine a creature
Felt no necessities of nature.
In summer, had she walked the town,
Her arm-pits would not stain her gown;
At country dances not a nose
Could in the dog-days smell her toes.
Her milk-white hands, both palms and backs,
Like ivory dry, and soft as wax.
Her hands the softest ever felt,
Though cold would burn, though dry would
melt . . .

Now Strephon sighed so loud and strong
He blew a settlement along
And brave drove his rivals down
With coach and six, and house in town.

The bashful nymph no more withstands,
Because her dear Papa commands.
The charming couple now unites.
Proceed we to the marriage rites . . .

The rites performed, the parson paid,
In state returned the grand parade
With loud huzzas from all the boys
That now the pair must crown their joys.

But still the hardest part remains.
Strephon had long perplexed his brains
How with so high a nymph he might
Demean himself the wedding night.
For as he viewed his person round,
Mere mortal flesh was all he found:
His hand, his neck, his mouth and feet
Were duly washed to keep 'em sweet
(With other parts that shall be nameless,
The ladies else might think me shameless).
The weather and his love were hot,
And should he struggle – I know what;
Why let it go, if I must tell it –
He'll sweat; and then the nymph may smell it.
While she a goddess dyed in grain
Was unsusceptible of stain
And, Venus-like, her fragrant skin
Exhaled ambrosia from within:
Can such a deity endure
A mortal, human touch impure?
How did the humbled swain detest
His prickled beard, and hairy breast!
His night-cap bordered round with lace
Could give no softness to his face.
Yet if the goddess could be kind,
What endless raptures must he find! . . .

While these reflections filled his head,
The bride was put with form to bed.
He followed, stripped, and in he crept –
But awfully his distance kept.

Now ponder well, ye parents dear:
Forbid your daughters guzzling beer,
And make them every afternoon
Forbear their tea, or drink it soon,
That e'er to bed they venture up
They may discharge it, every sup.
If not, they must in evil plight
Be often forced to rise at night.
Keep them to wholesome food confined,
Nor let them taste what causes wind . . .

Carminative and diuretick[1]
Will damp all passion sympathetic,
And love such nicety requires
One blast will put out all his fires.
Since husbands get behind the scene
The wife should study to be clean,
Nor give the smallest room to guess
The time when wants of nature press.

But after marriage, practise more
Decorum than she did before,
To keep her spouse deluded still
And make him fancy what she will.

In bed we left the married pair:
'Tis time to show how things went there.
Strephon, who had been often told
That fortune still assists the bold,
Resolved to make his first attack –
But Chloe drove him fiercely back.

[1]*carminative and diuretick* medicines to provoke wind and induce urination

How could a nymph so chaste as Chloe,
With constitution cold and snowy,
Permit a brutish man to touch her?
Even lambs by instinct fly the butcher.
Resistance on the wedding-night
Is what our maidens claim by right,
And Chloe, 'tis by all agreed,
Was maid in thought and word and deed.
Yet some assign a different reason:
That Strephon chose no proper season.

Say, fair ones, must I make a pause,
Or freely tell the secret cause?
Twelve cups of tea (with grief I speak)
Had now constrained the nymph to leak.
This point must needs be settled first:
The bride must either void, or burst.
Then see the dire effect of peas!
Think what can give the cholic ease.
The nymph, oppressed before, behind,
As ships are tossed by waves and wind,
Steals out her hand by nature led
And brings a vessel into bed –
Fair utensil, as smooth and white
As Chloe's skin, almost as bright.

Strephon, who heard the fuming rill
As from a mossy cliff distill,
Cried out: 'Ye gods, what sound is this?
Can Chloe, heavenly Chloe, piss?'
But when he smelt a noisome steam
Which oft attends that luke-warm stream,
He found her, while the scent increased,
As mortal as himself at least.
But soon with like occasions pressed
He boldly sent his hand in quest

(Inspired with courage from his bride)
To reach the pot on t'other side,
And as he filled the reeking vase,
Let forth a rouser in her face.

The little Cupids hovering round
(As pictures prove) with garlands crowned,
Abashed at what they saw and heard,
Flew off – nor evermore appeared.

Adieu to ravishing delights,
High raptures and romantic flights,
To goddesses so heavenly sweet,
Expiring shepherds at their feet,
To silver meads and shady bowers
Dressed up with amaranthine flowers.

How great a change! How quickly made!
They learn to call a spade a spade.
They soon from all constraint are freed,
Can see each other do their need:
On box of cedar sits the wife
And makes it warm for dearest life,
And, by the beastly way of thinking,
Finds great society in stinking.
Now Strephon daily entertains
His Chloe in the homeliest strains,
And Chloe, more experienced grown,
With interest pays him back his own.
No maid at court is less ashamed,
Howe'er for selling bargains famed,
Than she, to name her parts behind,
Or when a-bed, to let out wind . . .

O Strephon! e'er that fatal day
When Chloe stole your heart away,
Had you but through a cranny spied

On house of ease[1] your future bride,
In all the postures of her face
Which nature gives in such a case –
Distortions, groanings, strainings, heavings –
'Twere better you had licked her leavings
Than from experience find too late
Your goddess grown a filthy mate.
Your fancy then had always dwelt
On what you saw, and what you smelt –
Would still the same ideas give ye
As when you spied her on the privy,
And spite of Chloe's charms divine
Your heart had been as whole as mine . . .

On sense and wit your passion found,
By decency cemented round;
Let prudence with good nature strive
To keep esteem and love alive.
Then come old age whene'er it will
Your friendship shall continue still,
And thus a mutual, gentle fire
Shall never, but with life, expire.

JOHN OLDMIXON
(1673–1742)

To Cloe

Prithee, Cloe, not so fast –
Let's not run and wed in haste;
We've a thousand things to do:
You must fly, and I pursue;
You must frown, and I must sigh;
I entreat, and you deny.
Stay – if I am never crossed,

[1]*house of ease* lavatory

Half the pleasure will be lost;
Be, or seem to be, severe,
Give me reason to despair;
Fondness will my wishes cloy,
Make me careless of the joy.
Lovers may of course complain
Of their trouble and their pain,
But if pain and trouble cease,
Love without it will not please.

ANON
(c 1707)

Susannah and the Elders

Susannah the fair, with her beauties all bare
Was bathing herself in an arbour;
The elders stood peeping, and pleased with the dipping
Would fain have steered into her harbour.

But she in a rage swore she'd never engage
With monsters so old and so feeble.
This caused a great rout which had ne'er come about
Had the elders been sprightly and able.

JOHN WINSTANLEY
(1678?–1750)

An Epigram on Florio

Florio one evening, brisk and gay,
To pass the tedious hours away
With three young female rakes sat down
And played at whist for half a crown.
At length (if fame the truth can tell)

To questions and commands they fell.
'Florio', says Cloe, 'let me see
What Delia wears above her knee.'
The youth with ready hand obeyed
And by her garter caught the maid.
She kindled with affected heat
And rising vigorous from her seat
As if she thought him monstrous rude
Flew to her chamber. He pursued,
Then flung her softly on the bed,
'And now, my lovely girl', he said,
'I bar all squeakings and "O, fies!"'
'Go, bar the door you fool!' she cries.

THOMAS HAMILTON
6th Earl of Haddington
(1680–1735)

Tell Me, Friend John

'Tell me, friend John, do, if you can,
What is the reason, if a man
Attempts to take a lady fair
By you know what, lies you know where,
That while he lives he still shall find
The female, be she cross or kind,
Fret, frown, and push the hand away?
Tell me the reason, tell me, pray.'

Thoughtful and sage, John sat a while,
Then answered Thomas with a smile:
'Thomas, a case you never put
But it begins or ends in smut.
None but the wicked can applaud ye
Since all your thoughts still run on bawdy.
But yet, for once, my friend, I'll try

If I your doubts can satisfy.
Women still make a great pretence
To modesty and innocence,
And about virtue make a rout;
That is the reason, without doubt.'

'Ah, friend,' said Thomas with concern,
'I see you are but still to learn;
Your understanding's good for naught,
And you are better fed than taught.
Virtue and modesty's a story
As little thought on as John Dory.
Listen, you shall the reason know:
Whene'er you thrust your hand below
All women, be they foul or fair
Know that a hand is useless there.
But if, from May-day to December
You offer there the proper member
Push as you will to give them pain,
They'll neither wince, nor yet complain.'

JOHN GAY
(1685–1732)

from *An Epistle to the Rt Hon. William Pulteney, Esq.*

When the sweet-breathing spring unfolds the buds,
Love flies the dusty town for shady woods.
Then Tottenham fields with roving beauty swarm,
And Hampstead balls the city virgins warm;
Then Chelsea's meads o'erhear perfidious vows,
And the pressed grass defrauds the grazing cows.
'Tis here the same; but in a higher sphere,
For ev'n court ladies sit in open air.
What cit[1] with a gallant would trust his spouse

[1] *cit* tradesman

Beneath the tempting shade of Greenwich boughs?
What peer of France would let his duchess rove
Where Boulogne's closest woods invite to love?
But here no wife can blast her husband's fame –
Cuckold is grown an honourable name.
Stretched on the grass the shepherd sighs his pain,
And on the grass what shepherd sighs in vain?
On Chloe's lap here Damon laid along
Melts with the languish of her amorous song;
There Iris flies Palaemon through the glade,
Nor trips by chance – 'till in the thickest shade;
Here Celimene defends her lips and breast,
For kisses are by struggling closer pressed;
Alexis there with eager flame grows bold,
Nor can the nymph his wanton fingers hold.
Be wise, Alexis; what, so near the road!
Hark, a coach rolls, and husbands are abroad!
Such were our pleasures in the days of yore,
When amorous Charles Britannia's sceptre bore;
The nightly scene of joy the park was made,
And love in couples peopled every shade.
But since at court the rural taste is lost,
What mighty sums have velvet coaches cost!

Ballad

Of all the girls that e'er were seen,
   There's none so fine as Nelly,
For charming face, and shape, and mien,
   And what's not fit to tell ye.
Oh! the turned neck and smooth white skin
   Of lovely, dearest Nelly!
For many a swain it well had been
   Had she ne'er passed by Calais.

[224]

For when as Nelly came to France
   (Invited by her cousins)
Across the Tuilleries each glance
   Killed Frenchmen by whole dozens.
The King, as he at dinner sat,
   Did beckon to his hussar
And bid him bring his tabby cat
   For charming Nell to buss her.

The ladies were with rage provoked
   To see her so respected;
The men looked arch, as Nelly stroked,
   And puss her tail erected.
But not a man did look employ
   Except on pretty Nelly;
Then said the Duc de Villeroy,
   'Ah! qu'elle est bien jolie!'

But who's that grave philosopher
   That carefully looks a'ter?[1]
By his concern it should appear
   The fair one is his daughter.
'My foi!' (quoth then a courtier sly)
   'He on his child does leer too.
I wish he has no mind to try
   What some papas will here do.'

The courtiers all with one accord
   Broke out in Nelly's praises,
Admired her *rose*, and *lys sans farde*[2]
   (Which are your *termes françaises*).
Then might you see a painted ring
   Of dames that stood by Nelly;
She like the pride of all the spring,
   And they like *fleurs du palais*.[3]

[1] *a'ter* after her   [2] *rose, lys san farde* a pink and white complexion   [3] *fleurs du palais* most
beautiful in the court

In Marly's gardens, and St Cloud,
    I saw this charming Nelly,
Where shameless nymphs, exposed to view,
    Stand naked in each *allée*.[1]
But Venus had a brazen face
    Both at Versailles and Meudon,
Or else she had resigned her place
    And left the stone she stood on.

Were Nelly's figure mounted there
    'Twould put down all th'Italian.
Lord! how those foreigners would stare!
    But I should turn Pygmalion.
For spite of lips, and eyes, and mien,
    Me nothing can delight so
As does that part that lies between
    Her left toe and her right toe.

ANON
(c 1720)

Nae Hair On't

Yestreen I wed a lady fair,
    And ye wad believe me,
On her cunt there grows nae hair,
    That's the thing that grieves me.

It vexed me sair, it plagued me sair,
    It put me in a passion
To think that I had wed a wife
    Whase cunt was out o' fashion.

(collected by Robert Burns)

[1]*allée* a garden walk

[226]

ANON
(c 1741)

from *Consummation, or, The Rape of Adonis*

In vain her arts, her winning arts, she tries –
The froward boy her burning wish denies;
Averse he turns when heavenly charms invite,
Nor Venus' self can lure him to delight.
'Can'st thou,' said she, 'when prostrate beauty sues
For countless kisses given, one kiss refuse?
Mars, the fierce god of unrelenting arms,
Who none withstand, I conquered with my charms;
Prostrate that god, my captive and my slave,
Has begged for that which thou unasked shall have.
His lance and helmet o'er my altars hung,
The hero danced, as lisping Cupid sang;
For me in silks his warlike limbs he dressed,
And learned to wanton, dally, smile and jest.
Thus Mars armipotent I rule, who sues
For that which, freely offered, you refuse.
Let not thy charms in vain possess the might
To vanquish her who foils the god of fight.
Touch but my lips with those dear lips of thine –
The kiss shall be thy own as well as mine –
Look not thus blushing on the ground below
Where flowers unconscious of the blessing grow;
Look in my eyes, where all thy beauties play,
Where dying softness joins the pointed ray.
Bashful and coy art thou, afraid to kiss,
When none are present but who share the bliss?
Alone, unseen, of what art thou afraid?
Secure we wanton in the secret shade:
The flowers that bear our weight can never say
That here Venus beneath Adonis lay;
Can never whisper that my naked charms
They saw, or saw me clasp thee in my arms.

[227]

Be coy no more; from Nature learn that none
Live useless here, or for themselves alone.
Flowers are for smell, and fruits for taste designed,
For woman man, and man for womankind. . . .

Rapt as she spoke, for no reply she stayed,
Resolved that sense should act in reason's aid.
Her fair right hand, that trembled with delight,
Soft touched the mystic source of genial might.
The potent touch awaked the drowsy power
As the warm ray revives the drooping flower.
The wanton fair, in various nature wise,
Perceived the subject of enjoyment rise –
Perceived with rapture – and unfolds below
The source of bliss, where living waters flow;
There pleased receives it, while her eyes confess
The fit conjunction for the sweet excess.
With ardent haste her arms around him twined,
Her clasping hands the lovely bondage joined
And (kind compulsion) drew the blushing boy
To her soft bosom, panting for the joy.
Thus as she pressed him close and closer still,
Nature contents in spite a wayward will,
And skilled the mutual rapture to excite
She gently moved and urged the fierce delight.
By swift degrees the thrilling pleasures rise –
Blessed, and more blessed, the wondering stripling lies;
He faints; he melts; she feels the flowing bliss –
That bliss returns, and strains him with a kiss:
In mingled streams the mystic pleasures move,
And Beauty's goddess gives down all her love.

ANON
(c 1741)

The Resurrection

One morn as in bed with dear Cloe I lay,
Sleep stole on our eyes as the shades stole away.
But Miss, waking first, with the sports of the night
Not contented, but wishful for further delight,
With embraces and kisses my slumber destroyed,
And, says she, 'These dear moments should all be enjoyed.
Can you sleep while I'm waking, and wishing, and kind,
With the thoughts of past joys, to repeat I'm inclined?
When the morning, indulgent to either fond lover,
My beauties to thee, thine to me will discover?'

I waked, and looked up on the wanton with eyes
Which showed less desire by far than surprise,
And, says I, 'My dear Cloe', and looked very grave,
'Compose yourself, pray, for, believe me, you rave.
What – thinks my dear girl that a passion like mine
Is no more than mankind have in common with swine?
I'll never believe, though an angel should swear,
But that yours is a nobler, a purer by far.
Let us vie with the Beings in raptures Above –
My love's all seraphic; and such be *thy* love.'

'Oh, Jacky', the laughing young baggage replied,
'Talk this at the honeymoon's end to your bride!
I know – what I know. Let me see – aye, I'm right –
Your love is less now than I found it last night.
'Tis the most, without guilty ambition, you can,
While a man you continue, to love like a man.
Then tell me no more of the seraphs above,
And on earth be content without heavenly love –
For if, when they fought to be gods, angels fell,
Mankind, when they seek to be angels, rebel.'

Thus beat from my quarters, I shifted to new,
And allowed with a sigh all she said to be true.
'But to love till our deaths, my dear Cloe must know,
Is the utmost permitted to mortals below.
Nay, let me add further, than this to do more
No prude ever asked, and no rake ever swore;
And you know that o'ercome and oppressed with delight
I fainted and died on your bosom last night.
Till then sure I loved like a man; now the most
You can ask, or I do, is to love like a ghost.'

A moment she paused. 'Will you promise', said she,
'When again you're alive to love no-one but me?'
'That I do – for my soul –'tis enough, I don't doubt,
But to bring a complete resurrection about,
For a prophet of old (as I'm sure I have read)
Stretched himself o'er a child whom he raised from the dead.
Now of this I'm resolved to make trial, d'ye see,
And love, to that end stretch myself over thee.'

'Twas done in a moment, and o'er me she threw
A leg of such shape an Apelles ne'er drew.
Her lips to my lips, and her breast to my breast,
She joined with a sweetness which can't be expressed.
Her arms clasped me round – I grew warm in the strife
Till death gave me up, and I kindled to life.
But the nymph found her pleasure too great to restrain,
And with kindness excessive, she killed me again.
So true is that maxim – I sorrow, I sigh
To repeat it –'tis this: we live but to die.

JOHN WILKES
(1727–1797)

from *The Essay on Women, Book III*

The first fair she in Paradise was placed,
With each inciting charm by nature graced;
Love in her eyes, and kissing[1] in her mind,
She sought the place where Adam lay reclined.
His leg in her fair hand she gently took
And told him she had come to have – go-look.
Stout rose Sir Thomas with his mystic swell,
And Adam vowed that he would love her well.
After four times he found his spirits flag,
Yet Madam cried: 'Come, give me t'other bag.'
But all in vain; he could not make it stand,
Though Eve oft stroked it with her pretty hand.
This disappointment grieved her heart full sore,
And first determined her to be a whore.
But where to find a proper instrument
To please her heart, and give her full content,
She knew not, till at last the Devil she found,
Who kissed her ten times over – what a round!
Thus kissing first in Paradise began,
And the first cuckold was the earliest man.
The Devil so charmingly performed his part
That kissing fills alone each woman's heart.
This act of nature's most extensive plan
And used by fowl and fish, by beast and man,
Those great perpetrators of each race –
What diction can I find thy praise to grace?
Of all mankind, thou first supreme delight,
Our thoughts by day, our exercise by night;
How shall I all thy charms enumerate?
Or how thy praises justly celebrate?
The grasp divine, th'emphatic thrilling squeeze

[1]*kissing* coitus

The throbbing, panting breasts and trembling knees,
The tickling motion, th'enlivening flow,
The rapturous shiver, and dissolving *oh*!
These, thy attendant joys, more bliss bestow
Than aught besides which gives delight below.

ANON
(c 1765)

The Angler

Come listen awhile and I'll tell you a story,
'Tis of a staunch angler who loved the sport well;
Pray mark the contents which I here lay before ye,
The tale it is true that to you I shall tell.

The angler so staunch had a buxom young wife, sir,
Who oftentimes left her before break of day;
But she not approving his odd way of life, sir,
Would oft have a sigh while her spouse was away:

'Ah, why did I marry a man that loves fishing?
Yet Fair, be advised, for in this you'll agree –
That a right woman's man should love nothing but fleshing,
And with such a dear spouse how contented I'd be.'

Then straight to a buxom young fellow she went, sir,
Who often had blamed her for being too coy.
He viewed her fond eyes and found out her intent, sir,
And eagerly pressed her to grant him the joy.

Six times he put in and six times he pulled out, sir,
Till weary with sport he could angle no more;
Quoth he, 'Though I've caught neither barbel nor trout, sir,
I ne'er in my life had such angling before.'

'My dear', quoth the Fair, 'you may put in again, sir,
But first plumb your depth, or your art won't avail;
If you touch not the bottom, your angling's in vain, sir,
Fish deep to the ground, and of sport you'll not fail.'

Then straight with his plummet he felt for the ground, sir,
'Deeper yet', quoth the Fair, 'for you're never so near.'
'No bottom', quoth he, 'is there yet to be found, sir –
Zounds, why should I plumb, when no bottom is here?'

Then straight he pulled up, but the fish it was gone, sir,
His bait taken off and his line snapped in twain.
'See, my love', quoth the blade, 'I am quite broken down, sir,'
'Never mind it', quoth she, 'but put in once again.'

'Ah, no!' quoth the blade, 'see – my tackle's past using –
But tomorrow I'll come, so to that time adieu.'
'Go, foolish!' said she, 'for such pastime refusing –
Yet ah! could my spouse but angle like you!'

Observe, brother bobs, and take this as a warning –
The jest will hold good, for the moral is plain –
Ere ye part with your wives, give a hearty Good Morning
And as brisk a Good Night when you meet 'em again.

(from *The Choice Spirits' Museum* 1765)

ANON
(c 1780)

from *A Sapphic Epistle*

Dear lady, such is woman's state,
With Charlotte, or with Russia's Kate,
    Or Moll, or Peg, or Nan;
All sigh, as soon as fledged, to have
Some mere, male creature for a slave
    To prime their little pan.

[233]

Small's then the touch-hole, not being old,
The colour lead, or carrot gold,
   Or brown, or white, or black;
But think what a fair maid must bear
When some rough marksman to a hair
   Shoots at the little crack.

Ah, Kitty, Kitty, buxom wench
To let this creature make a trench
   Where Heaven but made a slit;
'Tis martyrdom, small wits declare,
To torture such a beauteous fair
   On such a monstrous spit.

To decency they've no pretence,
The want of that is want of sense,
   For say, what woman should
In such a case devote her life?
'Tis worse than stabbing with a knife
   To rip up flesh and blood.

But delicacy's fled the land!
They'll any thing now take in hand
   If they can shut their eyes;
Though it might make the dumb to speak
It cannot even make them squeak
   So well they manage size.

O would the sex pursue my plan
And turn upon the monster, man,
   What would they not escape?
A thousand woes, a thousand pains,
Swellings, distortions, cramps and strains
   The ruin of each shape.

Ah, hapless woman, to confide
In man, and sigh to be the bride,
   A vessel full of care;

Would you the wiser Sappho learn
You might your happiness discern
And shun a sharp dispair.

(from *The Bawd* 1782)

RICHARD BRINSLEY SHERIDAN
(1751–1816)

The Geranium

In the close covert of a grove
By nature formed for scenes of love,
Said Susan in a lucky hour:
'Observe yon sweet geranium flower.
How straight upon its stalk it stands,
And tempts our violating hands,
Whilst the soft bud, as yet unspread,
Hangs down its pale declining head.
Yet soon as it is ripe to blow,
The stems shall rise, the head shall glow.'
'Nature,' said I, 'my lovely Sue,
To all her followers lends a clue.
Her simple laws themselves explain
As links of one continued chain;
For her the mysteries of creation
Are but the works of generation.
Yon blushing, strong, triumphant flower
Is in the crisis of its power;
But short, alas, its vigorous reign;
He sheds his seed, and drops again.
The bud that hangs in pale decay
Feels not, as yet, the plastic ray.
Tomorrow's sun shall make him rise,
Then, too, he sheds his seed, and dies.

[235]

But words, my love, are vain and weak;
For proof, let bright example speak.'
Then straight before the wondering maid
The tree of life I gently laid.
'Observe, sweet Sue, his drooping head,
How pale, how languid, and how dead.
Yet let the sun of thy bright eyes
Shine but a moment, it shall rise.
Let but the dew of thy soft hand
Refresh the stem, it straight shall stand.
Already, see, it swells, it grows,
Its head is redder than the rose,
Its shrivelled fruit, of dusky hue,
Now glows – a present fit for Sue.
The balm of life each artery fills,
And in o'erflowing drops distils.'
'Oh, me!' cried Susan, 'When is this?
What strange tumultuous throbs of bliss!
Sure, never mortal till this hour
Felt such emotion at a flower!
Oh, serpent, cunning to deceive,
Sure 'tis this tree that tempted Eve.
The crimson apples hang so fair
Alas! what woman could forbear?'
'Well hast thou guessed, my love,' I cried,
'It is the tree by which she died –
The tree which could content her.
All nature, Susan, seeks the centre.
Yet let us still poor Eve forgive,
It's the tree by which we live.
For lovely women still it grows,
And in the centre only blows.
But chief for thee it spreads its charms,
For paradise is in thy arms . . .'
I ceased, for nature kindly here
Began to whisper in her ear,
And lovely Sue lay softly panting

While the geranium tree was planting,
'Till in the heat of amorous strife
She burst the mellow tree of life.
'Oh, heaven!' cried Susan with a sigh,
'The hour we taste – we surely die.
Strange raptures seize my fainting frame,
And all my body glows with flame.
Yet let me snatch one parting kiss
To tell my love I die with bliss –
That pleased thy Susan yields her breath;
Oh, who would live, if this be death?'

THOMAS ROWLANDSON
(1756–1827)

Carved on a Tombstone in one of his Cartoons

Here lies entombed
   Beneath these bricks
The scabbard of ten
   Thousand pricks.

WILLIAM BLAKE
(1757–1827)

from *Gnomic Verses*

Abstinence sows sand all over
The ruddy limbs & flaming hair,
But Desire Gratified.
Plants fruits of life & beauty there.

In a wife I would desire
What in whores is always found –
The lineaments of Gratified desire.

[237]

What is it men in women do require?
The lineaments of Gratified Desire.
What is it women do in men require?
The lineaments of Gratified Desire.

ANON
(c 1788)

To Mrs Hervey of No 21 Queen Anne Street, East

Behold those eyes that swim in humid fires
And trace her wanton thoughts and young desires;
Taste those sweet lips, with balmy nectar fraught,
And all the rich luxuriency of thought;
Press her soft bosom, seat of swelling joy,
Whose charms invite the rosy-pinioned boy,
Who fluttering here may point the unerring dart,
Flush in each eye, and revel in each heart,
Till bolder grown, your hand insatiate rove
O'er her delightful mount and sporting grove.
Then all her limbs unbound, her girdle loose,
There's nothing you can ask her, she'll refuse.

(from *Harris's List of Covent-Garden Ladies* for 1788)

ROBERT BURNS
(1759–1796)

Nine Inch Will Please a Lady

'Come rede[1] me, dame, come tell me, dame,
    My dame come tell me truly,
What length o' graith,[2] when weel ca'd[3] hame,
    Will sair[4] a woman duly?'

[1]*rede* advise [2]*graith* equipment [3]*ca'd* driven [4]*sair* serve

[238]

The carlin clew[1] her wanton tail,
    Her wanton tail sae ready –
'I learn'd a sang in Annandale,
    Nine inch will please a lady.

'But for a koontrie cunt like mine,
    In sooth we're nae sae gentle;
We'll tak tway[2] thumb-bread[3] to the nine,
    And that's a sonsy pintle:[4]
O leeze me on my Charlie lad,
    I'll ne'er forget my Charlie!
Tway roarin handfu's and a daud,[5]
    He nidge[6] it in fu' rarely.

'But weary fa' the laithron doup,[7]
    And may it ne'er be thrivin!
It's no the length that makes me loup,[8]
    But it's the double drivin.
Come nidge me, Tam, come nudge me, Tam,
    Come nidge me o'er the nyvel![9]
Come lowse & lug your battering ram,
    And thrash him at my gyvel!'[10]

Ode to Spring

When maukin bucks[11] at early fucks
    In dewy grass are seen, Sir,
And birds on boughs take off their mowes[12]
    Amand the leaves sae green, Sir,
Latona's son looks liquorish on
    Dame Nature's grand impétus
Till his pego[13] rise, then westward flies
    To roger Madame Thetis.

[1]*clew* fondled [2]*tway* two [3]*thumb-bread* thumb-breadths [4]*sonsy pintle* pretty prick
[5]*daud* lump [6]*nidge* squeeze [7]*laithron doup* lazy rump [8]*loup* leap [9]*nyvel* navel
[10]*gyvel* loins [11]*maukin bucks* hares [12]*mowes* copulations [31]*pego* prick

[239]

Yon wandering rill that marks the hill
    And glances o'er the brae, Sir,
Glides by a bower where many a flower
    Sheds fragrance on the day, Sir.
There Damon lay with Sylvia gay
    To love they thought no crime, Sir,
The wild-birds sang, the echos rang,
    While Damon's arse beat time, Sir.

First, wi' the thrush his thrust and push
    Had compass large and long, Sir,
The blackbird next, his tuneful text
    Was bolder, clear and strong, Sir.
The linnet's lay came then in play
    And the lark that soar'd aboon, Sir,
Till Damon, fierce, mistimed his arse,
    And fucked quite out of tune, Sir.

Our John's Brak Yestreen

Twa neebor wives sat i' the sun,
    A twynin'[1] at their rocks,[2]
An' they an argument began,
    An' a' the plea was cocks.

'Twas whether they were sinnens[3] strang,
    Or whether they were bane?[4]
An' how they row'd[5] about your thumb,
    And how they stand't themlane?[6]

First, Raichie gae her rock a rug,[7]
    An' syne she claw'd[8] her tail;
'When our Tam draws on his breeks,[9]
    It waigles[10] like a flail.'

[1]*twynin* weaving [2]*rocks* distaffs [3]*sinnens* sinews [4]*bane* bone [5]*row'd* rolled
[6]*themlane* by themselves [7]*rug* tug [8]*claw'd* scratched [9]*breeks* breeches [10]*waigles* waggles

Says Bess, 'They're bane I will maintain,
   And proof in han' I'll gie;
For our John's it brak yestreen,[1]
   And the margh[2] ran down my thie.'[3]

(attributed to Robert Burns)

ANON

Wad Ye Do That?

'Gudewife, when your gudeman's frae hame,
   Might I but be sae bauld
As come to your bed-chamber
   When winter nights are cauld?
As come to your bed-chamber
   When nights are cauld and wat,[4]
And lie in your gudeman's stead?
   Wad ye do that?'

'Young man, an ye should be so kind
   When our gudeman's frae hame,
As come to my bed-chamber
   Where I am laid my lane,[5]
And lie in our gudeman's stead,
   I will tell you want:
He fucks me five times ilka[6] night.
   Wad ye do that?'

(collected by Robert Burns)

[1]*yestreen* last night [2]*margh* marrow [3]*thie* thigh [4]*wat* wet [5]*my lane* alone [6]*ilka* every

GEORGE COLMAN?
(1762–1836)

from *Don Leon*

Leon and Nicolo

How many hours I've sat in pensive guise
To watch the mild expression of his eyes!
Or when asleep at noon, and from his mouth
His breath came sweet like odours from the south,
How long I've hung in rapture as he lay,
And silent chased the insect tribe away.
How oft at morn, when troubled by the heat,
The covering fell disordered at his feet,
I've gazed unsated at his naked charms
And clasped him waking to my longing arms.
How oft in winter, when the sky o'ercast
Capped the bleak mountains, and the ruthless blast
Moaned through the trees, or lashed the surfy strand,
I've drawn myself the glove upon his hand,
Thrown o'er his tender limbs the rough capote
Or tied the kerchief round his snowy throat.
How oft, when summer saw me fearless brave
With manly breast the blue transparent wave
Another Daedalus I taught him how
With spreading arms the liquid waste to plough.
Then brought him gently to the sunny beach
And wiped the briny moisture from his breech.
  Oh! how the happy moments seemed to fly,
Spent half in love and half in poetry!

(lines 592–618)

from *The Rodiad*

In towns and hamlets whipping clubs are formed
Where hearts and bottoms can alike be warmed;
Their families their infant felons bring
And publicly administer the sting,
Mixing the titillation with their tea,
And mid the sobbing gossip fair and free:
'Just to please you, as you've come late, my cousin,
I'll give my Emily another dozen.'
'As George's bottom's all I've got this week,
Suppose we share it – taking each a cheek.
We'll lay him down between us on his belly –
I'll bring first blood upon my cheek, I'll tell ye.'
There comes the besom-maker, and his right
Is to select a bottom for the night
On whose white skin he lavishes at will
His birchen bouquet, and enjoys his fill.
There too, poor parents clear a little sum
By letting out a child's attractive bum
To any wealthy whipper who may come –
'Here, sir's my Johnny – he's the lad to squeak –
He's not had his allowance for a week.'
'Oh, sir, I'm sure you'll like my William best –
I've brought him here, sir, at the squire's request,
Who says he's of a band of thieves the chief
And must be flogged till his behind's raw beef –
So work him well, and keep him in your power –
I'm sure he's cheap at eighteenpence an hour.'
Their love in various stages intervenes
And adds its raptures to these lively scenes;
O'er bleeding bottoms hardest hearts relent
And maiden arms impassioned youth content –
The Rod is Cupid's sweetest instrument.

THOMAS MOORE
(1779–1852)

Did Not

'Twas a new feeling – something more
Than we had dared to own before,
   Which then we hid not:
We saw it in each other's eye,
And wished, in every half-breathed sigh,
   To speak, but did not.

She felt my lips' impassioned touch –
'Twas the first time I dared so much,
   And yet she chid me not;
But whispered o'er my burning brow,
'Oh, do you doubt I love you now?'
   Sweet soul! I did not.

Warmly I felt her bosom thrill,
I pressed it closer, closer still,
   Though gently bid not,
Till – oh: the world hath seldom heard
Of lovers, who so nearly erred,
   And yet, who did not.

LORD BYRON
(1788–1824)

from *Don Juan*

Juan and Haidée

And thus they wandered forth, and hand in hand,
   Over the shining pebbles and the shells,
Glided along the smooth and hardened sand,
   And in the worn and wild receptacles

Worked by the storms, yet worked as it were planned,
    In hollow halls, with sparry roofs and cells,
They turned to rest; and, each clasped by an arm,
Yielded to the deep twilight's purple charm.

They looked up to the sky, whose floating glow
    Spread like a rosy ocean, vast and bright;
They gazed upon the glittering sea below,
    Whence the broad moon rose circling into sight;
They heard the waves splash, and the wind so low,
    And saw each other's dark eyes darting light
Into each other – and, beholding this,
Their lips drew near, and clung into a kiss;

A long, long kiss, a kiss of youth, and love,
    And beauty, all concentrating like rays
Into one focus, kindled from above;
    Such kisses as belong to early days,
Where heart, and soul, and sense, in concert move,
    And the blood's lava, and the pulse a blaze,
Each kiss a heart-quake – for a kiss's strength,
I think, it must be reckoned by its length.

By length, I mean duration; theirs endured
    Heaven knows how long – no doubt they never reckoned;
And if they had, they could not have secured
    The sum of their sensations to a second:
They had not spoken; but they felt allured,
    As if their souls and lips each other beckoned,
Which, being joined, like swarming bees they clung –
Their hearts the flowers from whence the honey sprung.

They were alone, but not alone as they
    Who shut in chambers think it loneliness;
The silent ocean, and the starlit bay,
    The twilight glow, which momently grew less,

The voiceless sands, and dropping caves, that lay
  Around them, made them to each other press,
As if there were no life beneath the sky
Save theirs, and that their life could never die.

They feared no eyes nor ears on that lone beach,
  They felt no terrors from the night; they were
All in all to each other; though their speech
  Was broken words, they *thought* a language there –
And all the burning tongues the passions teach
  Found in one sigh the best interpreter
Of nature's oracle – first love – that all
Which Eve has left her daughters since her fall.

(Canto II clxxxii–clxxxix)

JOHN KEATS
(1795–1821)

Song

O blush not so! O blush not so!
  Or I shall think you knowing;
And if you smile the blushing while,
  Then maidenheads are going.

There's a blush for won't, and a blush for shan't,
  And a blush for having done it:
There's a blush for thought, and a blush for naught,
  And a blush for just begun it.

O sigh not so! O sigh not so!
  For it sounds of Eve's sweet pippin;
By those loosened lips you have tasted the pips
  And fought in an amorous nipping.

[246]

Will you play once more at nice-cut-core,
    For it only will last our youth out?
And we have the prime of the kissing time,
    We have not one sweet tooth out.

There's a sigh for yes, and a sigh for no,
    And a sigh for I can't bear it!
O what can be done, shall we stay or run?
    O, cut the sweet apple and share it!

WALT WHITMAN
(1819–1892)

From Pent-Up Aching Rivers

From pent-up aching rivers,
From that of myself without which I were nothing,
From what I am determined to make illustrious, even if I stand
        sole among men,
From my own voice resonant, singing the phallus,
Singing the song of procreation,
Singing the need of superb children and therein superb grown
        people,
Singing the muscular urge and the blending,
Singing the bedfellow's song, (O resistless yearning!
O for any and each the body correlative attracting!
O for you whoever you are your correlative body! O it, more than
        all else, you delighting!)
From the hungry gnaw that eats me night and day,
From native moments, from bashful pains, singing them,
Seeking something yet unfound though I have diligently sought it
        many a long year,
Singing the true song of the soul fitful at random,
Renascent with grossest Nature or among animals,
Of that, of them and what goes with them my poems informing,
Of the smell of apples and lemons, of the pairing of birds,

[247]

Of the wet of woods, of the lapping of waves,
Of the mad pushes of waves upon the land, I them chanting,
The overture lightly sounding, the strain anticipating,
The welcome nearness, the sight of the perfect body,
The swimmer swimming naked in the bath, or motionless on his
        back lying and floating,
The female form approaching, I pensive, love-flesh tremulous
        aching,
The divine list for myself or you or for any one making,
The face, the limbs, the index from head to foot, and what it
        arouses,
The mystic deliria, the madness amorous, the utter abandonment,
(Hark close and still what I now whisper to you,
I love you, O you entirely possess me,
O that you and I escape from the rest and go utterly off, free and
        lawless,
Two hawks in the air, two fishes swimming in the sea not more
        lawless than we;)
The furious storm through me careering, I passionately trembling,
The oath of the inseparableness of two together, of the woman
        that loves me and whom I love more than
        my life, that oath swearing,
(O I willingly stake all for you,
O let me be lost if it must be so!
O you and I! what is it to us what the rest do or think?
What is all else to us; only that we enjoy each other and exhaust
        each other if it must be so;)
From the master, the pilot I yield the vessel to,
The general commanding me, commanding all, from him
        permission taking,
From time the programme hastening, (I have loitered too long as
        it is,)
From sex, from the warp and from the woof,
From privacy, from frequent repinings alone,
From plenty of persons near and yet the right person not near,
From the soft sliding of hands over me and thrusting of fingers
        through my hair and beard,

From the long sustained kiss upon the mouth or bosom,
From the close pressure that makes me or any man drunk,
               fainting with excess,
From what the divine husband knows, from the work of
               fatherhood,
From exultation, victory and relief from the bedfellow's embrace
               in the night,
From the act-poems of eyes, hands, hips and bosoms,
From the cling of trembling arm,
From the bending curve and the clinch,
From side by side the pliant coverlet off-throwing,
From the one so unwilling to have me leave, and me just as
               unwilling to leave,
(Yet a moment O tender waiter, and I return),
From the hour of shining stars and dropping dews,
From the night a moment I emerging flitting out,
Celebrate you act divine and you children prepared for,
And you stalwart loins.

from *I Sing the Body Electric*

5.

This is the female form,
A divine nimbus exhales from it from head to foot,
It attracts with fierce undeniable attraction,
I am drawn by its breath as if I were no more than a helpless
          vapour, all falls aside but myself and it,
Books, art, religion, time, the visible and solid earth, and what was
          expected of heaven or feared of hell, are now consumed,
Mad filaments, ungovernable shoots play out of it, the response
          likewise ungovernable,
Ebb stung by the flow and flow stung by the ebb, love-flesh
          swelling and deliciously aching,
Limitless limpid jets of love hot and enormous, quivering jelly of
          love, white-blow and delirious juice,

Bridgegroom night of love working surely and softly into the
      prostrate dawn,
Undulating into the willing and yielding day,
Lost in the cleave of the clasping and sweet-fleshed day.

This the nucleus – after the child is born of woman, man is born
      of woman,
This the bath of birth, this the merge of small and large, and the
      outlet again.

Be not ashamed women, your privilege encloses the rest, and is
      the exit of the rest,
You are the gates of the body, and you are the gates of the soul.

The female contains all qualities and tempers them,
She is in her place and moves with perfect balance,
She is all things duly veiled, she is both passive and active,
She is to conceive daughters as well as sons, and sons as well as
      daughters.

As I see my soul reflected in Nature,
As I see through a mist, One with inexpressible completeness,
      sanity, beauty,
See the bent head and arms folded over the breast, the Female I
      see.

9.

O my body! I dare not desert the likes of you in other men and
      women, nor the likes of the parts of you,
I believe the likes of you are to stand or fall with the likes of the
      soul (and that they are the soul),
I believe the likes of you shall stand and fall with my poems, and
      that they are my poems,
Man's, woman's, child's, youth's, wife's, husband's, mother's,
      father's, young man's, young woman's poems,

Head, neck, hair, ears, drop and tympan[1] of the ears,
Eyes, eye-fringes, iris of the eye, eyebrows, and the waking or
       sleeping of the lids,
Mouth, tongue, lips, teeth, roof of the mouth, jaws, and the
       jaw-hinges,
Nose, nostrils of the nose, and the partition,
Cheeks, temples, forehead, chin, throat, back of the neck,
       neck-slue,[2]
Strong shoulders, manly beard, scapula, hind-shoulders, and the
       ample side-round of the chest,
Upper-arm, armpit, elbow-socket, lower-arm, arm-sinews,
       arm-bones,
Wrist and wrist-joints, hand, palm, knuckles, thumb, fore-finger,
       finger-joints, finger-nails,
Broad breast-front, curling hair of the breast, breast-bone,
       breast-side,
Ribs, belly, backbone, joints of the backbone,
Hips, hip-sockets, hip-strength, inward and outward round,
       man-balls, man-root,
Strong set of thighs, well carrying the trunk above,
Leg-fibres, knee, knee-pan, upper-leg, under-leg,
Ankles, instep, foot-ball, toes, toe-joints, the heel;
All attitudes, all the shapeliness, all the belongings of my or your
       body or of any one's body, male or female,
The lung-sponges, the stomach-sac, the bowels sweet and clean,
The brain in its folds inside the skull-frame,
Sympathies, heart-valves, palate-valves, sexuality, maternity,
Womanhood and all that is a woman, and the man that comes
       from woman,
The womb, the teats, nipples, breast-milk, tears, laughter,
       weeping, love-looks, love-perturbations and risings,
The voice, articulation, language, whispering, shouting aloud,
Food, drink, pulse, digestion, sweat, sleep, walking, swimming,
Poise on the hips, leaping, reclining, embracing, arm-curving and
       tightening,

[1]*tympan* membrane   [2]*slue* change of position

The continual changes of the flex of the mouth, and around the
      eyes,
The skin, the sunburnt shade, freckles, hair,
The curious sympathy one feels when feeling with the hand the
      naked meat of the body,
The circling rivers the breath, and breathing it in and out,
The beauty of the waist, and thence of the hips, and thence
      downward towards the knees,
The thin red jellies within you or within me, the bones and the
      marrow in the bones,
The exquisite realisation of health;
O I say these are not the parts and poems of the body only, but
      of the soul,
O I say now these are the soul!

PIERRE CHARLES BAUDELAIRE
(1821–1867)

Jewels

My love was nude, but, knowing my desire,
Had donned her sounding jewels, an attire
That, with its air of triumph rich and brave,
Recalled some sultan's proud and favoured slave.

That radiant world of gem and metal dancing
Strikes forth a music mocking and entrancing;
I love it madly, for my chief delight
Is in the interplay of sound and light.

She lay there, then, and let herself be loved,
And from her couch she smiled down and approved
My deep, calm love that rose to her as if
It were an ocean mounting to a cliff.

Eyeing me like a well-tamed tigress there,
She posed with a distracted dreamy air,
And candour joined to lewdness lent a new
Strange charm to metamorphoses I knew.

Her oil-bright, swan-like arms, legs, loins and thighs,
All undulating, passed before my eyes
Clairvoyant and serene; those fruits of mine,
Her belly and breasts, the cluster on my vine,

Advanced like evil angels to cajole
And trouble the quiescence of my soul,
Dislodging her from the crystal rock where she
In solitude was resting peacefully.

She so thrust out her pelvis that it seemed
She made Antiope's plump hips combine
With the smooth bust of a youth in a new design.
On her tawny skin rouge exquisitely gleamed.

– And as the dead lamp left us half in gloom,
And now the hearth alone lit up the room,
With every flaming sigh there came a flood
Of light that drowned her amber skin in blood.

Afternoon Song

Though your eyebrows may give rise
To a strange malign impression,
(Unangelic's your expression,
Witch with the alluring eyes),

I'm your worshipper at least;
Perilous mad passion mine,
Wild one, yet for me divine,
You're the idol, I the priest!

[253]

Desert and thick forest scent
Your rude tresses; in your mien
Mysteries are dimly seen,
Secrets of the Orient;

Perfume floats about your form
As it floats about a censer,
Evening Nymph, adored dispenser
Of enchantments dark and warm.

Ah! no philtres known to men
With your indolence compare;
Your caresses are so rare
They'd revive the dead again!

By your hips your breasts are wooed,
You fill cushions with delight,
For they're ravished by the sight
Of your languid attitude.

Sometimes, seeking to assuage
Your mysterious sombre rage,
Pouring pain into my bliss,
You will bite me as you kiss;

From your mocking laugh I smart
As you tear me, then I swoon
When your gaze soft as the moon
Falls upon my tortured heart.

'Neath your soft and satin shoe,
'Neath your charming silken foot
All my happiness I put,
And my fate and genius too;

Healer of my soul, you are
Music, colour, living light!
Warm expression in the night
Of my black Siberia!

Tresses

O fleece that foams upon those shoulders bare!
O blissful locks! O languid fragrances!
Tonight, to people this dark alcove's air
With visions sleeping there, I'll wave your hair
To flutter like a banner in the breeze.

Exotic trances, tropic suns, the spell
Of all an absent world, nigh dead, remote,
In shadows of your scented forest dwell!
As other souls on seas of music sail
So mine, love, will upon your perfume float.

I'll rove where, full of sap, both men and tree
Swoon in the blazing heat of distant lands;
Strong tresses, be the swell that carries me!
Blinded, I dream, O sea of ebony,
Of masts and pennons, oarsmen, sails, and sands;

Of echoing ports where my soul drinks untold
Draughts of glittering colour, sound and scent;
Where ships gliding in shimmering moire and gold,
Stretch out their vast and eager arms to hold
The glory of a trembling firmament.

I'll plunge my drunken head in this black sea
In which the other ocean lies becalmed;
And there my subtle spirit will find *thee*,
Rich indolence, to lull me endlessly
In drowsing orient airs with spice embalmed.

O blue hair, tent of hanging darkness, veil
Of vaulted azure roofing skies afar!
The tangled meshes of your locks exhale
Blent odours that I drunkenly inhale
Of mingled coco-oil and musk and tar.

[255]

Oh, let my hand for ever in your mane
Sow rubies, sapphires, pearls, so you shall be
My loving sorceress again, again!
Oasis where I dream, gourd whence I drain
Long draughts of bliss – the wine of memory!

(tr Alan Conder)

The Cat

Come, my fine cat, against my loving heart;
Sheathe your sharp claws, and settle.
And let my eyes into your pupils dart
Where agate sparks with metal.

Now while my fingertips caress at leisure
Your head and wiry curves,
And that my hand's elated with the pleasure
Of your electric nerves,

I think about my woman – how her glances
Like yours, dear beast, deep-down
And cold, can cut and wound one as with lances;

Then, too, she has that vagrant
And subtle air of danger that makes fragrant
Her body, lithe and brown.

Poem

One night, when near a fearful Jewess lying,
As one corpse by another corpse, I sprawled –
Beside the venal body I was buying,
The beauty that was absent I recalled.

[256]

I pictured you in native majesty
With glances full of energy and grace,
Your hair, a perfumed casque, whose memory
Revives me for the amorous embrace.

For madly I'd have kissed your noble frame,
And from your cool feet to your great black tresses
Unleashed the treasure of profound caresses.

If with a single tear that gently came
You could have quenched, O queen of all the cruel!,
The blazing of your eyes, their icy fuel.

The Snake that Dances

I love to watch, while you are lazing,
   Your skin. It iridesces
Like silk or satin, smoothly-glazing
   The light that it caresses.

Under your tresses dark and deep
   Where acrid perfumes drown,
A fragrant sea whose breakers sweep
   In mazes blue or brown,

My soul, a ship, to the attraction
   Of breezes that bedizen
Its swelling canvas, clears for action
   And seeks a far horizon.

Your eyes where nothing can be seen
   Either of sweet or bitter
But gold and iron mix their sheen,
   Seem frosty gems that glitter.

To see you rhythmically advancing
    Seems to my fancy fond
As if it were a serpent dancing
    Waved by the charmer's wand.

Under the languorous moods that weight it,
    Your childish head bows down:
Like a young elephant's you sway it
    With motions soft as down.

Your body leans upon the hips
    Like a fine ship that laves
Its hull from side to side, and dips
    Its yards into the waves.

When, as by glaciers ground, the spate
    Swells hissing from beneath,
The water of your mouth, elate,
    Rises between your teeth –

It seems some old Bohemian vintage
    Triumphant, fierce, and tart,
A liquid heaven that showers a mintage
    Of stars across my heart.

(tr Roy Campbell)

ALGERNON CHARLES SWINBURNE
(1837–1909)

Love and Sleep

Lying asleep between the strokes of night
    I saw my love lean over my sad bed,
    Pale as the duskiest lily's leaf or head,
Smooth-skinned and dark, with bare throat made to bite,

Too wan for blushing and too warm for white,
    But perfect-coloured without white or red.
    And her lips opened amorously, and said –
I wist not what, saving one word – Delight.
And all her face was honey to my mouth,
    And all her body pasture to mine eyes;
        The long lithe arms and hotter hands than fire,
The quivering flanks, hair smelling of the south,
    The bright light feet, the splendid supple thighs
    And glittering eyelids of my soul's desire.

from *Dolores*

There are sins it may be to discover,
    There are deeds it may be to delight.
What new work wilt thou find for thy lover,
    What new passions for daytime or night?
What spells that they know not a word of
    Whose lives are as leaves overblown?
What tortures undreamt of, unheard of,
    Unwritten, unknown?

Ah beautiful passionate body
    That never has ached with a heart!
On thy mouth though the kisses are bloody,
    Though they sting till it shudder and smart,
More kind than the love we adore is,
    They hurt not the heart or the brain,
O bitter and tender Dolores,
    Our Lady of Pain.

As our kisses relax and redouble,
    From the lips and the foam and the fangs
Shall no new sin be born for men's trouble,
    No dream of impossible pangs?

[259]

With the sweet of the sins of old ages
  Wilt thou satiate thy soul as of yore?
Too sweet is the rind, say the sages,
  Too bitter the core.

Hast thou told all thy secrets the last time,
  And bared all thy beauties to one?
Ah, where shall we go then for pastime,
  If the worst that can be has been done?
But sweet as the rind was the core is;
  We are fain of thee still, we are fain,
O sanguine and subtle Dolores,
  Our Lady of Pain.

By the hunger of change and emotion,
  By the thirst of unbearable things,
By despair, the twin-born of devotion,
  By the pleasure that winces and stings,
The delight that consumes the desire,
  The desire that outruns the delight,
By the cruelty deaf as a fire
  And blind as the night,

By the ravenous teeth that have smitten
  Through the kisses that blossom and bud,
By the lips intertwisted and bitten
  Till the foam has a savour of blood,
By the pulse as it rises and falters,
  By the hands as they slacken and strain,
I adjure thee, respond from thy altars,
  Our Lady of Pain.

Wilt thou smile as a woman disdaining
  The light fire in the veins of a boy?
But he comes to thee sad, without feigning,
  Who has wearied of sorrow and joy;

Less careful of labour and glory
   Than the elders whose hair has uncurled;
And young, but with fancies as hoary
   And grey as the world.

*   *   *

Dost thou dream, in a respite of slumber,
   In a lull of the fires of thy life,
Of the days without name, without number,
   When thy will stung the world into strife;
When, a goddess, the pulse of thy passion,
   Smote kings as they revelled in Rome;
And they hailed thee re-risen, O Thalassian,
   Foam-white, from the foam?

When thy lips had such lovers to flatter;
   When the city lay red from thy rods,
And thine hands were as arrows to scatter
   The children of change and their gods;
When the blood of thy foemen made fervent
   A sand never moist from the main,
As one smote them, their lord and their servant,
   Our Lady of Pain.

On sands by the storm never shaken,
   Nor wet from the washing of tides;
Nor by foam of the waves overtaken,
   Nor winds that the thunder bestrides;
But red from the print of thy paces,
   Made smooth for the world and its lords,
Ringed round with a flame of fair faces,
   And splendid with swords.

There the gladiator, pale for thy pleasure,
   Drew bitter and perilous breath;
There torments laid hold on the treasure
   Of limbs too delicious for death;

[261]

When thy gardens were lit with live torches;
  When the world was a steed for thy rein;
When the nations lay prone in thy porches,
  Our Lady of Pain.

When, with flame all around him aspirant,
  Stood flushed, as a harp-player stands,
The implacable beautiful tyrant,
  Rose-crowned, having death in his hands;
And a sound as the sound of loud water
  Smote far through the flight of the fires,
And mixed with the lightning of slaughter
  A thunder of lyres.

Dost thou dream of what was and no more is,
  The old kingdoms of earth and the kings?
Dost thou hunger for these things, Dolores,
  For these, in a world of new things?
But thy bosom no fasts could emaciate,
  No hunger compel to complain
Those lips that no bloodshed could satiate,
  Our Lady of Pain.

As of old when the world's heart was lighter,
  Through thy garments the grace of thee glows,
The white wealth of thy body made whiter
  By the blushes of amorous blows,
And seamed with sharp lips and fierce fingers,
  And branded by kisses that bruise;
When all shall be gone that now lingers,
  Ah, what shall we lose?

Thou wert fair in the fearless old fashion,
  And thy lips are as melodies yet,
And move to the music of passion
  With lithe and lascivious regret.

What ailed us, O gods, to desert you
    For creeds that refuse and restrain?
Come down and redeem us from virtue,
    Our Lady of Pain.

from *The Flogging Block*

Rufus's Flogging

Dr Birkinshaw: Master Redmayne's posteriors, I see, are as tender
As plump – though so hardened and old an offender
Might by this time be almost expected to find
His skin, by much whipping, quite hardened behind.
But though all his backside is well seamed and well scarred
The skin is still tender, I see, and not hard.
Don't flinch, Master Rufus – don't stir! not an inch! for
If you do, sir, I'll *(swish)* give you something to flinch for.
                                            [*flogs Rufus*]
Now Rufus, my lad, can you tell me now, come,
Was the bum made for birch, or was birch for the bum?
Was the bottom by provident nature designed
That the birch might have matter to work on behind,
Or the birch providentially made for the part
Where it constantly makes all young gentlemen smart?
Should you guess, Master Rufus, that nature or God
First moulded the bottom – then thought of the rod?
Or after the birch, with its spreading green sprays,
Lithe twigs, and tough shoots, and rough buds, met the gaze
And approval (no doubt) of its fashioner – eh? –
Did the sight not suggest its right use – the one way
To make it of service, boy? What should you say?
Was the very first bottom – the very first boy
Ever born, made on purpose to find it employ?
Was that first-born of bottoms as chubby, I wonder,
As yours is? I doubt it: conjecture might blunder.
It's well, on the whole, you're a bad boy; for were you
A good boy, it wouldn't be easy to spare you.

It wouldn't, I may say, be proper to spare
So invitingly brawny a bottom, when bare –
So temptingly chubby a bottom as yours
Provokes the infliction it braves and endures.
Such a bum seems to challenge the birch that it feels
To cover its nakedness – covered with weals.
Its natural nakedness, covered with recent
Great bloody red weals, is no longer indecent.
The sight is improving and wholesome; I wish
It may prove so to all of your schoolfellows *(swish)*.
                    [*flogs Rufus soundly*]
I trust it may always impress them profoundly
To see such a big boy's bare bottom flogged soundly.

WILFRED SCAWEN BLUNT
(1840–1922)

On a Lost Opportunity

We might, if you had willed, have conquered heaven.
Once only in our lives before the gate
Of Paradise we stood, one fortunate even,
And gazed in sudden rapture through the grate,
And, while you stood astonished, I, our fate
Venturing, pushed the latch and found it free.
There stood the tree of knowledge fair and great
Beside the tree of life. One instant we
Stood in that happy garden, guardianless,
My hands already turned towards the tree,
And in another moment we had known
The taste of joy and immortality
And been ourselves as gods. But in distress
You thrust me back with supplicating arms
And eyes of terror, till the impatient sun
Had time to set and till the heavenly host
Rushed forth on us with clarions and alarms
And cast us out for ever, blind and lost.

JOHN ADDINGTON SYMONDS
(1840–1893)

from *Eudiades and a Cretan Idyll*

It was scarce the noon of night
When to his window in the pale starlight
Melanthias came, and pushed aside the boughs
Of blossoming rose, and, careful not to rouse
The sleeping boy, doffed cloak and shoes, and hid
His light of limbs beneath the coverlid.
Then the boy stirring in his dream was ware
Of that loved presence, feeling round his bare
Smooth ivory breast the warm arms laid; yet he
Feigned in his guile and wise simplicity
To sleep, and watched with fear what should befall.
But nought befell; nor was he moved at all
Save with new longing, for the lover kissed
His forehead with pure lips and gently pressed
The little swelling softness of his breast.
Then turned Eudiades, and laughed, and cried:
'Didst think me sleeping?' and to the man's side
Nestled, and lay there dreaming, half awake,
While wakeful birds of June sweet sounds did make
Among the cypresses. But at daybreak
Uprose Melanthias, and the boy could see
His beauty naked in the mystery
Of morning; and thenceforth, I ween, no dread
Stayed in his soul where love was harboured:
But day by day living with him he learned
New sweetness, and the fire divine that burned
In the man's heart was mirrored in the boy's,
So that he thirsted for the self-same joys,
And knew what passion was, nor could abide
To be one moment severed from the side
Of him in whom whatever maketh sweet
The life of man was centred and complete.

[265]

Yea, but the joy that grew between them wove
Their very bodies in a web of love,
So that they seemed to breathe one air and drew
The same delights dropping like honeydew
From all glad things – from scent of summer skies,
From sleep and toil and whispered melodies
Of music.

GERARD MANLEY HOPKINS
(1844–1889)

Harry Ploughman

Hard as hurdle arms, with a broth of goldish flue
Breathed round; the rack of ribs; the scooped flank; lank
Rope-over thigh; knee-nave; and barrelled shank –
    Head and foot, shoulder and shank –
By a grey eye's heed steered well, one crew, fall to;
Stand at stress. Each limb's barrowy brawn, his thew
That onewhere curded, onewhere sucked or sank –
    Soared or sank –,
Though as a beechbole firm, finds his, as at a roll-call, rank
And features, in flesh, what deed he each must do –
    His sinew-service where do.

He leans to it, Harry bends, look. Back, elbow, and liquid waist
In him, all quail to the wallowing o' the plough: 's cheek
                      crimsons; curls
Wag or crossbridle, in a wind lifted, windlaced –
    See his wind- lilylocks -laced;
Churlsgrace, too, child of Amansstrength, how it hangs or hurls
Them – broad in bluffhide his frowning feet lashed! raced
With, along them, cragiron under and culd furls –
    With-a-fountain's shining-shot furls.

THEODORE WRATISLAW
(fl 1850–90)

To a Sicilian Boy

Love, I adore the contours of thy shape,
Thine exquisite breasts and arms adorable;
The wonders of thine heavenly throat compel
Such fire of love as even my dreams escape:
I love thee as the sea-foam loves the cape,
Or as the shore the sea's enchanting spell:
In sweets the blossoms of thy mouth excel
The tenderest bloom of peach or purple grape.

I love thee, sweet! Kiss me, again, again!
Thy kisses soothe me, as tired earth the rain;
Between thine arms I find my only bliss;
Ah let me in thy bosom still enjoy
Oblivion of the past, divinest boy,
And the dull ennui of a woman's kiss!

A. G. RENSHAM
(fl 1850–90)

Jealousy

He loves me, but I would that he would die;
    I love him, but I would that he were dead,
And that he, silent, evermore should lie
    Where the soft earth enfolds his clustering head.

Yes! die before another's arm entwine
    His strong, white neck; die, ere his heartstrings throb
On other bosoms, and those firm lips pine
    For kisses and the soul's enraptured sob,

[267]

Not mine! I could not bear to lie alone,
　　Torn by fierce Jealousy's envenomed fang,
But I could sit beside his sculptured stone
　　Nursing sad Memory's keen but gentler pang.

Dead, ere he wearied of my burning love,
　　And those dear eyes had turned to one more dear;
Oh! better he should rest in Heaven above,
　　Than leave me in such Hell as that I fear!

I may not love him as his darling should,
　　I may not in his arms so happy lie;
I may not live the life of love I would,
　　And therefore pray I God that he may die.

GEORGE MOORE
(1852–1933)

Sonnet

Idly she yawned, and threw her heavy hair
Across her flesh-filled shoulders, called the maid,
And slipped her sweet blonde body out of bed,
Searching her slippers in the wintry air.

The fire shed over all a sullen glare, –
Then in her bath she sponged from foot to head,
Her body, arms, breasts, thighs, and things unsaid,
Powdered and dried herself with delicate care.

Then Zoë entered with Figaro,
The chocolate, the letters, and the cat,
And drew the blinds to show the falling snow,
Upon the sofa still her mistress sat
Drawing along her legs, as white as milk,
Her long stockings of finely-knitted silk.

[268]

OSCAR WILDE
(1854-1900)

From a Picture Painted by Miss V. T.

A fair slim boy not made for this world's pain,
With hair of gold thick clustering round his ears,
   And longing eyes half veil'd by foolish tears
Like bluest water seen through mists of rain;
Pale cheeks whereon no kiss hath left its stain,
     Red under-lip drawn in for fear of Love,
     And white throat whiter than the breast of dove –
Alas! alas! if all should be in vain.
Behind, wide fields, and reapers all a-row
In heat and labour toiling wearily,
To no sweet sound of laughter or of lute.
The sun is shooting wide its crimson glow,
Still the boy dreams: nor knows that night is nigh,
And in the night-time no man gathers fruit.

C. P. CAVAFY
(1863-1933)

Picture of a 23-Year-Old Youth Painted by his Friend of the
Same Age, an Amateur

He finished the painting   yesterday noon. Now
he studies it in detail.   He has painted him in a
gray unbuttoned coat,   a deep gray, without
any vest or tie.   With a rose-coloured shirt;
open at the collar,   so something might be seen
also of the beauty   of his chest, of his neck.
The right temple   is almost entirely
covered by his hair,   his beautiful hair
(parted in the manner   he prefers it this year).

There is the completely   voluptuous tone
he wanted to put into it   when he was doing the eyes,
when he was doing the lips . . .   His mouth, the lips
that are made for consummation,   for choice love-making.

Days of 1901

This he had in him that set him apart,
that in spite of all his dissoluteness
and his great experience in love,
despite the habitual harmony
that existed between his attitude and his age
there happened to be moments – however,
rarest moments, to be sure – when he gave the
impression of a flesh almost untouched.

The beauty of his twenty-nine years,
so tested by sensual delight,
at moments paradoxically recalled
a young man who – rather gawkily – surrenders
his pure body to love for the very first time.

Their Beginning

The fulfilment of their deviate, sensual delight
is done. They rise from the mattress,
and they dress hurriedly, without speaking.
They leave the house separately, furtively; and as
they walk somewhat uneasily on the street, it seems
as if they suspect that something about them betrays
into what kind of bed they fell a little while back.

But how the life of the artist has gained.
Tomorrow, the next day, years later, the vigorous verses
will be composed that had their beginning here.

To Remain

It must have been one o'clock in the morning,
or half past one.

       In a corner of the tavern;
behind the wooden partition.
Aside from the two of us the shop was completely deserted.
A kerosene lamp scarcely lighted it.
Dozing, at the doorway, the waiter dead for sleep.

No one would have seen us. But already
we had excited ourselves so much,
that we became unfit for precautions.

Our clothes were half-opened – they were not many
for a divine month of July was scorching hot.

Enjoyment of the flesh between
our half-opened clothes;
quick baring of the flesh – the vision of what
occurred twenty-six years ago; and has now come
to remain among these verses.

The Next Table

He must be scarcely twenty-two years old.
And yet I am certain that nearly as many
years ago, I enjoyed the very same body.

It isn't at all infatuation of love.
I entered the casino only a little while ago;
I didn't even have time to drink much.
I have enjoyed the same body.

If I can't recall where – one lapse of memory means nothing.

Ah, see, now that he is sitting down at the next table
I know every movement he makes – and beneath his clothes,
once more I see the beloved bare limbs.

(tr Rae Dalven)

W. B. YEATS
(1865–1939)

The Lover's Song

Bird sighs for the air,
Thought for I know not where,
For the womb the seed sighs.
Now sinks the same rest
On mind, on nest,
On straining thighs.

The Spur

You think it horrible that lust and rage
Should dance attendance on my old age;
They were not such a plague when I was young;
What else have I to spur me into song?

Politics

How can I, that girl standing there,
My attention fix
On Roman or on Russian
Or on Spanish politics?
Yet here's a travelled man that knows
What he talks about,
And there's a politician

That has read and thought,
And maybe what they say is true
Of war and war's alarms,
But O that I were young again
And held her in my arms!

ARTHUR SYMONS
(1865-1945)

White Heliotrope

The feverish room and that white bed,
The tumbled skirts upon a chair,
The novel flung half-open, where
Hat, hair-pins, puffs, and paints, are spread;

The mirror that has sucked your face
Into its secret deep of deeps,
And there mysteriously keeps
Forgotten memories of grace;

And you, half dressed and half awake,
Your slant eyes strangely watching me,
And I, who watch you drowsily,
With eyes that, having slept not, ache;

This (need one dread? nay, dare one hope?)
Will rise, a ghost of memory, if
Ever again my handkerchief
Is scented with White Heliotrope.

Bianca

Her cheeks are hot, her cheeks are white;
The white girl hardly breathes tonight,
So faint the pulses come and go,
That waken to a smouldering glow
The morbid faintness of her white.

What drowning heats of sense, desire
Longing and langourous, the fire
Of what white ashes, subtly mesh
The fascinations of the flesh
Into a breathing web of fire?

Only her eyes, only her mouth
Live, in the agony of drouth,
Athirst for that which may not be;
The desert of virginity
Aches in the hotness of her mouth.

I take her hands into my hands,
Silently, and she understands;
I set my lips upon her lips;
Shuddering to her finger-tips
She strains my hands within her hands.

I set my lips on hers; they close
Into a false and phantom rose;
Upon her thirsting lips I rain
A flood of kisses, and in vain;
Her lips inexorably close.

Through her closed lips that cling to mine,
Her hands that hold me and entwine,
Her body that abandoned lies,
Rigid with sterile ecstasies,
A shiver knits her flesh to mine.

Life sucks into a mist remote
Her fainting lips, her throbbing throat;
Her lips that open to my lips,
And, hot against my finger-tips,
The pulses leaping in her throat.

ERNEST DOWSON
(1867–1900)

Non Sum Qualis Eram Bonae
Sub Regno Cynarae

Last night, ah, yesternight, betwixt her lips and mine
There fell thy shadow, Cynara! thy breath was shed
Upon my soul between the kisses and the wine;
And I was desolate and sick of an old passion,
  Yea, I was desolate and bowed my head:
I have been faithful to thee, Cynara! in my fashion.

I have forgot much, Cynara! gone with the wind,
Flung roses, roses riotously with the throng,
Dancing, to put thy pale, lost lilies out of mind;
But I was desolate and sick of an old passion,
  Yea, all the time, because the dance was long:
I have been faithful to thee, Cynara! in my fashion.

I cried for madder music and for stronger wine,
But when the feast is finished and the lamps expire,
Then falls thy shadow, Cynara! the night is thine;
And I am desolate and sick of an old passion,
  Yea, hungry for the lips of my desire:
I have been faithful to thee, Cynara! in my fashion.

ALEISTER CROWLEY
(1875–1947)

'Dédicace'

You crown me king and queen. There is a name
  For whose soft sound I would abandon all
  This pomp. I liefer would have had you call
Some soft sweet title of beloved shame.

Gold coronets be seemly, but bright flame
   I choose for diadem; I would let fall
   All crowns, all kingdoms, for one rhythmical
Caress of thine, one kiss my soul to tame.

You crown me king and queen: I crown thee lover!
I bid thee hasten, nay, I plead with thee,
   Come in the thick dear darkness to my bed.
Heed not my sighs, but eagerly uncover
   As our mouths mingle, my sweet infamy,
   And rob thy lover of this maidenhead.

Lie close; no pity, but a little love.
   Kiss me but once and all my pain is paid.
Hurt me or soothe, stretch out one limb above
   Like a strong man who would constrain a maid.
Touch me; I shudder and my lips turn back
   Over my shoulder if so be that thus
My mouth may find thy mouth, if aught there lack
   To thy desire, till love is one with us.

God! I shall faint with pain, I hide my face
   For shame. I am disturbed, I cannot rise,
I breathe hard with thy breath; thy quick embrace
   Crushes; thy teeth are agony – pain dies
In deadly passion. Ah! you come – you kill me!
Christ! God! Bite! Bite! Ah Bite! Love's fountains fill me!

PAUL-JEAN TOULET
(1867–1920)

The First Time

'Mother! – I wish I could die of it!'
She loudly cried.
'That's because it's your first time,
Madame, and the best.'

[276]

But she, with ingenious elbow
Adjusting her shoulder-strap,
'No, I was dreaming', said.
'Ah! but you were naked . . .'

STEFAN GEORGE
(1868–1933)

For Maximin

You slim and pure as flame
You crystal and bright as morning
You lively branch of a noble tree
You strange and simple secret stream

You surround me in sunny meadows
You the smoky haze of sunset
Lighting my path in the shadow
You cool wind you warm breath

You are my lust and my thought
With every breath I breathe you
With every drink I sip you
With every scent I kiss you

You lively branch of a noble tree
You strange and simple secret stream
You slim and pure as flame
You crystal and bright as morning.

GUILLAUME APOLLINAIRE
(1880–1918)

The Ninth Secret Poem

I worship your fleece which is the perfect triangle
    Of the Goddess
I am the lumberjack of the only virgin forest
    O my Eldorado
I am the only fish in your voluptuous ocean
    You my lovely Siren
I am the climber on your snowy mountains
    O my whitest Alp
I am the heavenly archer of your beautiful mouth
    O my darling quiver
I am the hauler of your midnight hair
    O lovely ship on the canal of my kisses
And the lilies of your arms are beckoning me
    O my summer garden
The fruits of your breast are ripening their honey for me
    O my sweet-smelling orchard
And I am raising you O Madeleine O my beauty above the earth
    Like the torch of all light

(tr Oliver Bernard)

D. H. LAWRENCE
(1885–1930)

'She Said as Well to Me'

She said as well to me: 'Why are you ashamed?
That little bit of your chest that shows between
the gap of your shirt, why cover it up?
Why shouldn't your legs and your good strong thighs
be rough and hairy? – I'm glad they are like that.
You are shy, you silly, you silly shy thing.
Men are the shyest creatures, they never will come

[278]

out of their covers. Like any snake
slipping into its bed of dead leaves, you hurry into your clothes.
And I love you so! Straight and clean and all of a piece is the
body of a man,
such an instrument, a spade, like a spear, or an oar,
such a joy to me –'
So she laid her hands and pressed them down my sides,
so that I began to wonder over myself, and what I was.

She said to me: 'What an instrument, your body!
single and perfectly distinct from everything else!
What a tool in the hands of the Lord!
Only God could have brought it to its shape.
It feels as if his handgrasp, wearing you
had polished you and hollowed you,
hollowed this groove in your sides, grasped you under the breasts
and brought you to the very quick of your form,
subtler than an old, soft-worn fiddle-bow.

'When I was a child, I loved my father's riding-whip
that he used so often.
I loved to handle it, it seemed like a near part of him.
So did his pens, and the jasper seal on his desk.

Something seemed to surge through me when I touched them.
'So it is with you, but here
The joy I feel!
God knows what I feel, but it is joy!
Look, you are clean and fine and singled out!
I admire you so, you are beautiful: this clean sweep of your sides,
this firmness, this hard mould!
I would die rather than have it injured with one scar.
I wish I could grip you like the fist of the Lord
and have you –'

So she said, and I wondered,
feeling trammelled and hurt.
It did not make me free.

[279]

Now I say to her: 'No tool, no instrument, no God!
Don't touch me and appreciate me.
It is an infamy.
You would think twice before you touched a weasel on a fence
as it lifts its straight white throat.
Your hand would not be so flig and easy.
Nor the adder we saw asleep with her head on her shoulder,
curled up in the sunshine like a princess;
when she lifted her head in delicate, startled wonder
you did not stretch forward to caress her
though she looked rarely beautiful
and a miracle as she glided delicately away, with such dignity.
And the young bull in the field, with his wrinkled, sad face,
you are afraid if he rises to his feet,
though he is all wistful and pathetic, like a monolith, arrested,
                                                                    static.

'Is there nothing in me to make you hesitate?
I tell you there is all these.
And why should you overlook them in me? –'

Figs

The proper way to eat a fig, in society,
Is to split it in four, holding it by the stump,
And open it, so that it is a glittering, rosy, moist, honied, heavy-
                    petalled four-petalled flower.

Then you throw away the skin
Which is just like a four-petalled calex,
After you have taken off the blossom with your lips.

But the vulgar way
Is just to put your mouth to the crack, and take out the flesh in
                    one bite.

Every fruit has its secret.

[280]

The fig is a very secretive fruit.
As you see it standing growing, you feel at once it is symbolic:
And it seems male.
But when you come to know it better, you agree with the Romans,
                                it is female.

The Italians vulgarly say, it stands for the female part; the
                                fig-fruit:
The fissure, the yoni,
The wonderful moist conductivity towards the centre.

Involved,
Inturned,
The flowering all inward and womb-fibrilled;
And but one orifice.

The fig, the horse-shoe, the squash-blossom.
Symbols.

There was a flower that flowered inward, womb-ward;
Now there is a fruit like a ripe womb.
It was always a secret.
That's how it should be, the female should always be secret.

There never was any standing aloft and unfolded on a bough
Like other flowers, in a revelation of petals;
Silver-pink peach, venetian glass of medlars and sorb-apples,
Shallow wine-cups on short, bulging stems
Openly pledging heaven:
Here's to the thorn in flower! Here is to Utterance!
The brave, adventurous rosaceae.

Folded upon itself, and secret unutterable,
And milk-sapped, sap that curdles milk and makes *ricotta*,
Sap that smells strange on your fingers, that even goats won't
                                taste it;
Folded upon itself, enclosed like any Mohammedan woman,
Its nakedness all within-walls, its flowering forever unseen,

[281]

One small way of access only, and this close-curtained from the
                                    light;
Fig, fruit of the female mystery, covert and inward,
Mediterranean fruit, with your covert nakedness,
Where everything happens invisible, flowering and fertilisation,
                              and fruiting
In the inwardness of your you, that eye will never see
Till it's finished, and you're over-ripe, and you burst to give up
                              your ghost.

Till the drop of ripeness exudes,
And the year is over.

That's how the fig dies, showing her crimson through the purple
                              slit
Like a wound, the exposure of her secret, on the open day.
Like a prostitute, the bursten fig, making a show of her secret.

That's how women die too.

The year is fallen over-ripe,
The year of our women.
The year of our women is fallen over-ripe.
The secret is laid bare.
And rottenness soon sets in.
The year of our women is fallen over-ripe.

When Eve once knew *in her mind* that she was naked
She quickly sewed fig-leaves, and sewed the same for the man.
She'd been naked all her days before,
But till then, till that apple of knowledge, she hadn't had the fact
                              on her mind.

She got the fact on her mind, and quickly sewed fig-leaves.
And women have been sewing ever since.
But now they stitch to adorn the bursten fig, not to cover it.
They have their nakedness more than ever on their mind,
And they won't let us forget it.

[282]

Now, the secret
Becomes an affirmation through moist, scarlet lips
That laugh at the Lord's indignation.

What then, good Lord! cry the women.
We have kept our secret long enough.
We are a ripe fig.
Let us burst into affirmation.

They forget, ripe figs won't keep.
Ripe figs won't keep.

Honey-white figs of the north, black figs with scarlet inside, of
                  the south.
Ripe figs won't keep, won't keep in any clime.
What then, when women the world over have all bursten into
                  self-assertion?
And bursten figs won't keep?

Film Passion

If all those females who so passionately loved
the film face of Rudolf Valentino
had had to take him for one night only, in the flesh,
how they'd have hated him!

Hated him just because he was a man
and flesh of a man.
For the luscious filmy imagination loathes the male substance
with deadly loathing.

All the women who adored the shadow of the man on the screen
helped to kill him in the flesh.
Such adoration pierces the loins and perishes the man
worse than the evil eye.

[283]

Bawdy Can be Sane

Bawdy can be sane and wholesome,
in fact a little bawdy is necessary in every life
to keep it sane and wholesome.

And a little whoring can be sane and wholesome.
In fact a little whoring is necessary in every life
to keep it sane and wholesome.

Even sodomy can be sane and wholesome
granted there is an exchange of genuine feeling.

But get any of them on the brain, and they become pernicious:
bawdy on the brain becomes obscenity, vicious.
Whoring on the brain becomes really syphilitic
and sodomy on the brain becomes a mission,
all the lot of them, vice, missions, etc., insanely unhealthy.

In the same way, chastity in its hour is sweet and wholesome.
But chastity on the brain is a vice, a perversion.
And rigid suppression of all bawdy, whoring or other such

          commerce

is a straight way to raving insanity.
The fifth generation of puritans, when it isn't obscenely profligate,
is idiot. So you've got to choose.

EZRA POUND
(1885–1972)

The Temperaments

Nine adulteries, 12 liaisons, 64 fornications and something
          approaching a rape
Rest nightly upon the soul of our delicate friend Florialis,
And yet the man is so quiet and reserved in demeanour

That he passes for both bloodless and sexless.
Bastidides, on the contrary, who both talks and writes of nothing
                                                but copulation,
Has become the father of twins,
But he accomplished this feat at some cost;
He had to be four times cuckold.

Phyllidula

Phyllidula is scrawny but amorous,
Thus have the gods awarded her,
That in pleasure she receives more than she can give;
If she does not count this blessed
Let her change her religion.

Night Song

And have you thoroughly kissed my lips?
   There was no particular haste,
And are you not ready when evening's come?
   There's no *particular* haste.

You've got the whole night before you,
   Heart's-all-beloved-my-own;
In an uninterrupted night one can
   Get a good deal of kissing done.

The Encounter

All the while they were talking the new morality
Her eyes explored me.
And when I arose to go
Her fingers were like the tissue
Of a Japanese paper napkin.

Me happy, night, night full of brightness;
Oh couch made happy by my long delectations;
How many words talked out with abundant candles;
Struggles when the lights were taken away;
Now with bared breasts she wrestled against me,
     Tunic spread in delay;
And she then opening my eyelids fallen in sleep,
Her lips upon them; and it was her mouth saying:
   Sluggard!

In how many varied embraces, our changing arms,
Her kisses, how many, lingering on my lips.
'Turn not Venus into a blinded motion,
     Eyes are the guides of love,
Paris took Helen naked coming from the bed of Menelaus,
Endymion's naked body, bright bait for Diana,'
   – such at least is the story.

While our fates twine together, sate we our eyes with love;
For long night comes upon you
                         and a day when no day returns.
Let the gods lay chains upon us
                    so that no day shall unbind them.

Fool who would set a term to love's madness,
For the sun shall drive with black horses,
     earth shall bring wheat from barley,
The flood shall move toward the fountain
     Ere love know moderations,
     The fish shall swim in dry streams.
No, now while it may be, let not the fruit of life cease.

          Dry wreaths drop their petals,
             their stalks are woven in baskets,
          To-day we take the great breath of lovers,
             to-morrow fate shuts us in.

Though you give all your kisses
                           you give but few.

Nor can I shift my pains to other,
      Hers will I be dead,
If she confer such nights upon me,
                           long is my life, long in years,
If she give me many,
           God am I for the time.

ALDO PALAZZESCHI
(1885–   )

Pornography

Taken by this thing
So much talked about
The wish comes to everyone
To see what it is,
And getting for myself certain magazines
Which publicize this tedious argument
I could even admire on the cover
A woman as Our Lord made her
And he didn't do badly
To tell the truth.
And inside others competed
To exhibit completely
Their exuberant beauty.
And a man and a woman as well,
Who seemed ready for that act
Commanded by Our Lord
In order that our species should not be extinguished.
So much that at this point
A suspicion flashed through my mind
Whether the real pornographer
Was not the Creator of humanity.

Having arrived at a more accessible peak
I said to myself:
'In the end I have understood: pornography is only the truth.'

(tr Ronald Bottrall)

RUPERT BROOKE
(1887–1915)

Lust

How should I know? The enormous wheels of will
  Drove me cold-eyed on tired and sleepless feet.
Night was void arms and you a phantom still,
  And day your far light swaying down the street.
As never fool for love, I starved for you;
  My throat was dry and my eyes hot to see.
Your mouth so lying was most heaven to view,
  And your remembered smell most agony.

Love wakens love! I felt your hot wrist shiver,
  And suddenly the mad victory I planned
    Flashed real, in your burning bending head . . .
My conqueror's blood was cool as a deep river
  In shadow; and my heart beneath your hand
    Quieter than a dead man on a bed.

VINCENZO CARDARELLI
(1887–1959)

Adolescent

Over you, young virgin, broods
a holy shadow.
Nothing is more mysterious
and adorable and becoming

[288]

than your naked flesh.
But you keep shut in your careful dress
and live aloof and far off
with your favours
not knowing who will reach you there.
Surely not me, who turn giddy
if I see you pass by
at such a proud distance,
with your hair loose
and your whole person guarded:
sleek tight-skinned creature
whose very breath comes heavy
with an obscure rapture of flesh
that can hardly bear its fullness.
In your blood suffusing
your face like a burn
the laughter of the cosmos darts
as in the swallow's black eyes.
Your pupils are branded
with the sun that hives there.
Your lips are locked.
Your white hands are innocent
of the shameful sweats of contact.
And I think how your body
unbending and wanted
makes love despair
in a man's heart!

Still, someone will deflower you,
mouth of a wellspring.
Some undiscerning
sponge fisher
will find this rare pearl –
to him the grace and good luck
not to have searched for you
and not to know what you are
nor how to enjoy you

with the subtle knowledge
that offends a grudging God.
Yes, the brute will be
simple enough not to
die sooner than touch you.
And it's always like this.
Even you don't know who you are.
You will let yourself be taken
only to see how the game goes,
and laugh together a while.
Like a flame fading in daylight,
in the starkness of truth
your promised mysteries
dissolve into nothing.
So much unconsumed
pleasure will slip by!
You'll give yourself, you'll be lost
to the first one who charms you,
for a whim that will never guess why.
Time loves the joke
in its favour, not the cautious
will that lags and considers.
So it's youth
Must keep the world rolling.
And the wisest man is just a boy
who grieves that he's grown up.

(tr Sonia Raiziss and Alfredo de Palchi)

WALTER JAMES TURNER
(1889-1946)

Epithalamium

Can the lover share his soul,
   Or the mistress show her mind;
Can the body beauty share,
   Or lust satisfaction find?

Marriage is but keeping house,
   Sharing food and company,
What has this to do with love
   Or the body's beauty?

If love means affection, I
   Love old trees, hats, coats and things,
Anything that's been with me
   In my daily sufferings.

That is how one loves a wife –
   There's a human interest too,
And a pity for the days
   We so soon live through.

What has this to do with love,
   The anguish and the sharp despair,
The madness roving in the blood
   Because a girl or hill is fair?

I have stared upon a dawn
   And trembled like a man in love,
A man in love I was, and I
   Could not speak and could not move.

Hymn to Her Unknown

In despair at not being able to rival the creations of God
I thought on her
Whom I saw on the twenty-fourth of August nineteen thirty-four
Having tea on the fifth storey of Swan and Edgar's
In Piccadilly Circus.

She sat facing me with an older woman and a younger
And a little boy aged about five;
I could see that she was his mother,
Also she wore a wedding-ring and one set with diamonds.

[291]

She was about twenty-five years old,
Slim, graceful, disciplined;
She had none of the mannerisms of the suburbs,
No affectations, a low clear speech, good manners,
Hair thick and undyed.

She knew that she was beautiful and exceedingly attractive,
Every line of her dress showed it;
She was cool and determined and laughed heartily,
A wide mouth with magnificent teeth.

And having said this I come to the beginning of my despair,
Despair that I in no way can describe her
Or bring before the eyes of the present or the future
This image that I saw.

Hundreds and hundreds of women do I see
But rarely a woman on whom my eyes linger
As the eyes of Venus lingered on Adonis.

What is the use of being a poet?
Is it not a farce to call an artist a creator,
Who can create nothing, not even re-present what his eyes have
                                        seen?

She never showed a sign that she saw me
But I knew and she knew that I knew –
Our eyes fleeting past, never meeting directly
Like that vernal twinkling of butterflies
To which Coleridge compared Shakespeare's *Venus and Adonis.*

And, like Venus, I lavished my love upon her
I dallied with her hair, her delicate skin and smooth limbs,
On her arms were heavy thick bangles
Like the ropes of my heart's blood.

Could I express the ecstasy of my adoration?
Mating with her were in itself a separation!
Only our bodies fusing in a flame of crystal

Burning in an infinite empyrean
Until all the blue of the limitless heaven were drunken
In one globe of united perfection
Like a bubble that is all the oceans of the world ascending
To the fire that is the fire of fires, transcending
The love of God, the love of God, the love of God –
Ah! my pitiful efforts now ending
I remember a bough of coral
Flower of the transparent sea
Delicate pink as though a ray of the sun descending
Pathless into the ocean
Printed the foot of Venus
Where bloomed this asphodel.

HUGH MACDIARMID
(1892–1978)

O Wha's the Bride

O wha's the bride that cairries the bunch
O' thistles blinterin'[1] white?
Her cuckold bridegroom little dreids[2]
What he sall ken this nicht.

For closer than gudeman can come
And closer to'r than hersel'
Wha didna need her maidenheid
Has wrocht his purpose fell.

O wha's been here afore me, lass,
And hoo did he get in?
– *A man that deed or was I born*
This evil thing has din.

And left, as it were on a corpse,
Your maidenheid to me?
– *Nae lass, gudeman, sin' Time began*
'S hed ony mair to gi'e.

But I can gi'e ye kindness, lad,
And a pair o' willin' hands,
And you shall he'e my breists like stars,
My limbs like willow wands.

And on my lips ye'll heed nae mair,
And in my hair forget,
The seed o' a' the men that in
My virgin womb ha'e met. . . .

EDNA ST VINCENT MILLAY
(1892–1950)

Sonnet XLI

I, being born a woman and distressed
By all the needs and notions of my kind,
Am urged by your propinquity to find
Your person fair, and feel a certain zest
To bear your body's weight upon my breast:
So subtly is the fume of life designed,
To clarify the pulse and cloud the mind,
And leave me once again undone, possessed.
Think not for this, however, the poor treason
Of my stout blood against my staggering brain,
I shall remember you with love, or season
My scorn with pity – let me make it plain:
I find this frenzy insufficient reason
For conversation when we meet again.

e.e. cummings
(1894–1962)

i like my body when it is with your

i like my body when it is with your
body. It is so quite new a thing.
Muscles better and nerves more.
i like your body. i like what it does,
i like its hows. i like to feel the spine
of your body and its bones, and the trembling
-firm-smooth ness and which i will
again and again and again
kiss, i like kissing this and that of you,
i like, slowly stroking the, shocking fuzz
of your electric fur, and what-is-it comes
over parting flesh. . . . And eyes big love-crumbs,
and possibly i like the thrill
of under me you so quite new

she being Brand

she being Brand

-new; and you
know consequently a
little stiff i was
careful of her and(having

thoroughly oiled the universal
joint tested my gas felt of
her radiator made sure her springs were O.

K.)i went right to it flooded-the-carburetor cranked her

up,slipped the
clutch(and then somehow got into reverse she

[295]

kicked what
the hell)next
minute i was back in neutral tried and
again slo-wly;bare,ly nudg. ing(my

lev-er Right-
oh and her gears being in
A 1 shape passed
from low through
second-in-to-high like
greasedlightning)just as we turned the corner of Divinity

avenue i touched the accelerator and give

her the juice,good
                                    (it
was the first ride and believe i we was
happy to see how nice she acted right up to
the last minute coming back down by the Public
Gardens i slammed on
the
internalexpanding
&
externalcontracting
brakes Bothatonce and

brought allof her tremB
-ling
to a:dead.

stand-
;Still)

       may i feel said he

         may i feel said he
         (i'll squeal said she
         just once said he)
         it's fun said she

(may i touch said he
how much said she
a lot said he)
why not said she

(let's go said he
not too far said she
what's too far said he
where you are said she)

may i stay said he
(which way said she
like this said he
if you kiss said she

may i move said he
is it love said she)
if you're willing said he
(but you're killing said she

but it's life said he
but your wife said she
now said he)
ow said she

(tiptop said he
don't stop said she
oh no said he)
go slow said she

(cccome? said he
umm said she)
you're divine! said he
(you are Mine said she)

I'll Tell You a Dream

i'll tell you a dream i had once i was away up in the
sky Blue,everything:a bar the bar was made of brass

hangIng from strings (or)someThing i was lying on
the bar it was cOOl i didn't have anything on and I
was hot all Hot and the bar was
COOl
O My lover,

          there's just room for me in You
my stomach goes into your Little Stomach My legs
are in your legs Your arms

                        under me around;my head
fits(my head)in your Brain – my, head's
big
she(said laughing
)with your head.all big

Sonnet

O It's Nice To Get Up In, the slipshod mucous kiss
of her riant belly's fooling bore
– When The Sun Begins To(with a phrasing crease
of hot subliminal lips,as if a score
of youngest angels suddenly should stretch neat necks
just to see how always squirms
the skilful mystery of Hell)me suddenly

grips in chuckles of supreme sex.

In The Good Old Summer Time.
My gorgeous bullet in tickling intuitive flight
aches,just,simply,into,her.   Thirsty
stirring.   (Must be summer.   Hush.   Worms.)
But It's Nicer To Lie In Bed
                    – eh?   I'm

not. Again. Hush. God. Please hold. Tight.

Poem

mr youse needn't be so spry
concernin questions arty

each has his tastes but as for i
i likes a certain party

gimme the he-man's solid bliss
for youse ideas i'll match youse

a pretty girl who naked is
is worth a million statues

Poem

sh estiffl
ystrut sal
lif san
dbut sth
epoutin(gWh.ono:w
s li psh ergo
wnd ow n,
                    r
Eve

aling 2 a
-sprout eyelands)sin
uously&them&twi
tching,begins

unununun?
butbutbut??
tonton???
ing????

```
            – Out-&
                steps;which
        flipchucking
        .grins
        gRiNdS

        d is app ea r in gly
        eyes grip live loop croon mime
        nakedly hurl asquirm the
        sips&giveswoop&swoon&ingly

        seethe firm swirl hips whirling climb to
        GIVE
        (yoursmine mineyours yoursmine
        !
        i()t)
```

ROBERT GRAVES
(1895–   )

Down, Wanton, Down

Down, wanton, down! Have you no shame
That at the whisper of Love's name,
Or Beauty's, presto! up you raise
Your angry head and stand at gaze?

Poor bombard-captain, sworn to reach
The ravelin and effect a breach –
Indifferent what you storm or why,
So be that in the breach you die!

Love may be blind, but Love at least
Knows what is man and what mere beast;
Or Beauty wayward, but requires
True delicacy from her squires.

Tell me, my witless, whose one boast
Could be your staunchness at the post,
When were you made a man of parts
To think fine and profess the arts?

Will many-gifted Beauty come
Bowing to your bald rule of thumb,
Or Love swear loyalty to your crown?
Be gone, have done! Down, wanton, down!

The Metaphor

The act of love seemed a dead metaphor
For love itself, until the timeless moment
When fingers trembled, heads clouded,
And love rode everywhere, too numinous
To be expressed or greeted calmly:
O, then it was, deep in our own forest,
We dared revivify the metaphor,
Shedding the garments of this epoch
In scorn of time's wilful irrelevancy;
So at last understood true nakedness
And the long debt to silence owed.

PAUL ÉLUARD
(1897–1952)

Lover

Lover, secretly behind your smile
The words of love nakedly
Discover your breasts and your neck
And your hips and your eyelids
Discover every caress
So that the kisses in your eyes
Reveal entire the whole of you.

FEDERICO GARCIA LORCA
(1898–1936)

Thamár and Amnón

The moon whirls in the sky
above lands in drought
while summer distributes
rumours of tigers and flame.
Over the roofs
nerves of metal rang.
Heat-crisped air
drifted with woolly bleatings.
The earth displayed itself
all scars,
or shuddered, searingly,
cauterised with white lights.

Thamár dreamed of birds
beating in her throat
accompanied by tambourines
and cool, moon-cool citherns.
Her body, naked on the roof,
exquisite pointer of palm,
invites snowflakes on her belly
and hailstones on her shoulders.
Thamár sang
naked on the terrace.
At her feet
were five frozen pigeons.
Amnón, slender, concrete,
watched from the tower,
spume at his groin,
his beard erect.
His glowing nakedness
spread upon the terrace,
with, murmuring between his teeth,

a quivering new arrow.
Amnón watched
The low, round moon,
and saw in the moon
the firm breasts of his sister.

Amnón, at half past three,
flexed his body on his bed.
The whole room suffered
as he fluttered his eyelashes.
The thick light buries
villages in brown sand,
or discovers transitory
coral of roses and dahlias.
Troubled water from the well
blossomed silently in jars.
In the moss of tree-trunks
the cobra, flexing, sings.
Amnón groans between
his bed's chill sheets.
A shiver creeps like ivy
over his burning flesh.
Thamár came silently
into the silent room,
the colour of vein and Danube,
troubled with distant traces.
'Thamár, stop my eyes
with your sure dawn.
The skeins of my blood
weave frills upon your lap.'
'Leave me in peace, brother.
Your kisses on my shoulder
are wasps breezing
in a double swarm of flutes.'
'Thamár, in your peaked breasts
two fishes call me,
and at your fingers' tips
a rumour of an unopened rose.'

The hundred horses of the king
neighed in the courtyard.
The slender vine resisted
the deluge of the sun.
He takes her by the hair,
he tears at her shift,
warm coral runs
rivulets on a fair map.

Oh, what screams
soar over the rooftops!
What a gathering of daggers
and rent tunics.
On the sad stairways
slaves come and go.
Thighs pump and play
beneath still clouds.
Around Thamár
gipsy virgins scream,
and others gather drops
of her martyrised flower.
White cloths redden
in the locked rooms.
The first rumours of dawn
colour vines and fishes.
Infuriated rapist,
Amnón flies on his mare.
Negroes aim arrows
from walls, from towers.
And when the four hooves
were only four echoes,
David, with scissors,
severed his harpstrings.

The Faithless Wife

Thinking her to be a virgin
I took her to the river,
but she had a husband.
It was the night of St James,
and as though I was forced.
They switched off the streetlamps;
the crickets blazed.
At the last corner
I touched her sleeping breasts,
and they like spikes of hyacinth
immediately blossomed.
Her stiff petticoat
crackled in my ear
like a piece of silk
slashed by ten knives.
With no silver light on their tops
the trees were magnified,
and a horizon of dogs
barks miles from the river.

Past the blackberry bushes,
the reeds and hawthorns,
under the net of her hair
I scooped a bed in the sand.
I took off my tie.
She took off her dress.
I, my belt and revolver.
She, her four bodices.
Not a rose, not a shell
has so fine a skin,
mirrors of crystal
do not shine so bright.
Her thighs escaped me
like frightened fish,
one half aflame

one half of ice.
That night I rode
the best of roads
on a mare of pearl
without bridle or stirrups.
As a man, I won't repeat
the things she cried to me,
the light of understanding
has made me discreet.
Freckled with sand and kisses
I brought her from the river.
Lilies like swords
were carving the air.

I was my very self.
Like a real gipsy.
I gave her a sewing-basket
of straw-coloured satin.
But I stopped myself from loving her
because although she was married
she told me she was a virgin
as I took her to the river.

Serenata

The night soaks itself
along the shore of the river
and in Lolita's breasts
the branches die of love.

The branches die of love.

Naked the night sings
above the bridges of March.
Lolita bathes her body
with salt water and roses.

The branches die of love.

The night of anise and silver
shines over the rooftops.
Silver of streams and mirrors.
Anise of your white thighs.

The branches die of love.

VICENTE A. EIXANDRE
(1900–   )

To a Naked Girl

How tenderly she looks
at me – you, girl with the dark eyes!
From the bank of that river, with waves mid-stream,
I can see your outline sharp above a harmony of green.
It is no nakedness come to sear the grass like a flame,
or like the startling fallen ember, foreteller of ashes,
but rather you are set there in stillness, freshest
of morning primroses, come to perfection in a breath.
Fresh image of the softly blowing primrose.
Your body has a bed of secluded virgin turf
whose verges lie like a river flowing at peace.
Stretched out you lie, and your dear nakedness sings,
sweetly composed by the breezes of a valley.
Ah, girl of music, so graciously offered, and
the gift denied, there on that far-off shore!
Wild waves intervene, dividing me from you,
my sweet everlasting desire, body, bond of happiness,
resting like a heavenly star upon that grass.

(tr Edwin Morgan)

STEVIE SMITH
(1902–1971)

Seymour and Chantelle
or *Un Peu De Vice*

In memory of A. Swinburne and Mary Gordon

Pull my arm back, Seymour,
Like the boys do,
Oh Seymour, the pain, the pain,
Still more then, do.
I am thy schoolboy friend, now I
Am not Chantelle any more but mi.
Say 'sweet mi', 'my sweet mi'. Oh, the pain, the pain,
Kiss me and I will kiss you again.

Tell me, Seymour, when they . . . when . . .
Does it hurt as much as this
And this and this? Ah what pain.
When I do so I feel
How very painful it is for you,
No I will, so, again and again,
Now stuff the dockleaves in your mouth
And bite the pain.

Seymour, when you hold me so tight it hurts
I feel my ribs break and the blood spurt,
Oh what heaven, what bliss,
Will you kiss me, if I give you this
Kiss, and this and this? Like this?

Seymour, this morning Nanny swished me so hard
(Because I told her she had the face
Of an antediluvian animal that had
Become extinct because of being so wet)
She broke her hair-brush. What bliss.
No, don't stop me crying now with a kiss, oh God it was pain-
Ful, I could not stop crying.

[308]

Oh darling, what heaven, how did you think
Of doing that? You are my sweetest angel of a
Little cousin, and your tears
Are as nice as the sea, as icy and salt as it is.

ROY CAMPBELL
(1902–1957)

The Sisters

After hot loveless nights, when cold winds stream
Sprinkling the frost and dew, before the light,
Bored with the foolish things that girls must dream
Because their beds are empty of delight,

Two sisters rise and strip. Out from the night
Their horses run to their low-whistled pleas –
Vast phantom shapes with eyeballs rolling white
That sneeze a fiery stream about their knees:

Through the crisp manes their stealthy prowling hands,
Stronger than curbs, in slow caresses rove,
They gallop down across the milk-white sands
And wade far out into the sleeping cove:

The frost stings sweetly with a burning kiss
As intimate as love, as cold as death:
Their lips, whereon delicious tremors hiss,
Fume with the ghostly pollen of their breath.

Far out on the grey silence of the flood
They watch the dawn in smouldering gyres expand
Beyond them; and the day burns through their blood
Like a white candle through a shuttered hand.

Suite from Catullus

*. . . uerum si quid ages statim iubeto: nam pransus
iaceo et satur supinus pertundo tunicamque palliumque*

Sometimes when you are gone
he stirs and grows like an enchanted tree,
catching himself in a bow and throbbing,
then creeping up and up inside my clothes
until he stands at his full height
hard as the horn of a steer
beating and beating for you

At the first secret movement of your hand
he leaps like a young salmon,
shaking himself for joy
Roll him and press him and fondle him:
he will squirm under your touch like a puppy alive with love
But when you clasp him tight
he stands like a tower in the warm ring of your fingers

He knows your skin as an infant with closed eyes knows his
                                                    mother
He lies against your small soft belly
and seeks your warm crevices,
nuzzling into the little bramble patch of your pubic hair
as if he would hide in it like a rabbit
He pretends to be shy
Do not trust him
He is as fierce as a lion

A creature of fire like the phoenix,
he swims into the hot dark cave that receives him throbbing with
                                                    parted lips,

and ascends the river of fire to his source
Quietly stirring in the darkness,
he nudges at the tender walls,
exploring each soft inch a thousand times
for the opening into the last dark room;
then in a slow masterful fury swells and strikes,
lunging with all his power into the shuddering dark,
coiling and uncoiling over his whole length
and expelling his fire into the sweet fire that drowns him

He is peaceful now
He lies soft against your flank,
the tired warrior wearing out his rest

When he wakes for love again
he is like a boy waking on Saturday
At first he does not know what day it is;
he hunches and rolls over
If I call him he will not answer
You call him
See him spring up as he remembers all the happy things he
                                       meant to do with you

You are wise to demand great works of him
This sulky dog
who can doze in some women's presence without lifting an ear
comes bright awake at a look from you
Do not spare him
Beat him until he is too weak
even to beg

In the cold weather
when I take him to perform his other office
he lies pale and shrivelled in my fingers
like an old king out of sorts with the world
You would not know him then:
he is a business man
and his business is bad

PABLO NERUDA
(1904–1973)

Body of a Woman . . .

Body of a woman, white hills, white thighs,
you look like a world, lying in surrender.
My rough peasant's body digs in you
and makes the sun leap from the depth of the earth.

I only was a tunnel. The birds fled from me,
and night swamped me with its crushing invasion.
To survive myself I forged you like a weapon,
like an arrow in my bow, a stone in my sling.

But the hour of vengeance falls, and I love you.
Body of skin, of moss, of eager and firm milk.
Oh the goblets of the breast! Oh the eyes of absence!
Oh the roses of the pubis! Oh your voice, slow and sad!

Body of my woman, I will persist in your grace.
My thirst, my boundless desire, my shifting road.
Dark river-beds where the eternal thirst flows
and weariness follows, and the infinite ache.

(tr W. S. Merwin)

Single Gentleman

The young homosexuals and the amorous girls
and widows, past it, delirious, sleepless,
the young wives thirty hours pregnant,
the hoarse cats sliding through the shadowy garden
like a necklace of throbbing sexual oysters
surround my lonely house

like enemies dug in against my soul
like pajamaed conspirators
swopping long, sticky kisses in secret.

The radiant summer attracts the lovers
in matching identical regiments
composers of flaccid and plump, happy and mournful pairs:
under elegant palm-trees, along the moonlit beach
trousers and skirts are continually excited,
the rumour of touched-up silk thighs
nipples lively as eyes.

The unimportant clerk, bored to tears,
bored for a week, a week of paperback trash,
has at last bedded his neighbour
and takes her to the cheap cinema
where the heroes are either young studs or romantic princes:
his palm feels the soft down of her legs,
his sweaty palms, smelling of cigarillos.

The quick afternoons of seducers, nights in legal beds,
fold around me like neat sheets,
the lunchtime hours when young boys and girls,
students, as well as priests, toss themselves off,
the animals fuck like crazy
bees smell of blood, flies angrily buzz,
and boy cousins play strange games with girl cousins
and doctors stare furiously at their young patient's husband,
and the professor, absentmindedly in the morning
takes a quick marital fuck and then breakfasts,
and then the truly loving fornicators lovingly fornicate
on beds high and lengthy as ocean liners –
securely, eternally, I'm surrounded by this vast
breathing forest with flowers like mouths, and with teeth,
their black roots shaped like hoofs and shoes.

JOHN BETJEMAN
(1906–   )

The Olympic Girl

The sort of girl I like to see
Smiles down from her great height at me.
She stands in strong, athletic pose
And wrinkles her *retroussé* nose.
Is it distaste that makes her frown,
So furious and freckled, down
On an unhealthy worm like me?
Or am I what she likes to see?
I do not know, though much I care.
Εἴθε γενοίμην . . . would I were
(Forgive me, shade of Rupert Brooke)
An object fit to claim her look.
Oh! would I were her racket press'd
With hard excitement to her breast
And swished into the sunlit air
Arm-high above her tousled hair
And banged against the bounding ball
'Oh! Plung!' my taunten'd strings would call,
'Oh! Plung! my darling, break my strings
For you I will do brilliant things.'
And when the match is over, I
Would flop beside you, hear you sigh;
And then, with what supreme caress,
You'ld tuck me up into my press.
Fair tigress of the tennis courts,
So short in sleeve and strong in shorts,
Little, alas, to you I mean,
For I am bald and old and green.

A. D. HOPE
(1907–   )

Imperial Adam

Imperial Adam, naked in the dew,
   Felt his brown flanks and found the rib had gone.
Puzzled, he turned and saw where, two and two,
   The mighty spoor of Jahweh marked the lawn.

Then he remembered through mysterious sleep
   The surgeon fingers probing at the bone,
The voice so far away, so rich and deep:
   'It is not good for him to live alone.'

Turning once more, he found Man's counterpart
   In tender parody, breathing at his side.
He knew her at first sight; he knew by heart
   Her allegory of sense unsatisfied.

The pawpaw drooped its golden breasts above
   Less generous than the honey of her flesh;
The innocent sunlight showed the place of love;
   The dew on its dark hairs winked crisp and fresh.

This plump gourd severed from his virile root,
   She promised on the turf of Paradise
Delicious pulp of the forbidden fruit;
   Sly as the snake she loosed her sinuous thighs,

And waking, smiled up at him from the grass.
   Her breasts rose softly, and he heard her sigh –
From all the beasts, whose pleasant task it was
   In Eden to increase and multiply,

Adam had learned the jolly deed of kind:
   He took her in his arms, and there and then,
Like the clean beasts, embracing from behind,
   Began in joy to found the breed of men.

Then from the spurt of seed within her broke
  Her terrible and triumphant female cry,
Split upward by the sexual lightning stroke.
  It was the beasts now who stood watching by.

The gravid elephant, the calving hind,
  The breeding bitch, the she-ape big with young,
Were the first gentle midwives of mankind:
  The teeming lioness rasped her with her tongue,

The proud vicuña nuzzled her as she slept
  Lax on the grass – and Adam, watching too,
Saw how her dumb breasts at their ripening wept,
  The great pod of her belly swelled and grew,

And saw its water break, and saw, in fear,
  Its quaking muscles in the act of birth,
Between her legs a pigmy face appear –
  And the first murderer lay upon the earth.

RONALD McCUAIG
(1908–   )

The Hungry Moths

Poor hungry white moths
That eat my love's clothing,
Who says very soon
Ye'll leave her with nothing,
Here under the moon
I make bold to persuade ye,
Ye may eat all her clothes
So ye leave me milady,
Poor
    hungry
        white
            moths.

[316]

I'm living with a commercial traveller;
He's away, most of the time;
Most I see of him's his wife; as for her:
I'm just home from a show,
And there I am undressing, in my shirt;
I hear midnight chime,
And up flares the curtain at the window;
The door's opened; it's Gert,
That's the wife; her hair's hanging down;
She's only got her nightgown
Blowing up against her in the wind;
She's fat, and getting fatter;
I said, 'What's the matter?'
'Jack,' she said, 'now's your chance';
'What chance?' I said. 'You out of your mind?'
She goes over to the bed;
I grab my pants;
'That's enough of that,' I said. 'Now, go on; you get out.'
'But, Jack,' she said, 'don't you love me?'
'I don't know what you're talking about,'
I said, 'besides, Jim –
What about him?'
'Yes; Jim,' she said; 'there's always Jim, but he's
Always away; and you don't know
What it's like. I can't stand it. And anyhow,
Jack, don't you want me?' 'Oh, don't be an ass',
I said; 'look at yourself in the glass.'
She faced the mirror where she stood
And sort of stiffened there;
Her eyes went still as knots in a piece of wood,
And it all seemed to sigh out of her;
'All right,' she said; 'all right, all right, good-night,'
As though she didn't know if I'd heard,
And shuffled out without another word.
Well, I was tired; I went to bed and slept.

In the morning
I thought I'd dreamed the whole thing;
But at breakfast, I could have wept;
Poor Gert, clattering the dishes
With a dead sort of face
Like a fish's.
I'll have to get a new place.
I'm going out today to have a look.
Trouble is, she's a marvellous cook.

Music in the Air

There was music in the air
  And the moon shone bright
When Jack had his girl
  On Friday night.

He closed his desk
  At the close of day;
As he passed the counter
  They gave him his pay:

> *There was music in the air*
>   *And the moon shone bright*
> *As he walked down town*
>   *On Friday night:*

She was a typist
  Down at the bank;
Her mother was religious;
  Her father drank:

> *There was music in the air*
>   *And the moon shone bright*
> *As they drank and prayed*
>   *On Friday night:*

[318]

Her boss was a beast;
   He kept her late;
Jack got a headache,
   Having to wait:

        There was music in the air
          And the moon shone bright
        When she came at last
        On Friday night:

They went to a café;
   The soup was cold;
The beef was scraggy,
   The prunes full of mould:

        There was music in the air
          And the moon shone bright
        As they ate their dinner
        On Friday night:

They sat very still
   In the rattle and hum.
Jack said, 'Mary,
   I want to go home':

        There was music in the air
          And the moon shone bright
        When he spoke her name
        On Friday night:

'I want to go home
   And go to bed:
Besides, you remember
   What you said':

        There was music in the air
          And the moon shone bright
        When Mary remembered
        On Friday night:

[319]

She picked up her bag,
　　Made no reply;
She pushed back her chair
　　With a quiet sigh:

> *There was music in the air*
> 　*And the moon shone bright*
> *When they left the café*
> 　*On Friday night:*

He took her arm
　　Through a traffic jam;
They stood on the corner
　　To wait for a tram:

> *There was music in the air*
> 　*And the moon shone bright*
> *As they stood on the corner*
> 　*On Friday night:*

Their faces were pale
　　In the crimson spite
Of the shop-signs' whorish
　　Beckoning light:

> *There was music in the air*
> 　*And the moon shone bright*
> *When the tram crawled by*
> 　*On Friday night:*

They got in the tram
　　It jolted them down
To the end of the section
　　On the edge of town:

> *There was music in the air*
> 　*And the moon shone bright*
> *As they crossed the road*
> 　*On Friday night:*

[320]

Jack had a room
  On the second floor;
They climbed the stairs
  And opened the door:

> *There was music in the air*
>   *And the moon shone bright*
> *Through the open door*
>   *On Friday night:*

They closed the door;
  Mary hung
Lax in his arms;
  His fierce lips stung:

> *There was music in the air*
>   *And the moon shone bright*
> *When they closed the door*
>   *On Friday night:*

His fierce lips stung
  At her throat like a bee;
Like a snake, like a sleek
  Lithe leopard was he:

> *There was music in the air*
>   *And the moon shone bright*
> *When his fierce lips stung*
>   *On Friday night;*

Like a leopard, and she
  Was placid prey;
She'd dreamed it for months
  All night and day:

> *There was music in the air*
>   *And the moon shone bright*
> *When her dreams came true*
>   *On Friday night:*

He loosened her blouse
  And mad waist bands;
She tried to help
  His clumsy hands:

> *There was music in the air*
>   *And the moon shone bright*
> *When he loosened her blouse*
>   *On Friday night:*

She loved his hands;
  She said, 'Oh, mind;
I'll do it myself;'
  He drew the blind:

> *There was music in the air*
>   *And the moon shone bright*
> *As he drew the blind*
>   *On Friday night:*

The whore next door
  Had a radio set,
And she was seeing
  What she could get:

> *There was music in the air*
>   *And the moon shone bright*
> *As she screwed at the dial*
>   *On Friday night:*

A loud voice sang
  From Heaven above
With a screeching scratch
  Of the joys of love:

> *There was music in the air*
>   *And the moon shone bright*
> *As the loud voice sang*
>   *On Friday night:*

[322]

Of the joys of love;
  Pale in the gloom
She was deaf to the world
  In her wild blood's boom:

> *There was music in the air*
>   *And the moon shone bright*
> *Through her booming blood*
>   *On Friday night:*

Like the boom of trams
  Outside, and the squeal
Of nerves on the curves
  Of shrieking steel:

> *There was music in the air*
>   *And the moon shone bright*
> *In curving nerves*
>   *On Friday night:*

Like shrieking steel
  In his shaking embrace
Through a slit in the blind
  Light streamed on her face:

> *There was music in the air*
>   *And the moon shone bright*
> *Through a slit in the blind*
>   *On Friday night:*

On her anguished face
  And tight-shut eyes;
Jack won't forget it
  Until he dies:

> *There was music in the air*
>   *And the moon shone bright*
> *When Jack had his girl*
>   *On Friday night.*

[323]

GEORGE BARKER
(1912–   )

Secular Elegy – V

O Golden Fleece she is where she lies tonight
Trammelled in her sheets like midsummer on a bed,
Kisses like moths flitter over her bright
Mouth, and, as she turns her head,
All space moves over to give her beauty room.

Where her hand, like a bird on the branch of her arm,
Droops its wings over the bedside as she sleeps,
There the air perpetually stays warm
Since, nested, her hand rests there. And she keeps
Under her green thumb life like a growing poem.

My nine-tiered tigress in the cage of sex
I feed with meat that you tear from my side
Crowning your nine months with the paradox:
The love that kisses with a homicide
In robes of red generation resurrects.

The bride who rides the hymenaeal waterfall
Spawning all possibles in her pools of surplus,
Whom the train rapes going into a tunnel,
The imperial multiplicator nothing can nonplus:
My mother Nature is the origin of it all.

At Pharaoh's Feast and in the family cupboard,
Gay corpse, bright skeleton, and the fly in amber,
She sits with her laws like antlers from her forehead
Enmeshing everyone, with flowers and thunder
Adorning the head that destiny never worried.

DOUGLAS STEWART
(1913–   )

The Dosser in Springtime

The girl from the sun is bathing in the creek,
Says the white old dosser[1] in the cave.
It's a sight worth seeing though your old frame's weak;
Her clothes are on the wattle[2] and it's gold all over,
And if I was twenty I'd try to be her lover,
Says the white old dosser in the cave.

If I was twenty I'd chase her back to Bourke,
Says the white old dosser in the cave.
My swag[3] on my shoulder and a haughty eye for work,
I'd chase her to the sunset where the desert burns and reels,
With an old blue dog full of fleas at my heels,
Says the white old dosser in the cave.

I'd chase her back to Bourke again, I'd chase her back to Alice,
Says the white old dosser in the cave.
And I'd drop upon her sleeping like a beauty in a palace
With the sunset wrapped around her and a black snake keeping
                                            watch –
She's lovely and she's naked but she's very hard to catch,
Says the white old dosser in the cave.

I've been cooling here for years with the gum-trees wet and weird,
Says the white old dosser in the cave.
My head grew lichens and moss was my beard,
The creek was in my brain and a bullfrog in my belly,
The she-oaks washed their hair in me down all the gloomy gully,
Says the white old dosser in the cave.

My eyes were full of water and my ears were stopped with
                                            bubbles,

[1]*dosser* tramp [2]*wattle* mimosa tree [3]*swag* roll of bedding

[325]

Says the white old dosser in the cave.
Yabbies[1] raised their claws in me or skulked behind the pebbles.
The water-beetle loved his wife, he chased her round and round –
I thought I'd never see a girl unless I found one drowned,
Says the white old dosser in the cave.

Many a time I laughed aloud to stop my heart from thumping,
Says the white old dosser in the cave.
I saw my laugh I saw my laugh I saw my laugh go jumping
Like a jaunty old goanna[2] with his tail up stiff
Till he dived like a stone in the pool below the cliff,
Says the white old dosser in the cave.

There's a fine bed of bracken, the billy boils beside her,
Says the white old dosser in the cave.
But no one ever ate with me except the loathsome spider,
And no one ever lay with me beside the sandstone wall
Except the pallid moonlight and she's no good at all,
Says the white old dosser in the cave.

But now she's in the creek again, that woman made of flame,
Says the white old dosser in the cave.
By cripes, if I was twenty I'd stop her little game.
Her dress is on the wattle – I'd take it off and hide it;
And when she sought that golden dress, I'd lay her down beside it,
Says the white old dosser in the cave.

DYLAN THOMAS
(1914–53)

On the Marriage of a Virgin

Waking alone in a multitude of loves when morning's light
Surprised in the opening of her nightlong eyes
His golden yesterday asleep upon the iris

[1]*yabbies* freshwater crayfish [2]*goanna* Australian monitor lizard

[326]

And this day's sun leapt up the sky out of her thighs
Was miraculous virginity old as loaves and fishes,
Though the moment of a miracle is unending lightning
And the shipyards of Galilee's footprints hide a navy of doves.

No longer will the vibrations of the sun desire on
Her deepsea pillow where once she married alone,
Her heart all ears and eyes, lips catching the avalanche
Of the golden ghost who ringed with his streams her mercury bone,
Who under the lids of her windows hoisted his golden luggage,
For a man sleeps where fire leapt down and she learns through
                                                        his arm
That other sun, the jealous coursing of the unrivalled blood.

Lament

    When I was a windy boy and a bit
    And the black spit of the chapel fold,
    (Sighed the old ram rod, dying of women),
    I tiptoed shy in the gooseberry wood,
    The rude owl cried like a telltale tit,
    I skipped in a blush as the big girls rolled
    Ninepin down on the donkey's common,
    And on seesaw sunday nights I wooed
    Whoever I would with my wicked eyes,
    The whole of the moon I could love and leave
    All the green leaved little weddings' wives
    In the coal black bush and let them grieve.

    When I was a gusty man and a half
    And the black beast of the beetles' pews
    (Sighed the old ram rod, dying of bitches),
    Not a boy and a bit in the wick-
    Dipping moon and drunk as a new dropped calf,
    I whistled all night in the twisted flues,
    Midwives grew in the midnight ditches,

And the sizzling beds of the town cried, Quick! –
Whenever I dove in a breast high shoal,
Wherever I ramped in the clover quilts,
Whatsoever I did in the coal-
Black night, I left my quivering prints.

When I was a man you could call a man
And the black cross of the holy house
(Sighed the old ram rod, dying of welcome),
Brandy and ripe in my bright, bass prime,
No springtailed tom in the red hot town
With every simmering woman his mouse
But a hillocky bull in the swelter
Of summer come in his great good time
To the sultry, biding herds, I said,
Oh, time enough when the blood creeps cold,
And I lie down but to sleep in bed
For my sulking, skulking, coal black soul!

When I was a half of the man I was
And serve me right as the preachers warn,
(Sighed the old ram rod, dying of downfall),
No flailing calf or cat in the flame
Or hickory bull in milky grass
But a black sheep with a crumpled horn,
At last the soul from its foul mousehole
Slunk pouting out when the limp time came;
And I gave my soul a blind, slashed eye,
Gristle and rind, and a roarer's life,
And I shoved it into the coal black sky
To find a woman's soul for a wife.

Now I am a man no more no more
And a black reward for a roaring life,
(Sighed the old ram rod, dying of strangers),
Tidy and cursed in my dove cooed room
I lie down thin and hear the good bells jaw –

For, oh, my soul found a sunday wife
In the coal black sky and she bore angels!
Harpies around me out of her womb!
Chastity prays for me, piety sings,
Innocence sweetens my last black breath,
Modesty hides my thighs in her wings,
And all the deadly virtues plague my death!

GAVIN EWART
(1916–   )

To the Virgins, to Make Much of Time

Now, listen.
I want you new girls, every morning,
To sprinkle an oral contraceptive on your cornflakes.
I've got my eye on you, I want to marry into you,
To fluffle you up a bit, then dive right in
Smoothly.

I'm a potentate. Don't be too girlish,
Don't bother to name those breasts Maria and Matilda
Or call your favourite ball-point Clarence.
None of this interests me. Wear a bra if you want to
And panties if you want to. It's immaterial.

In this establishment, my will holds.
If you are naughty, there's a cane in the corner.
I don't believe in God, I can do what I like.

Every morning there's naked bathing
And then at least two hours of horse-back riding
To promote a well-developed, rounded bottom.
The only lessons are Theory and Practice;
All my instructresses are big harsh Lesbians
So watch your step.

Night duty begins at eight. A roster will be published.
My favourite girls have a really marvellous time.
I hope you will be happy here. Never forget
These are the best years of your life.
Go to your rooms now. Goodnight.

Sonnet: The Womansmell of Sex

It's interesting how the sexual smell of women,
when they are excited by their lovers,
has never found its way into romantic literature
(nor, for that matter, into any other literature).
One poem by Donne. I can't think of much else.
The taboo must be very strong. Even pornography
describes visual and tactile but not the olfactory.
Some readers would go mad if it were even mentioned.

Of course, you can't describe a smell. Yet even hypocrites
would admit that for a man in love
this is an important factor in the physical attraction.
It should have, as it were, at least a footnote.
People don't like admitting that they're animals –
they turn their minds away from the fact and its proving.

The Lover Reflects: Afterwards

Perhaps I was greedy. I know I should be grateful.
You wanted a snack and I wanted a plateful.

ALEX COMFORT
(1920–   )

After You, Madam

There are no upper hands in love
though one is under, one above:
the man who said so lied –

[330]

it is a choice for human mates
lacking in other vertebrates
   that you or I should ride.

Adam, that Freudian figurehead,
considered his prestige in bed –
   taking their cue from that
the Moslem schoolmen who believe
in the delinquency of Eve
   extend her like a mat:

The casuists of the Vatican
in placing women under man
   take Paul *au pied de la lettre*.
Before the medieval *conte*
made it a source of *mauvaise honte*.
   Petronius knew better.

Lady, the whimsical restraints
imposed by inexperienced saints
   on modes of procreation
have little interest for us.
We share the honours without fuss
   by frequent alternation.

Communication

Babies' and lovers' toes express
ecstasies of wantonness.
It's a language which we lose
with the trick of wearing shoes.

ANTONÍN BARTUŠEK
(1921–1975)

Simonetta Vespucci

Breasts beaten by thunder
like cymbals.
It's only a short step, sir,
to my room.
You may, if you wish,
copulate with me.
Gently run your hand
over my shimmering skin,
the envy of alabaster.
Small veins showing blue
on opened thighs,
as in quartz.
Empty the sky
around my halo.
Bone laid to bone
by the gravedigger
as he digs a fresh grave.
That proud profile in the landscape
with the river Lethe,
with the river and an unknown
Italian lake.

The scream of your throat
reaches the belly's cavern.
The flame's spearpoint
has cut right through your middle.
The dress, slipped off the shoulder,
no longer conceals anything.
And again May
with bleary eyes
is exploring your loins.

There's nothing ruin cannot do.
All that's left is a gold
serpent necklace,
time biting its own tale.

Man looks about,
his eyes wandering,
as if looking for
someone he knows.

(tr Ewald Osers)

VERNON SCANNELL
(1922–   )

Act of Love

This is not the man that women choose,
This honest fellow, stuffed to the lips with groans,
Whose passion cannot even speak plain prose
But grunts and mumbles in the muddiest tones.
His antics are disgusting or absurd,
His lust obtrusive, craning from its nest
At awkward times its blind reptilian head;
His jealousy and candour are a pest.

Now here is the boy that women will lie down for,
The snappy actor, skilled in the lover's part,
A lyric fibber and subvocal tenor
Whose pleasure in the play conceals his art;
Who, even as he enters her warm yes,
Hears fluttering hands and programmes in the vast
Auditorium beyond her voice
Applauding just one member of the cast.

KINGSLEY AMIS
(1922–   )

Nothing to Fear

All fixed: early arrival at the flat
Lent by a friend, whose note says *Lucky sod*;
Drinks on the tray; the cover-story pat
And quite uncheckable; her husband off
Somewhere with all the kids till six o'clock
(Which ought to be quite long enough):
And all worth while: face really beautiful,
Good legs and hips, and as for breasts – my God.
What about guilt, compunction and such stuff?
I've had my fill of all that cock;
It'll wear off, as usual.

Yes, all fixed. Then why this slight trembling,
Dry mouth, quick pulse-rate, sweaty hands,
As though she were the first? No, not impatience,
Nor fear of failure, thank you, Jack.
Beauty, they tell me, is a dangerous thing,
Whose touch will burn, but I'm asbestos, see?
All worth while – it's a dead coincidence
That sitting here, a bag of glands
Tuned up to concert pitch, I seem to sense
A different style of caller at my back,
As cold as ice, but just as set on me.

An Ever-Fixed Mark

Years ago, at a private school
Run on traditional lines,
One fellow used to perform
Prodigious feats in the dorm:
His quite undevious designs
Found many a willing tool.

[334]

On the rugger field, in the gym,
Buck marked down at his leisure
The likeliest bits of stuff;
The notion, familiar enough,
Of 'using somebody for pleasure'
Seemed handy and harmless to him.

But another chap was above
The diversions of such a lout.
Seven years in the place
And he never got to first base
With the kid he followed about.
What interested Ralph was love.

He did the whole thing in style:
Letters three times a week,
Sonnet-sequences, Sunday walks.
At last, during one of their talks,
The youngster caressed his cheek,
And that made it all worth while.

Nowadays, for a quid pro quo,
Ralph's chum does what, and with which;
Buck's playmates, family men,
Eye a Boy Scout now and then.
Sex is a momentary itch,
Love never lets you go.

ANON
(c 1940)

Auld Lang Syne

Busts and bosoms have I known
    Of various shapes and sizes,
From grievous disappointments
    To jubilant surprises.

PAUL BLACKBURN
(1926–   )

The Once-Over

The tanned blonde
                    in the green print sack
in the center of the subway car
                              standing
though there are seats
                    has had it from
1   teen-age hood
1   lesbian
1   envious housewife
4   men over fifty
(& myself), in short
the contents of this half of the car

                    Our notations are:
long legs, long waist, high breasts (no bra), long
neck, the model slump
                        the handbag drape and how the skirt
cuts in under a very handsome
                              set of cheeks
'stirring dull roots with spring rain' sayeth the preacher

            Only a stolid young man
            with a blue business suit and the New York Times
            does not know he is being assaulted

So.
She has us and we her
all the way to downtown Brooklyn
Over the tunnel and through the bridge
            to DeKalb Avenue we go
all very chummy

She stares at the number over the door
and gives no sign

                    yet the sign is on her

JOYCE MANSOUR
(1928–   )

Two Poems

Your hands ransacked my gaping breast
Looping blond loops
Pinching nipples
Grating on my veins
Clotting my blood
Your tongue was plump with hate in my mouth
Your hand bruised my cheek with pleasure
Your teeth clawed swearwords on my back
The marrow of my bones dripped out between my legs
And the car roared off along the sneering road
Running down my family as it went

Let me love you
I love the taste of your thick blood
I savour it in my toothless mouth
Its heat scorches my throat
I love your sweat
I love to stroke your armpits
Dripping down joy
Let me love you
Let me lick your closed eyes
Let me pierce them with my pointed tongue
And feel their hollows with my spittle
Let me blind you

(tr Graham Martin)

[337]

GAEL TURNBULL
(1928–   )

Thighs Gripping

Thighs gripping
moving in pace – her face
suffused – each breath
short and quick
through spread lips,
she is possessed
and lost in the act

alas, trotting
her horse down the lane.

JONATHAN WILLIAMS
(1929–   )

A Little Tumescence

This time I mean it:
twice tonight!
        (*omne animal*, always
        The Hope

Triste, triste
situation, such outrageous
limitation,
limp,
    simply

JOHN ARDEN
(1930–   )

I'll Make My Love a Breast of Glass

I'll make my love a breast of glass
And a heart of the porcelain white
The red blood seen through this clear window
Will stain it now dark now light.
I will make my love a head of gold
With hair of the black crow's feather
Her eyeballs of diamonds set therein
To crackle like thundery weather.

I'll make my love two arms of ice
Two hands of the rigid snow
I'll make my love two legs of flame
That will char the grass as they go.
I will make her a belly of the round moonlight
And the secret parts beneath
I will make of stars in a rainy night
Now hidden now gleaming like teeth.

To travel thereunder is my hope and my joy
To travel thereunder alone
An uncertain ride on a pitching road
Between black mire and sharp stone.
But what I will make, I will make and set up
In the corner of my love's crooked room
That she may regard it and learn from its shape
With what contrast of lust I consume.

I will make my love this image to love
And upon its hard brow I will write:
'This dream is my love yet you are my love
And who can tell which in the night?'

[339]

I will serve her in duty with flesh like an oak
And yet she will never know
How strong and how often I am serving the other
Stark naked in fire and in snow.

ADRIAN MITCHELL
(1932–   )

Celia Celia

When I am sad and weary,
When I think all hope has gone,
When I walk along High Holborn
I think of you with nothing on.

PHILIP HOBSBAUM
(1932–   )

A Lesson in Love

Sitting straightbacked, a modest Irish miss,
Knees clenched together – even then I knew
Your full mouth would open under my kiss,
The line under your eyes gave me my clue.

Now on the floor, legs thrashing your dress
Over your stocking-tops, your tight blue pants
Bursting to be off at my caress,
This is the underside of our romance.

Which is the truer? I, speaking of Donne,
Calling the act a means and not an end,
Or at your sweet pudenda, sleeking you down:
Was there no other way to be your friend?

None, none. The awkward pauses when we talk
The literary phrases, are a lie.
It was for this your teacher ran amock:
Truth lies between your legs, and so do I.

MAUREEN DUFFY
(1933–   )

A Dream of Fair Woman

I am beset with a dream of fair woman,
Lunatic for Venus flesh
So sweet in the night.
I do not know if I have woven her,
Pygmalion, out of my desires
Or if indeed those hours she lay
Beside, under me.
Happy the hand that touches her,
The cloth that drapes her,
The eyes and words that catch hers.
Where she is the skies are
Clouded with loves, the minutes dove drawn.
I whisper in this waking sleep
Remembering as dogs run down past quarry,
Hunter and snared by my dream of fair woman,
Lunatic for your Venus flesh.

Eureka

Turning to sponge a flank
In the bath, a new manoeuvre
Out of laziness, flue, old age,
I discover a big brown mole
That you must often have met
And wonder what else you know

Of me secret from even myself,
What other blemishes of mind
Or body you caress lovingly
Behind my back.

FLEUR ADCOCK
(1934–   )

Against Coupling

I write in praise of the solitary act:
Of not feeling a trespassing tongue
Forced into one's mouth, one's breath
Smothered, nipples crushed against the
Ribcage, and that metallic tingling
In the chin set off by a certain odd nerve:

Unpleasure. Just to avoid those eyes would help –
Such eyes as a young girl draws life from,
Listening to the vegetal
Rustle within her, as his gaze
Stirs polypal fronds in the obscure
Seabed of her body, and her own eyes blur.

There is much to be said for abandoning
This no longer novel exercise –
For not 'participating in
A total experience'– when
One feels like the lady in Leeds who
Had seen 'The Sound of Music' eighty-six times;

Or more, perhaps, like the school drama mistress
Producing 'A Midsummer Night's Dream'
For the seventh year running, with
Yet another cast from 5B.
Pyramus and Thisbe are dead, but
The hole in the wall can still be troublesome.

I advise you, then, to embrace it without
Encumbrance. No need to set the scene,
Dress up (or undress), make speeches.
Five minutes of solitude are
Enough – in the bath, or to fill
That gap between the Sunday papers and lunch.

ROGER McGOUGH
(1937–   )

The Act of Love

The Act of Love lies somewhere
Between the belly and the mind
I lost the love sometime ago
Now I've only the act to grind

Brought her back from a party
Don't bother swapping names
Identity's not needed
When you're only playing games

High on bedroom darkness
We endure the pantomime
Ships that go bang in the night
Run aground on the sands of time

Saved in the nick of dawn
It's cornflakes and then goodbye
Another notch on the headboard
Another day wondering why

The Act of Love lies somewhere
Between the belly and the mind
I lost the love sometime ago
Now I've only the act to grind

PETE BROWN
(1940–   )

Vision

Wow! 2
small virgins
carrying
a gigantic
mattress!

DAVE CUNLIFFE
(1941–   )

That Awfully Nice Young Man

There's some things I just don't understand.
Like the time that beautiful young lady
entered a train carriage & took off
her clothes;   cupped those firm young
breasts in both hands;   stuck out a
fine white arse;   bristled her deep black
pubic hairs;   stroked a soft moist
cunt;   laid back & stretched those long
lovely legs out wide & invitingly . . .
& the only man in that compartment
threw down his paper,   leapt to his
feet, & draped his overcoat around her.

TOM PICKARD
(1946–   )

Shag

canny bord ower there
sharrap man yi think i nowt but tarts

divin na though
wouden mind a bash arrit

hoo pet can a yek yi yem?
am a big streng lad
al luk after yi

a na ya not owld inuff ti suck a dummy

hoo lads tommys scored
whats ya name pet
howear gis a kiss
gis a bit feel pet
di yi fancy a meat injectin?
well jump on the end i this

suck me plums
gis a suck off

o yi commin fora walk wis?
will gan ower the quarry
a nas a shortcut

leave is alen

sharrap or all belt yi

grab a
gis a bit feel
pull a doon
lets have a bit tit
howear man am forst

am warnin yis all git the coppas

sharrap or al kick ya teeth in

pull a doon
rip a skort off
hurry up an stuff it tom
its me next

are man quick
stick it in the get
howld a doon
shi winnit keep still
well hit the twat
please keep still pet an a winnit be a minit
go on man go on
a-a-r-r-r- thatsnice

howear well
its me next

MARILYN HACKER
(1942-   )

Elektra on Third Avenue

At six, when April chills our hands and feet
walking downtown, we stop at Clancy's Bar
or Bickford's, where the part-time hustlers are
scoffing between the mailroom and the street.
Old pensioners appraise them while they eat,
and so do we, debating half in jest
which piece of hasty pudding we'd like best.
I know you know I think your mouth is sweet
as anything exhibited for sale,
fresh coffee cakes or boys fresh out of jail,
which tender hint of incest brings me near
to ordering more coffee or more beer.
The homebound crowd provides new youth to cruise.
We nurse our cups, nudge knees, and pick and choose.

[346]

JULIAN ENNIS
( )

Strip Club

Sweetly disordered, the dresses drop
Like waterfalls down each glossy back
To shimmer, pools of silk, on the bawdy floor,
Until, with cheeky, Charleston flick
High heels heave them to the laundry
In the wings, and the girls gleam, pinned up
For the business, advertising underwear
And long legs. Then, modelling, slowly
They unwind their pink selves to the travellers
Who, land-locked with the same wives in every
Port of call, watch hands crawl like crabs across
Breasts, the fingers, small truncated men,
Scuttle up thighs, those dark peninsulas,
To unhitch and unroll the nylon skin,
Then untie the true-love, granny knot.

At last, the naked Eves stand, spotlit
And still, observing the law with a cute wink,
Briefly clapped and vanishing in the moist
Blackness of the room; and the old Adams,
Who have paid so lavishly to see
What oft they've seen but ne'er so well undressed,
Wake up from their evening-out dreams
And take their solitary way to the bar
To swap and drown their choices in strong drink.

INDEX OF FIRST LINES

[349]

[355]

INDEX OF POETS